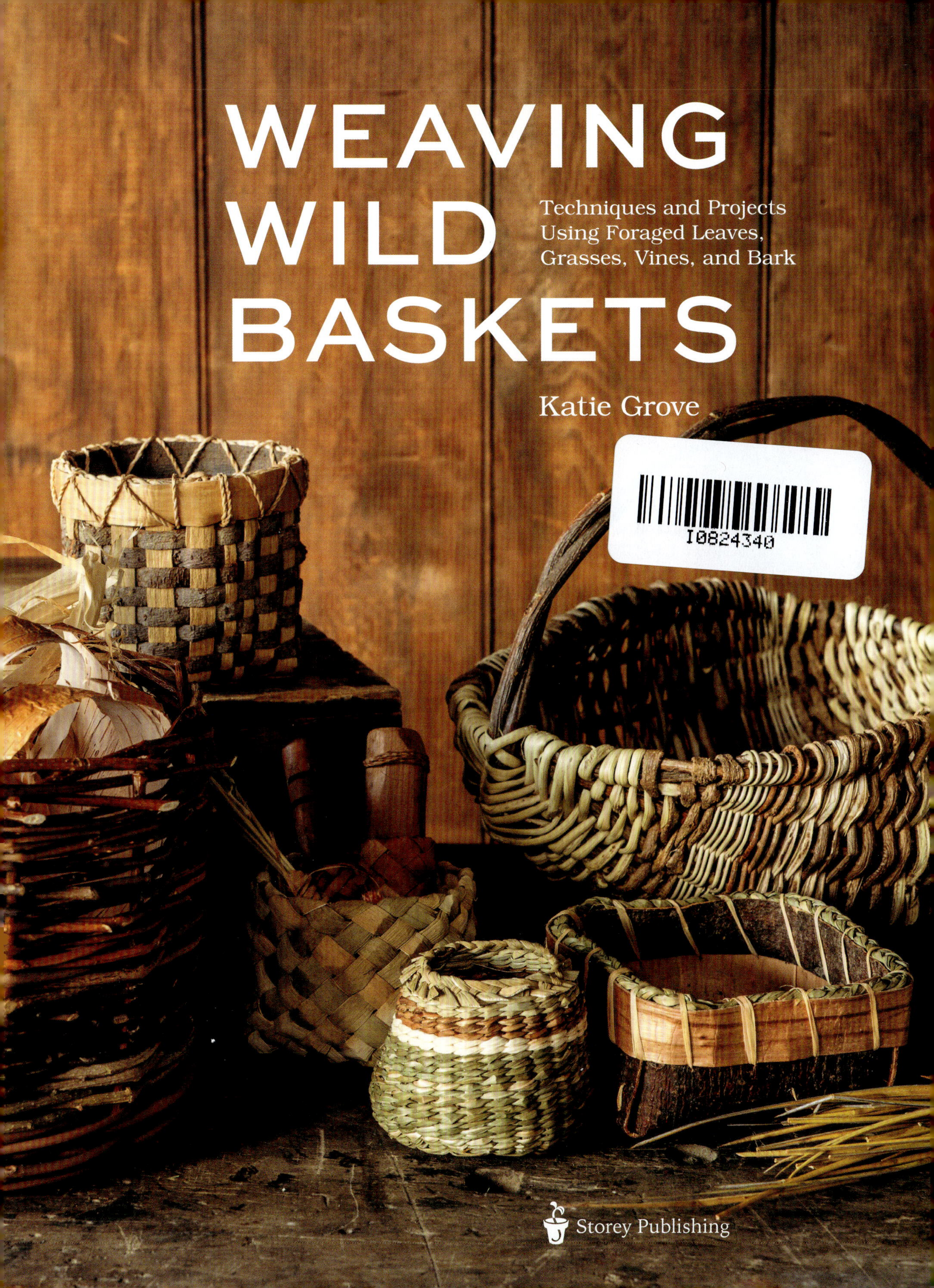

WEAVING WILD BASKETS

Techniques and Projects Using Foraged Leaves, Grasses, Vines, and Bark

Katie Grove

Storey Publishing

The mission of Storey Publishing is to serve our customers by publishing practical information that encourages personal independence in harmony with the environment.

EDITED BY Alethea Morrison and Melanie Falick
ART DIRECTION AND BOOK DESIGN BY Alethea Morrison
BACK COVER DESIGN BY Bredna Lago
TEXT PRODUCTION BY Jennifer Jepson Smith

COVER PHOTOGRAPHY BY © Andrew Frasz, except front, back t.r., b.r., 3rd fr. t.l., author by Mars Vilaubi © Storey Publishing
INTERIOR PHOTOGRAPHY BY © Andrew Frasz, i, 8, 120 b., 126, 133, 138, 143–144, 152, 156, 164, 172, 182, 190 t., 194, 198, 210, 214, 224, 232, 237, 239–240, 244, 249 t.r., 252, 258, 263 b., 269–270, 274, 279–280, 284, 290, 294; Mars Vilaubi © Storey Publishing, iv–vi, 2–4, 5 main, 6, 11, 13–14, 18, 20–23, 25, 40, 46–48, 50, 56, 58–62, 68, 70, 72, 79–80, 83–86, 88 l., 89 b.r., 90–92, 94–97, 102, 105–106, 108–119, 120 t., 121–122, 123 main, 124, 129–132, 134–137, 141, 146–151, 155, 157–163, 166, 169–171, 174–181, 184–189, 190 b.l. & b.r., 191–193, 200–209, 213, 215–223, 226–231, 235, 238, 241–243, 246–248, 249 all but t.r., 250–251, 255–256, 260–262, 263 t.l. & t.r., 264–268, 272–273, 277, 281–283, 286–288, 289 t., 293, 296–304, 306
ADDITIONAL PHOTOGRAPHY BY © A_Lesik/Shutterstock.com, 26; © ap-studio/Shutterstock.com, 54 l.; © Bradley D. Saum /Shutterstock.com, 39; © captureandcompose/Shutterstock .com, 5 & 123 inset; © ClubhouseArts/Shutterstock.com, 100 l.; Costa Boutsikaris, 88 r., 89 all but b.r.; © Donna Bollenbach/Shutterstock.com, 45, 75 r.; © Elmar Langle /Shutterstock.com, 99; © fotokate/stock.adobe.com, 65; © Gerry Bishop/Alamy Stock Photo, 76; © High Mountain /Shutterstock.com, 52 r.; © iPlantsman/Shutterstock.com, 101 l.; © Irene Fox/Shutterstock.com, 44 r.; © Iv-olga /Shutterstock.com, 98 l.; © julie deshaies/Shutterstock.com, 64; © K Steve Cope/Shutterstock.com, 55 l.; Katelyn Grove, 57, 66–67, 87, 289 b.; © Kevinr4/Shutterstock.com, 38; © Krzysztof Bubel/Shutterstock.com, 100 r.; © Mary Swift/ Shutterstock.com, 101 r.; © MT.PHOTOSTOCK/ Shutterstock.com, 75 l.; © Paul Maguire/Shutterstock.com, 55 r.; © piemags/nature/Alamy Stock Photo, 98 r.; © SHARKY PHOTOGRAPHY/Shutterstock.com, 42 l.; © Stock for you/Shutterstock.com, 31 t.; © stsvirkun/ stock.adobe.com, 42 r.; © Tetiana A/Shutterstock.com, 31 b.; © This_is_JiHun_Lee/Shutterstock.com, 52 l.; © ToffeePhoto/Shutterstock.com, 74; © UbjsP/Shutterstock .com, 44 l.; © Vlad Siaber/Shutterstock.com, 77 l.; © Wollwerth Imagery/stock.adobe.com, 54 r.; © xxcxxc/ Shutterstock.com, 43; © youli zhao/stock.adobe.com, 53; © zedspider/Shutterstock.com, 77 r.
PHOTO STYLING BY Alison Pebworth

Storey books may be purchased in bulk for business, educational, or promotional use. Special editions or book excerpts can also be created to specification. For details, please contact your local bookseller or the Hachette Book Group Special Markets Department at special.markets@hbgusa.com.

Storey Publishing
210 MASS MoCA Way
North Adams, MA 01247
storey.com

Storey Publishing is an imprint of Workman Publishing, a division of Hachette Book Group, Inc., 1290 Avenue of the Americas, New York, NY 10104. The Storey Publishing name and logo are registered trademarks of Hachette Book Group, Inc.

ISBNs: 978-1-63586-888-3 (paperback);
978-1-63586-889-0 (ebook)

Printed in China by Imago on paper from responsible sources
10 9 8 7 6 5 4 3 2 1

IM

Library of Congress Cataloging-in-Publication Data on file

Be sure to read all the instructions thoroughly before undertaking any of the projects in this book.
Please use caution when using sharp tools.

To my basketry students, friends,
and community who inspired and encouraged me
to write this book.

CONTENTS

INTRODUCTION

WHAT ARE WILD BASKETS?

I believe that connecting to the natural world is the most important thing we can do as human beings and that creating meaningful objects, including baskets, using natural materials is one of the most profound ways we can do this. I call this wild basketry.

Wild basketry is a way to get to know the natural world and the plants growing in it as you would a friend, by spending quality time together to develop a deep and meaningful relationship. Discovering the bounty of my local land and returning to the same spots every year to forage has become a ritual. My awareness of nature has grown slowly, plant by plant, and the feeling that we are parts of a whole has grown alongside it.

Nature is alive and abundant, offering weaving material that anyone can forage ethically and sustainably. My favorite aspect of basketry starts long before weaving, when I walk a quiet trail in autumn, pausing to harvest milkweed stems, or stand alone in a cattail marsh amid birdsong. During these moments I am deeply connected to myself and my surroundings. Exploring this feeling of connection—and weaving my love for the land into my baskets—motivates my creative practice. I am passionate about sharing a mindset of curiosity, resourcefulness, sustainability, and playfulness with others and inspiring people to reciprocate nature's generosity with care.

Wild basketry is also a way to slow down and work with one's hands, which has immense meditative and healing potential in a world where we've grown accustomed to disposable goods and fast results.

And it's a way to connect to our ancestors, all of whom were basket makers. It's true! Every single person on this earth has ancestors who harvested plants and made baskets, just as we all have ancestors who made stone tools and built fires. In every environment, from deserts to the arctic, people have been using local plants to make baskets—for survival, ritual, cultural expression, and beauty—for tens, possibly even hundreds, of thousands of years.

This book is my way of sharing everything I've learned since I made my first basket out of pine needles in 2009. In the pages that follow I've tried to present each step in the most accessible way possible, from identifying plants you can forage to the finished basket. I demonstrate each technique and project with specific plants that grow near me in New York's Hudson Valley, and I also describe a range of other plant materials you can use instead. That way, no matter where you live, you will be able to find excellent materials with which to work.

There is a lot of information here—as much as I could squeeze in—but don't let the scope of this book intimidate you, because beginning is easy. If you don't know where to start, I suggest you skim these pages to see what catches your eye and inspires you the most. If you are most excited about foraging, read Part One to understand what makes a plant suitable

for basketry. And then, of course, go for a walk and observe the plants around you! If you want to start a project right away, I recommend trying cordage on page 128, which can be made with all sorts of different plant materials and is an essential technique. Other great projects for beginners are the Coiled Bowl (page 145), Bark Necklace Pouch (page 239), Looped Cordage Pouch (page 155), Grapevine Market Basket (page 279), and Tension Tray (page 271).

The information in this book is gathered from my personal experience: spending thousands of hours foraging, processing, and creating baskets with plants. Along this journey I've engaged in deep historical research, studied with great teachers, and learned from fellow basket makers, but much of what I've chosen to include comes from good old dirt time: digging in, exploring with an open mind, and trying new things. And that is what I hope you will do.

You are your own best teacher. As I always tell students in my classes: Do not believe—or disbelieve—anything I tell you until you try it yourself. There are so many plants waiting to be discovered, and there are many right ways to achieve the same result. Use this book as a jumping-off point, then go outside, look around, and put your own spin on the deep and exciting world of wild basketry.

PART ONE

GATHERING AND PREPARING PLANTS FOR WILD BASKETS

Wild basketry begins with cultivating awareness of the natural world. And it all starts in your own backyard and neighborhood. Observing which plants are nearby and how they change throughout the year invites us to live in sync with the seasons.

One of my favorite parts of being a basket maker is that there is always something exciting happening right outside the front door. Over time I've learned to notice when new leaves emerge, vines feel most flexible, grasses begin to dry. Plants are continually beckoning their readiness for basketry.

I will help you learn which plants are growing around you, how to forage them, and what to do with the materials to prepare them for basketmaking. Chapter 1 gives an overview of the tools you need, as well as the basics of foraging and caring for plant materials. In Chapter 2, learn more about identifying plants and foraging them ethically, then try the exercises I share to build familiarity with your local landscape. Consult the foraging calendar on pages 16–17 to see which plants are in season right now. What is available and ready to be harvested at any given time in your environment will determine which types of baskets you can make at that moment. Chapters 3 through 7 offer specifics about how to forage, dry, store, and prepare different types of plants so that you can have a stash of materials ready to get out and make baskets with all year round.

My goals are to inspire you to get outside and look around with new eyes and to provide you with the information you need to gather plants for basketmaking with confidence and sensitivity. You may find, like me and so many of my students, that learning to forage sustainably and then creating beautiful baskets with your bounty is a deeply profound, life-changing experience. And all you really need to get started is a pair of scissors and a good measure of curiosity.

CHAPTER 1

TOOLS AND MATERIALS

Acquiring a tool kit and gathering plant material are essential to the basketry journey. As basket makers, we learn the best times to forage for our materials, which means when it is healthiest for the plant and most useful for our process. And we learn how to handle the materials once we've gathered them—which ones we can use fresh, which ones must be dried and rehydrated, which ones require peeling and splitting or some other type of manipulation—and how to store our materials so they will be in good condition when we are ready to create a basket.

Tools for Foraging and Basketmaking

You only need a few basic tools to get started, some of which you probably have on hand already. If you're sure you want to set up a full basketmaking studio, go ahead and gather everything listed here. Alternatively, choose a project and assemble only the tools and supplies listed in the tools list.

Many of these tools should be easy to find locally, and others are sold at specialty basketry or leather-working stores and websites. (See Resources on page 305.) I recommend buying quality tools. Take good care of them, and many will last a lifetime.

basic tools

The following tools are the basis of a good basketry tool kit and will get you started with most foraging and basketmaking projects covered in this book.

① **Basketry scissors.** Use these to cut bark, grasses, and other plant materials. My favorite kind are red-and-white-handled basketry shears, readily available on most basketry-supply websites. They are sharp and strong, and their slim profile makes it easy to cut accurately. The next best thing would be any pair of strong all-purpose scissors.

② **Pruning shears.** These are necessary for foraging vines, woody stems, and all thicker branches. I recommend getting a high-quality pair from a reputable brand like Felco, which last indefinitely with good care. Those old, rusty pruning shears in your shed will not do the trick.

③ **Knife with 2- to 5-inch fixed blade.** This is your all-purpose cutting, whittling, harvesting, and splitting tool. I recommend Morakniv knives, with their Companion model being an affordable option. Do not use a folding blade; it is not sturdy enough for most jobs. Keep the blade sharp and clean.

④ **Utility knife with retractable blade.** This tool is great for splitting bark and other thin materials into fine strips or for jobs where being able to retract the blade between uses is helpful. Change the blade often for clean, safe cutting.

⑤ **Tapestry and chenille needles.** I keep an assortment of these large-eyed needles in different sizes on hand for sewing coiled baskets, threading materials into baskets, and more. Tapestry needles have rounded, dull points, and chenille needles have sharp points.

⑥ **Awls.** These pointy pieces of metal are for poking holes, opening spaces, and many other essential tasks. I have three awls: a sharp, narrow one for poking small holes, a medium-size one for poking larger holes and inserting ribs in ribbed baskets, and a wider, longer one for willow work.

⑦ **Needle-nose pliers.** A long, thin pair with a slim profile is great for tightening lashing, reaching into narrow spaces, and many other tasks.

⑧ **Packing tools.** These basketry-specific tools have many uses, including packing down rows of weaving and opening spaces for inserting materials. (See Understanding Packing on page 178.) They come in many different sizes and lengths with straight or bent tips. To start, I recommend that you get three variations: a heavy-duty bent tip; a regular straight tip; and a small straight tip for detail work. Packing tools can be improvised—a dull screwdriver or whittled stick will work in a pinch—but don't use anything with a sharp point or edges, which is dangerous for both you and your basket.

1
2
FELCO 8
SWISS MADE
3
MORAKNIV
4
5
6
7
8
9
10

(9) **Spring clamps.** A half dozen in 2-inch and 4-inch sizes are essential for clamping materials while making baskets and storing plant material.

(10) **Micro alligator clips.** Small steel clips with smooth jaws are essential for holding little pieces in place as you make baskets. Clothespins often do the trick, but a clip with a thinner profile is usually better.

Spray bottle. You will need to spray baskets with water to keep them damp while working.

Nine- to 12-inch reusable zip ties. Use these to secure bundles of materials. Regular strong string is an alternative.

Gardening gloves. I recommend wearing gloves with a tight fit for work that is hard on the hands, such as harvesting—especially vines—and digging roots.

studio tools

Rehydrating and processing plant material are key aspects of basketry. The following supplies will give you a great home setup.

Large stockpots. Get a few large ones dedicated to basketry only. They will become quite dirty and won't be usable for food preparation afterward. A standard 5-gallon enamel-coated canning pot is fine to start, but a larger one will fit more materials. My 20-gallon pot is a prized possession. Stainless steel is always best because it is nonreactive and lasts a long time, but it can be pricey, especially if purchased new. To save money, keep your eyes peeled at yard sales and thrift shops.

Stove. For indoor work, I use a portable countertop induction burner. Choose one capable of holding at least 45 pounds. A professional-level burner is sturdy and heats large amounts of water quickly. For outdoor work I use a heavy-duty, stand-alone, single-burner propane stove. A kitchen stove is always an option, but keep in mind that basketry work can get messy.

Electric kettle. This is a great tool for quickly heating a bit of water when rehydrating plant material.

Two-gallon buckets. Having two or three is enough to start.

Old towels. I can never have enough towels for holding wet materials and cleaning up.

Plastic shower curtain liner. Such a liner or a lightweight tarp keeps plant material moist and flexible. Also use it for mellowing willow and cattails.

Large plastic bin. A 30-gallon bin or larger is a good place to soak bendy grasses or keep already soaked vines pliable.

bark harvesting and processing tools

The pruning shears, knife, and scissors from your basic tool kit are effective for harvesting the bark of saplings and branches. For harvesting larger pieces of bark and processing them into neat, even pieces, the following tools are extremely helpful.

(1) **Drawknife.** Also called a draw shave, this tool has a blade between two handles that you draw toward your body. Used for shaving thick outer bark from trees, it needs to have a straight blade between 9 and 12 inches long. Finding one at an antique shop with a straight, intact blade and solidly attached handles will save you money, and the quality is likely to be excellent. A good, new drawknife will cost more than buying one used. Beware of the cheapest new versions; in my experience, they never work.

(2) **Leather strap cutter.** Designed for leather, this tool works wonderfully in basketry for cutting inner bark down to size, one strip at a time, and is a good introductory tool to use before investing in a tabletop leather lace cutter.

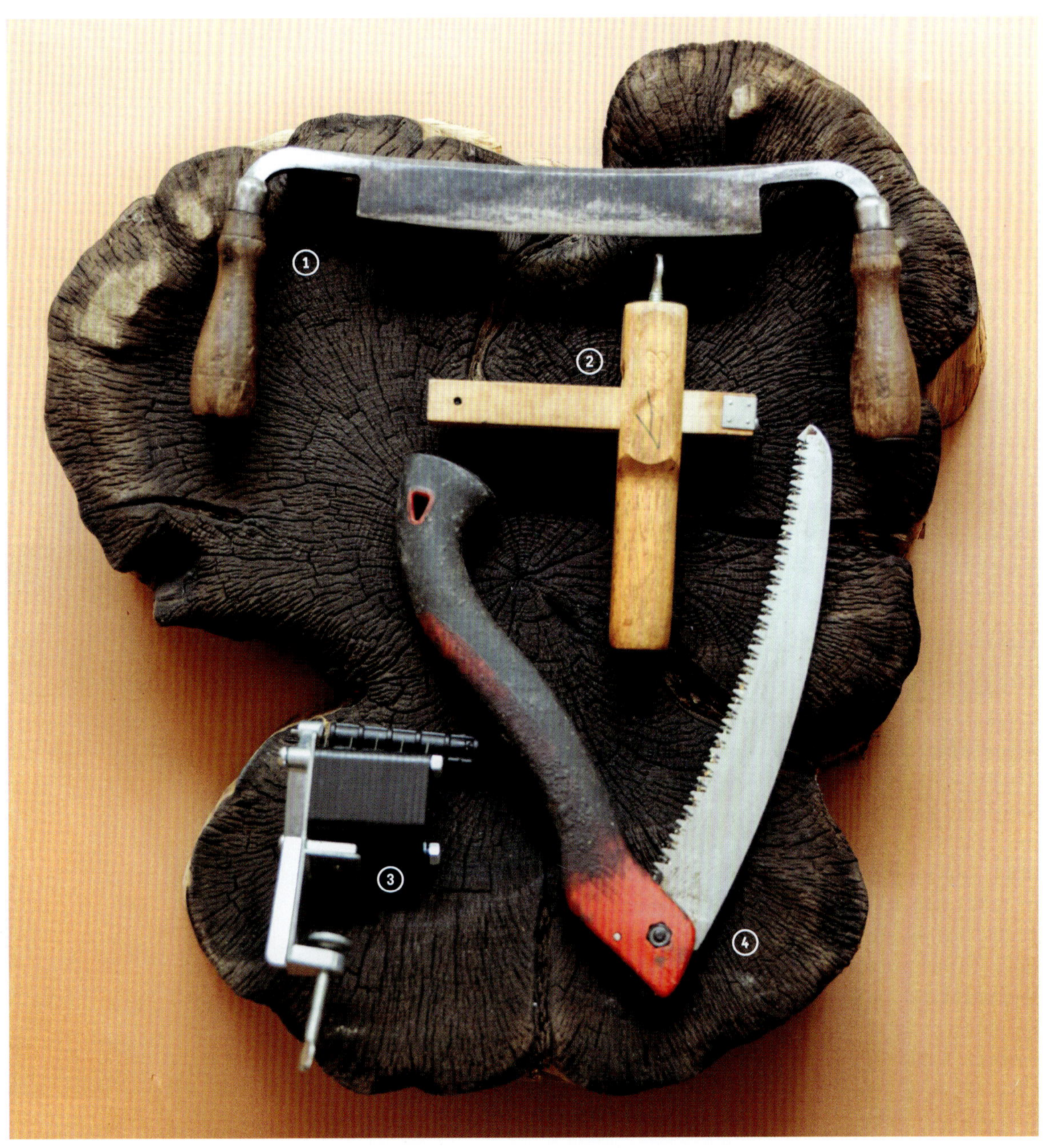

③ **Tabletop leather lace cutter.** This leatherworking tool is faster than the leather strap cutter and can cut multiple strips of inner bark at the same time, which results in straighter strips. You attach it to a solid, immobile table and pull the bark through it.

④ **Folding saw.** Use for cutting branches, felling saplings, and making circumference cuts when removing inner bark.

Loppers. Requiring two hands to operate, loppers are long handled with large blades and can cut branches and vines that are bigger than your pruning shears can handle.

Foraging for Plant Materials

I have never felt more at home in my skin than when I am outside foraging for basketry plants. During these moments I am deeply connected to myself and my surroundings. It feels uncannily familiar and comforting, like shrugging into a favorite sweater. I first experienced this feeling while rinsing fiber in the slow-moving waters of a summer river and have gone on to feel it time and time again since then—in fields, backyards, marshes; under old trees; and even in the brambly undergrowth next to my home in New York's Hudson Valley. These experiences are deeply nourishing, and it has become my passion in life to inspire others to start their own journeys in the natural world and to care for the natural world through the process.

where to forage

There are places to forage for basketmaking everywhere, whether you live in a city, suburb, or rural area. The first step is to look around. Are there weeds in the lot behind your apartment? Are there vines covering the neighbor's fence? What are all those interesting plants growing in the hedgerow? The second step is to build relationships with your local community. Tell people that you are learning basketry and looking for places to pick plants. You will be surprised at how often they will invite you to explore on their land. I've even left kind notes in strangers' mailboxes, inviting them to email me if they are open to sharing.

Following is a list of foraging resources that exist in many communities. You can reach out by emailing, writing letters, putting up flyers, and talking to folks in person. I find it always helps to have a basket or some photos of baskets on hand to help describe what you do. While foraging, be respectful of their property and be sure you and the property owner communicate clearly about what they will allow you to pick. Building a community network is one of the richest parts of being a basket maker and has led to some of my closest friendships.

OBVIOUS (AND NOT-SO-OBVIOUS) PLACES TO FORAGE

Almost any natural environment—from wetlands, forests, and meadows to shrublands and deserts—holds riches for the basket maker. Areas where human activity has altered the natural landscape—from gardens, parks, and yards to roadsides and abandoned lots—all contain suitable plant material. Edge areas (zones where two types of ecosystems meet and overlap, such as where a field turns into forest) tend to be particularly bountiful.

Private yards and gardens, community gardens, transfer stations, and parks. Many homeowners are thrilled to have a basket maker appreciate and make good use of their plants, such as grasses that need to be cut back at the end of a season. This extends to businesses, community gardens, parks, and even plant piles at local transfer stations. Of course, always ask for permission first.

Landscapers and arborists. These professionals often have access to a treasure trove of materials. For example, landscapers working on a redesign might need to remove a cattail patch on a pond or clear the woods of wisteria vines. During yearly maintenance they're regularly asked to cut back ornamental grasses and leafy plants, such as irises. Arborists regularly cut down great basketry trees, such as tulip poplar.

Local environmental groups. Invasive plants are species that are not native to the ecosystem in which they are growing and whose introduction causes harm to the environment or human health. There are often local initiatives to remove invasive plants from parks and rail trails. Reach out to the groups that manage these lands and see if you can join in or organize an event both to help the ecosystem and source basketry materials.

Social media. Every spring, when I am looking for bark, I ask my online community if trees have fallen in their yards recently or if they're planning to cut down any trees that are good sources for bark. These posts have yielded some of my best hauls. You could do the same, or you might ask people if they're cutting back leafy garden plants in fall or vines in winter.

when to forage

We harvest most plants for basketry while they are still living. Dead and dry plants or those that have begun to die back and compost will not be suitable for weaving. In addition, each plant species needs to be harvested at a certain time in its life cycle. The timing is based on what is best for the plant and the surrounding ecosystem as well as the stage in development that suits its use in basketry. For example, for basketry purposes, daylily leaves could be used in summer; however, I will only forage them in fall, after the plant has flowered and is just starting to die back, to avoid depleting the root system. I forage at the right time for the plant and then store materials for year-round use. Guidelines for harvesting, processing, and storing plants vary depending on the type of material. For detailed information, both generally by material type and specifically by plant species, see Chapters 3 to 7.

HARVEST TIMES CHEAT SHEET

The foraging calendar on the following pages gives detailed information about peak and acceptable harvest times for many of my favorite basketry plants. For plants not on that list, here are some general guidelines for choosing the season to harvest.

Barks: Late spring–summer

Leaves and grasses: Early fall

Vines: Late fall–winter

Woody stems: Early winter–late winter

Roots: Late spring–early fall

Foraging Calendar

PLANT	PLANT TYPE	PLANT PART	SEASON		
Refer to the plant profiles in each chapter for more details on harvest times.			WINTER		
			Early	Mid	Late
Akebia	Vine	Vine			
Basswood	Tree	Bark and bark fiber			
Birch	Tree	Bark			
Bittersweet	Vine	Vine			
Black walnut	Tree	Bark			
Brambles	Shrub	Woody stems			
Cattail	Herbaceous	Leaves			
Corn	Herbaceous	Leaves			
Dandelion	Herbaceous	Soft stems			
Daylily	Herbaceous	Leaves			
Dogbane	Herbaceous	Stalk fiber			
Elm	Tree	Bark and bark fiber			
Grapevine	Vine	Vine			
Hickory	Tree	Bark			
Honeysuckle	Vine	Vine			
Iris	Herbaceous	Leaves			
Kudzu	Vine	Vine			
Milkweed	Herbaceous	Stalk fiber			
Nettle	Herbaceous	Stalk fiber			
Ornamental grasses	Herbaceous	Soft stems and leaves			
Palms	Tree	Leaves			
Pine	Tree	Needles (leaves)			
Porcelain berry	Vine	Vine			
Red osier dogwood	Shrub	Woody stems			
Snake plant	Herbaceous	Leaf fiber			
Soft rush	Herbaceous	Soft stems			
Softstem bulrush	Herbaceous	Soft stems			
Spruce	Tree	Roots			
Sumac	Tree	Bark			
Tulip poplar	Tree	Bark			
Virginia creeper	Vine	Vine			
Water sprouts	Tree	Woody stems			
Western red cedar	Tree	Bark, bark fiber, and roots			
White pine	Tree	Bark and roots			
Willow	Tree or shrub	Woody stems, bark, and fiber			
Wisteria	Vine	Vine			
Yucca	Herbaceous	Leaf fiber			

- **PEAK** (easiest to gather, most abundant, best quality, and often best for plant's health)
- **OFTEN ACCEPTABLE** (depends on geographic location, weather, plant health, and other factors)
- **SOMETIMES ACCEPTABLE** (depends on the factors above; quality and ease of harvest will vary)

SPRING			SUMMER			FALL		
Early	Mid	Late	Early	Mid	Late	Early	Mid	Late

safe foraging and making

Safety comes first. Here are some general guidelines to follow.

Be aware of harmful plants. Research how to identify poisonous, thorny, and otherwise dangerous plants, as well as where they grow. I am always on the lookout for poison ivy where I live.

Watch out for ticks. If you forage in a region with tick-borne illnesses, consider wearing light-colored clothes (so ticks will be visible on them) and applying repellent before you head out. Afterward, remove your clothes immediately and give yourself a thorough, full-body check since ticks are mobile and can get into all sorts of crevices. As an added precaution, some people put their clothes in the dryer for 10 minutes right after they take them off to kill any ticks.

Avoid chemicals. Don't forage in areas sprayed with chemicals or polluted with farm runoff. Invasive vines on roadsides, such as kudzu, for example, are often sprayed. You don't want to expose yourself to poisons.

Proceed with caution on roadsides. If you are tempted to gather plant material on the roadside, be careful, as drivers are not expecting to see you there.

Be wary of dead vines. Before pulling vines, check to see if the trees they are climbing are alive. Never pull vines intertwined with dead or dying branches. Stop completely or proceed with caution. Dead or dying branches can easily break and fall on you or someone else nearby.

Practice knife safety. Follow these guidelines when using any kind of blade or other sharp tool, including awls, scissors, and saws.

- Never use a knife or sharp object while another person is within arm's reach.
- Never walk around with your knife or pruning shears open.
- Before cutting, make sure your fingers and your body are out of the way.

Always angle a knife away from your body (never toward it) while working.

- Always angle the knife away from your body (never toward it) while working.
- When whittling, make small, controlled cuts, rather than one big one.
- Retract the blade on your utility knife every time you put it down.
- Keep knives in their sheaths when not in use.
- Keep knives sharp and rust-free. Cutting dirty objects will dull them.

ethical and respectful foraging

One of the most rewarding parts of wild basketry is the opportunity to come to know and care for the land. For me, this means developing a relationship with natural places and the plants that live there. When we treat the natural world as something alive (which it is) and worthy of respect and care, just like our friends and family, we are more likely to protect it. In fact, this is our privilege and responsibility as human beings—and basketmaking is a beautiful way to begin!

There are many deeply important, time-tested best practices for foraging. Indigenous groups around the world have embodied these principles for many thousands of years. Contemporary environmental movements likewise encourage sustainable approaches and protecting nature. The intentions I focus on are care, respect, and reciprocity with the natural world. Robin Wall Kimmerer's book *Braiding Sweetgrass* is an excellent source for learning more about this approach.

Practice gratitude. All plants deserve our respect, even invasive ones. Practice gratitude by thanking the plant and the land throughout the foraging process.

Ask the plant for permission. This practice may seem strange at first, but it is deeply empowering. Ask the plant for permission out loud or pose the question internally. Either way, stop and pay attention to what you feel in your body in response. You may be surprised by what comes through—trust it.

Harvest plants with care and kindness. Forage thoughtfully, intentionally, and slowly, being mindful of the multitude of other plants and creatures living in the area. I find that when I center myself as I work, the process goes more smoothly and is much more meaningful than when I rush or work haphazardly.

Ask the land's stewards or owners for permission. If you're harvesting on public land, get permission from the current stewards. They will know the management plan in place for that location. If you're harvesting on private land, always get permission from the landowner.

Be resourceful and opportunistic. Choose cultivated plants (those already growing in people's yards) or invasive plants. Actively reroute plant waste resulting from storms, property development, maintenance, and municipal roadwork.

Correctly identify plants. To avoid waste, identify whether a plant is suitable for your intended purpose before you remove it from its ecosystem. If you find a plant with seemingly good basketry qualities whose identity you are unsure of (and you are certain it is not poisonous), harvest a small amount to test before taking more.

ETHICAL BASKETMAKING

Beyond caring for the land, I believe in making choices with intention and respect for other people. Mimicking Indigenous basket designs can be a form of cultural appropriation—defined as the use without permission of a people's traditional dress, music, culture, food, knowledge, ways of being, and other traditions by someone of another culture. There is no checklist of ways to ensure that your basketmaking is authentic to you and not appropriative, but I encourage you to research, talk, and think about your practices and do your best to be an ally to Indigenous peoples.

Learn about and care for the ecosystem. The plant you are harvesting may provide food, nesting material, a spot for laying eggs, and shelter for other inhabitants, such as birds and insects. Learning more about your local ecosystems and the interconnectedness between species will help inform your foraging practice.

Take only a small portion. Take a small percentage of what is available until you understand how your harvest affects a particular ecosystem. Be especially conservative if other individuals may be foraging in the same place. It takes many years for certain plant populations to regenerate; others don't regenerate at all. Notable exceptions are plants that are invasive or aggressive in their growing tendencies.

Never take the first or the last plant. Explore an area to find different populations of the plant. Choose the healthiest and most abundant area to harvest from. If there is only one tiny white pine tree, don't cut it! Find a spot where they are plentiful or choose a different species that is more plentiful. As always, invasive plants are an exception.

Use everything you take. Whether it is an entire tree or grasses that grow again every year, every plant's life is valuable, and basket makers are responsible for honoring and appreciating our plants by not letting any part go to waste. Understanding how to prepare and store plant material and being realistic about how much time we can dedicate to working with it helps a lot. If you are not able to work with all the material you take, compost it and learn for next time.

Leave no trace. When you are finished collecting, spread out any leftover trimmings, fill any holes, and, of course, be sure to take all your tools or anything else you might have brought to the area. Try to leave the area better than you found it.

Give back. Reciprocity is at the heart of developing a relationship with the land. Giving back to a plant or the earth in which it grows could mean removing litter from the area, clearing invasive plant species, spreading the seeds of the plant that you are harvesting (unless it's an invasive one), and even returning to care for the new plants as needed. Be creative when developing your own practice of reciprocity.

Check back. Return to harvest spots every year or multiple times a year and observe how your actions have affected the ecosystem. Take notes, make videos, and build your knowledge of how to develop the most regenerative practices for your area.

Share. Be generous in sharing both the materials you gather as well as the knowledge you are gaining as a practicing basket maker. Sharing stories and experiences is an excellent way to open people's hearts to the beauty and importance of caring for the natural world.

The more notes you take in the first few years, the more you will learn and the better off you will be going forward. I know from personal experience how gratifying it is to wonder when I can harvest cattails again, consult my journal, and be reminded of the exact dates and the quality of the materials I gathered in previous years.

Drying, Storing, and Rehydrating Plant Materials

While it's tempting to forage for plant material and make a basket right away, it is usually better to allow the material to dry and then rehydrate it to make it malleable again. Freshly cut plant material is filled with moisture that evaporates over time; this causes the material to shrink and the weaving to loosen. Of course, there are exceptions and workarounds. Certain plants, such as grapevine, don't retain a lot of moisture, so it's fine to weave them fresh. Or, in some cases, you can dry your freshly foraged materials just enough—so most of the moisture is gone but they're still flexible enough to manipulate—then make a basket with them within just a few days.

While each plant has its own nuances, what follows are some basic guidelines for drying, storing, and rehydrating. For more specific recommendations and requirements by type of material, see Chapters 3 to 7.

drying plant materials

The goal is to remove moisture from the material so that it won't attract mold in storage or shrink when you use it to make baskets. The following principles apply to any material you gather.

Materials such as these grasses will dry fastest on elevated screens in a cool, dry, indoor environment.

Start drying plant material as soon as possible after harvest. An indoor, dry, climate-controlled environment is ideal. This might be an air-conditioned room, a garage space with a dehumidifier running, or a cool, dry attic. If possible, run an electric fan to keep air circulating and to speed up the drying process. Don't leave your material outside, in the trunk of your car, or on a porch, because it will start to compost.

Spread material in a single layer. Use elevated screens or lay the plant material directly on a table or the floor; screens are helpful because they allow air to flow underneath. Alternatively, tie your harvested plants in small bundles and hang them from the ceiling.

Shuffle and turn the materials once or twice a day. Drying time will vary depending on the material's consistency and the conditions. A fair estimate for most plants is a few days to 2 weeks. Exceptions include stems, such as willow, which take many weeks or even months to dry completely. Your material is dry if it cracks or snaps when bent. Leaves will make a rustling sound when shuffled and will be visibly smaller in size.

If space or electricity is lacking, do what you can to meet these conditions and check for mold regularly to avoid wasting material.

storing plant materials

How you store your hard-earned plant material can have a big effect on how likely you are to use it and whether it's resistant to mold and breakage. A huge pile of unsorted grasses and vines in a cardboard box in the corner does not welcome creativity. Take the time to organize and store your materials well, and when you want to make a basket each component will be easily accessible and ready to go. General guidelines for storage include the following.

Keep your harvested plants in a cool, dry environment. Giving space around the materials with good air circulation is key. Depending on the climate, you may need to run a dehumidifier or an air conditioner seasonally or year-round.

Label everything. Note what it is, when and where it was foraged, and maybe even what you intend to use it for. (For example, while processing bark, I often know I want to use certain bundles for stakes and others for weavers. Leaving a note for my future self helps me remember.)

Bundle small amounts. Heaps of material are inaccessible, while small quantities are easy to pull out and soak to use.

Choose clear containers. If using boxes, I prefer clear tote bins or bags so I can easily see the contents.

DEALING WITH MOLD

Don't continue to store or make baskets with materials that have developed green surface mold or black mold spots. Compost leafy plant materials like grasses and corn husks, since the mold will be difficult to clean off completely. For other materials without extensive damage, try removing the mold using one of the methods below. Sometimes black mold spots leave a stain, but the material can still be used.

Boiling in water, applying vinegar, and exposing materials to sunlight and fresh air are the best remedies for mold. While cleaning, always wear a mask and rubber gloves to avoid breathing in and otherwise coming in contact with the mold spores.

- **If the material is tough enough to boil:** Place vines or thicker unsplit barks in a large pot and fill it with enough water to cover. Boil for a few minutes to kill the mold spores. Using tongs, carefully transfer the material to a work surface in the bright sun. Spray the material with vinegar and wipe it down to make sure all spores are removed. Spray the material again and let it dry in fresh air very thoroughly. Afterward, store the material in a drier place with better ventilation.
- **If boiling isn't an option:** Soak a rag in white vinegar, use the rag to wipe down the moldy material, then dry it. This works best for flat materials with no cracks or crevices for mold to grow; thin materials that might be damaged by boiling; or materials that won't fit in a pot, such as willow.

rehydrating plant materials

The goal when rehydrating is to make the materials flexible enough to manipulate without waterlogging them. Each plant requires different soaking times and conditions, but generally, the thicker and woodier the material, the longer it will take to soak and the more it will benefit from heat. Chapters 3 to 7 detail soaking methods and times for specific types of materials and plant species, but the following outline gives the big picture. Use all the instructions in this book for rehydrating as a starting point and be prepared to adjust.

Note that leafy materials rehydrate best through a method called mellowing (see page 49) rather than submerging them in water. Mellowing allows them to absorb just enough water without becoming oversoaked.

Test and observe. After something has been soaking for a while, take it out of the water and evaluate its condition. Is it flexible? When you try to weave with it, does it crack? If it's inflexible, put it back in the water for another 10 minutes, then try again. Listen to what the material is telling you rather than getting too attached to how long you think it should take to get ready.

Rehydrate just enough. As you work, keep in mind that plants left in the water too long begin to break down and get mushy. Also, most plant materials degrade if they are rehydrated and dried out too many times, so aim to rehydrate only as much as you need for your current project.

Use hot water, if possible. Hot water speeds up the rehydrating process, but lukewarm or even cold water can work, especially for thinner materials. When using hot water, be careful not to cook the material; just put it in hot water in a pot and let it sit (or heat the water over low heat to steam). The only exceptions are vines and thicker sheets of bark, which may require a low simmer.

Store-Bought Materials

There are many store-bought natural materials that can be used for the projects in this book. In fact, there is a whole discipline of basketry dedicated to using processed natural materials that are widely available in basketry-supply stores. They may lack the character of wild foraged plants, but they are easy to obtain and are a good resource for those who are not able to forage or need to supplement their stash or practice their techniques.

Rattan. Reed and cane, both products from rattan plants, are the most widespread natural weaving materials available in stores. They come from a large group of spiny, vinelike, climbing palms native to Southeast Asia. Rattan is used for all manner of woven, twined, and ribbed baskets.

Raffia. This is a leaf fiber that comes from the leaves of the raffia palm, which is grown primarily for basketry in Madagascar. The tree keeps growing after the leaves are harvested, making this practice sustainable. Use raffia for cordage, coiling, and twining.

Other fibers and recycled materials. Jute, hemp, ramie (which is in the nettle family), and sisal are all natural fibers available online. Most of the projects in this book can also be completed with human-made and recycled materials, such as strips of fabric, paper, rope, plastic, or even wire.

Get creative! There is so much room for experimentation and upcycling.

Thinking Outside the Box

The natural world is filled with materials and objects that have interesting shapes, textures, and forms. These unconventional materials can be used creatively in baskets that are either utilitarian or artistic. Twisted driftwood or antlers can become the handle of a gathering basket. Intriguing roots or vines can become a random-weave sculpture. Seedpods, shells, and handmade beads can decorate the outside of coiled baskets. As an artist, I am constantly collecting from nature or gathering scraps from my studio to repurpose in wall hangings, in sculptures, or as embellishments on regular baskets.

Experiment with whatever you find that inspires you. Look at the qualities of what you gather. Is it flexible or stiff? Delicate or strong? Use the qualities you observe to experiment with the best ways to integrate it into a basket or sculptural piece. When approaching basketry from a sculptural, creative, and experimental viewpoint, the final products don't even have to resemble traditional baskets. They can be sinuous structures, or even take the form of a non-vessel object, such as a book or an animal. Some unconventional materials to try:

- Seashells
- Driftwood
- Twisted vines
- Acorns and other nuts
- Bark
- Antlers
- Clay
- Stones
- Roots
- Feathers
- Seedpods
- Bone
- Leather
- Wool and yarn
- Handmade paper
- Seaweed

When thinking experimentally, you also don't have to limit yourself to unconventional materials. Typical basketry materials can be used in sculptural forms with great success. Remember that there is no right or wrong. Just have fun!

CHAPTER 2

PLANT IDENTIFICATION

After learning to identify a few plants, you will never be able to drive down the road or go on a walk without noticing the bounty surrounding you. Where once you saw only a wall of green, suddenly the species you learned about will seem to appear everywhere. Not only is this empowering, but getting to know new plants is fun—like meeting a neighborhood friend. The journey starts with learning how to classify key features of the plants that you find so that you can assess whether they are candidates for basketmaking and eventually identify them. Whether or not you become passionate about plant identification or botany, even a little bit of knowledge will help immensely in the basketmaking process.

How to Start Seeing Plants

Starting to differentiate the plants within the "wall of green" outside doesn't have to be overwhelming. You can steadily acquire skill if you slow down, use your own senses in firsthand observation, learn to identify plants one at a time, and study some basic botany.

Pay attention. Practice looking at plants and describing what they look like. Ask yourself questions. For example, how do the leaves connect to the branches? What shape is the leaf? What is the texture of the leaf? What does the edge of the leaf look like? Are there flowers? What do they look like? (See Basic Botany for Wild Basketry on page 31 for some options of how you might describe these things.) Also, consider how a plant looks or behaves from a different perspective. For example, you might notice how a plant moves, smells, feels, and sounds when the wind passes over it. (Tasting it is not necessary for basketry.)

Sit with plants and observe them over time. Notice how they change through the seasons, when they flower, when they drop their leaves, what their seeds look like, and more. Sometimes identifying a plant is easiest when it is leafing, flowering, or fruiting, but that isn't necessarily the right time to harvest it for basketry. Therefore, it's important to note the location during that season and come back to visit during other times of year. Soon you'll be able to identify basketry plants throughout their growth cycle and especially at harvest time.

Walk with friends who are interested in plants. Ask them to tell you stories about a couple of plants they know well. Ask how they recognize these plants and what they mean to them. Most of us retain information more easily when we learn through positive experiences and storytelling rather than academic study.

Keep a journal. Record your observations. Write descriptions, draw, press leaves, take photos, whatever makes sense for you. Your journal doesn't have to be elaborate or even consistent, but everything you record there will help you grow as a basket maker. The exercises on pages 29–30 can help get you in the groove of the journal practice.

Refer to regional field guides and books. Keep them around and flip through them often. I find that field guides written specifically for your state or region will have the best and most comprehensive descriptions and photos, although there are some with larger scopes that are great, too. Alternatively, there are many plant videos and online archives to follow. See Resources on page 305 for suggestions. I would only use plant identification apps as a starting point since they are not always accurate, especially when plants don't have obvious distinguishing characteristics. They also encourage learners to get a quick answer, rather than developing their own ability to observe and deduce.

Research a plant's natural and cultural history. Once you know a plant's name, you can research its natural history—how it functions as a part of an ecosystem and in what kind of environments you will find it. Additionally, you can find out its cultural history—how people have interacted with and used it over time. Plants are an essential part of human culture, and many basketry plants are or have been used not only for weaving but also as medicine, food, building materials, and tools.

KEEP A FORAGING JOURNAL

Journaling is an incredibly valuable practice not only for identifying plants but also for taking foraging notes. I prefer to use one that is unlined so I can include drawings and paste in images, but any type that you like will work. Make an entry for every plant you forage, noting the date and characteristics of the plant and the experience. For example:

> **May 20, 2024.** Peeled bark from a 7-inch-diameter basswood tree. It wasn't easy, but I was able to get the bark off without tearing. Have noticed that it was much easier to peel from basswood in June last year. Basswood might have a later peeling season than other deciduous trees. Also noted that the leaves were very small. Perhaps leaf size is a better indicator of when the bark will be ready than the date. Pay attention to this next year!

journal exercises

These are some of the first assignments I give students in my wild basketry workshops. By the end of the year, students are amazed to look back and see where they started. The exercises are progressive and build upon each other.

Map Your Area

Begin looking at your surroundings with new eyes by making a basic map of your yard or a nearby natural location.

1. Walk around your area to get a sense of its layout or use a map app to see the shape of the area and draw a basic overhead view in your journal.

2. Note on the map where different kinds of plants or groups of plants are growing. The notes can be very simple. For example, "wet field with grasses" or "fence covered in vines."

3. Unless you want to, there is no need to identify species. The goal is just to see what *types* of plants are growing in your space.

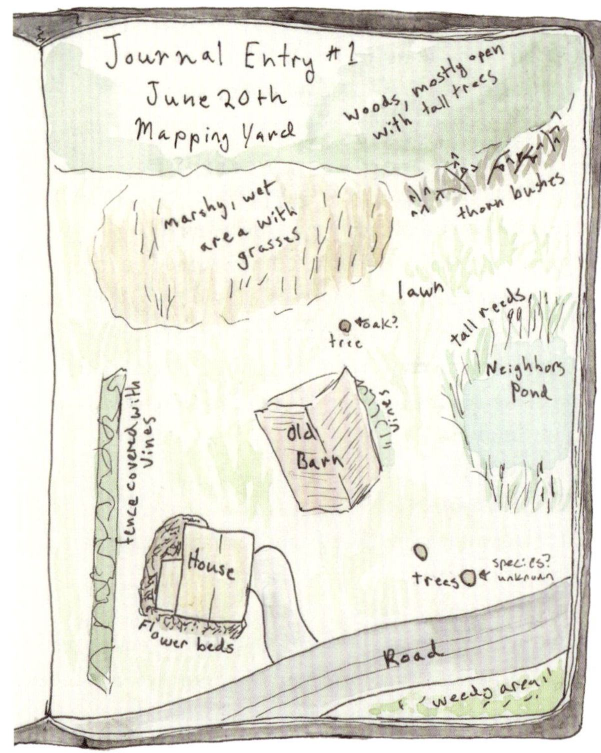

Using a map app for assistance with an aerial view, start with a sketch of a natural area.

Sit with a Plant

Next, practice awareness and observation while spending time with a particular plant. Make sure you have at least 30 minutes to sit with this exercise.

1. Pick one plant or type of plant from your map to focus on. It doesn't have to be a basketry plant, and it doesn't matter if you know what species it is.

2. Sit next to the plant. Don't get out your journal yet. Spend some undisturbed time observing the plant and getting curious. Look very closely at its form and observe the details. The following questions are just a few to get you started. What shape and texture are the leaves? Are they soft or hard? What is the exact texture of the bark or stem? How would you describe the color of the flowers? What are the tiniest details you can notice? Close your eyes. What does it smell like? How does it sound in the wind? Open your heart to simply observe and be with the plant.

3. After observing for at least 10 minutes, begin to record in your journal what you are observing and experiencing. This can look many ways. You might sketch, make notes, or write, even abstractly. You can create a poem or record your feelings. If you are not sure where to start, write down the characteristics you observed in the plant, make a quick sketch, and then go from there.

Dive Deeper

The next step is to identify and learn more about this plant.

1. If you aren't familiar with the plant species, get out some field guides, consult the internet, or—even better—reach out to a friend to help decipher what it is. Sometimes positively identifying a plant takes more than one method.

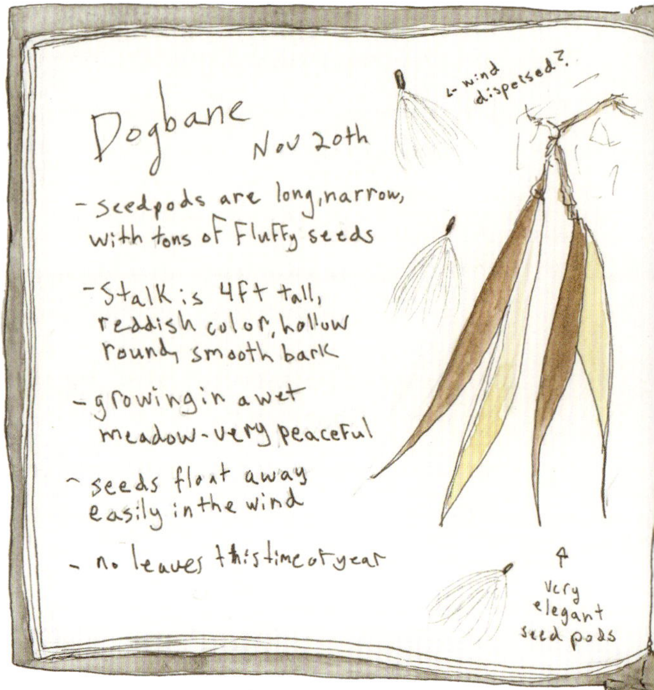

2. Spend some time researching the plant. What is the geographical range in which it grows? Is the plant native to the area or was it introduced? Does it have any uses, such as food, medicine, or even basketry? If it has been used for basketry, what types of baskets did it make, and what groups of people used it? Try to find someone you know who is familiar with it and ask them what they know or what they like about the plant. Stories are a great way to internalize knowledge.

3. Record what you learn in your journal. Write down at least a few things that you found particularly interesting or curious about the plant.

Repeat these exercises with many plants throughout your basketry journey! This is one way to begin to know individual plants and develop a relationship with the land.

Basic Botany for Wild Basketry

Learning some terminology for categorizing plants and describing their physical characteristics is very helpful for navigating field guides and other resources. Since botany is an enormous field of study, let's focus on what is most useful for basketry.

The place to start is noting where the plant is growing geographically (e.g., town, state) and in what ecosystem (e.g., marsh, grassland, forest). The location helps you find the appropriate field guide or online resource to consult.

Conifer (white pine)

forms of growth

The growth form of a plant determines what kind of baskets you can make with it and which field guide will provide the most support with identification.

Trees

Trees are woody plants that usually have a single trunk and are more than 15 feet tall at maturity. There is overlap between trees and shrubs, and sometimes a species can grow as either. There are two main types: deciduous trees, which lose their leaves in winter, and conifers, which keep their leaves—known as needles—all year round. The primary tree part used for basketry is the bark, which is generally woven and folded for bark baskets. Some other parts useful in basketmaking are roots, needles from pine trees, and water sprouts, which are shoots that grow from the trunk or branch of a tree.

Deciduous tree (basswood)

Shrubs

Shrubs are woody plants that are typically smaller than a tree and have multiple stems coming out of the roots. The stems are usually smaller than 3 to 4 inches in diameter. The bark is excellent for weaving, twining, and cordage, and the first-year stems of some species—such as willow or red osier dogwood—are perfect for wickerwork.

BASIC PARTS OF A PLANT

Vines

A vine has long stems that trail along the ground or climb another structure for support. The stems can either be woody, like grapevines, or soft, like bindweed. Vines of all types have many applications in many types of basketry.

Herbaceous Plants

These plants generally have soft, flexible stems instead of woody stems. The pliability makes them suitable for coiling, twining, and cordage, but some are good for braiding, diagonal plaiting, and weaving as well. Most of the ones used for basketry are perennials that grow back year after year, but a few—particularly some grasses—are annuals, lasting only one season. This is a very large category with many different groups, but here are a few ones that are notable for basketry.

Grasses. An annual or perennial plant that has narrow leaves; very narrow, slightly stiff hollow stems; and flowers that are tiny, green, and inconspicuous. They often grow in clumps or spread out over fields. I use them most for coiling, although they could be used in cordage and twining as well.

Bast fiber stalks. Not an official botanical designation, I use this term for a group of unrelated perennial herbaceous plants that happen to have bast—or inner bark fibers—that are particularly strong and run the entire length of their stalks. You can process these fibers for cordage, twining, or weaving. The most common North American species are milkweed, nettle, and dogbane.

Rushes. Rushes have slender, straight, flexible, soft, unbranched round stems and are found in wet habitats. They often look like a clump of green straws sticking out of the water. Leaves are typically small and clustered at the base of the plant. *Juncus* is the largest genus in this group and contains the plants used for basketry, which offer excellent materials for twining, coiling, braiding, and weaving.

arrangement of branch, leaf, and bud

The next aspect to look at in identifying plants is how the buds—and therefore the leaves that emerge from them in spring—are arranged on a plant's twigs, branches, and stems. There are only a few options, but look very closely. Sometimes from a distance they look alike. As the twigs and branches of a tree develop, they will have this same arrangement.

Alternate

Leaves and buds are alternately arranged so that their placement zigzags up the stem.

LEAF ARRANGEMENTS

Opposite

Leaves and buds are directly opposite one another.

Whorled

Leaves and buds emerge from points all around the circumference of one point on a stem.

leaf characteristics

Leaves are one of the most obvious parts of the plant we look at for identification. Even though some basketry plants are harvested in winter when there are no leaves, you can identify the plants when the leaves are present and make a mental note to return when they are dormant. The illustrations that follow show a selective list of characteristics.

PARTS OF A LEAF

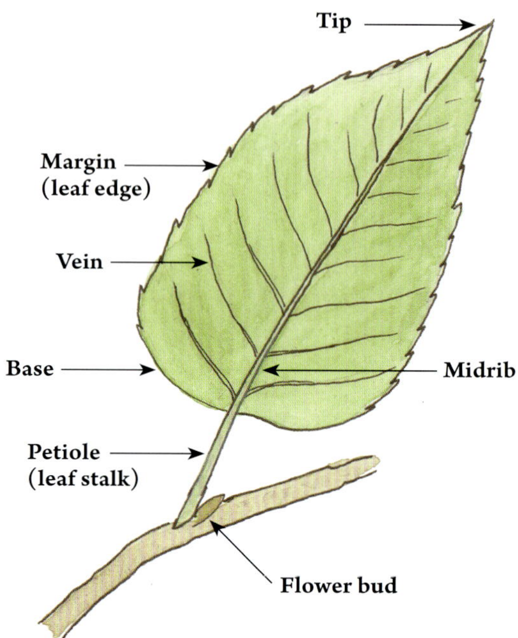

LEAF SHAPES

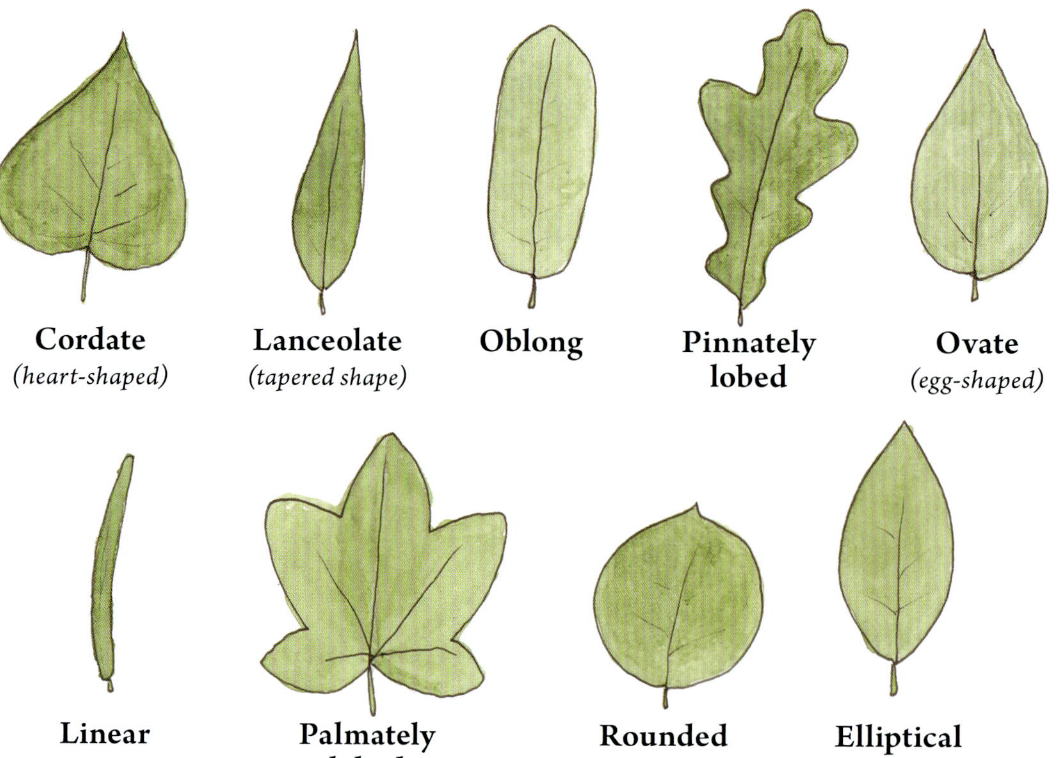

LEAF TYPES

Simple

The leaf has only one part.

Compound

The leaf consists of a central midrib with many leaflets coming out of a bud. There are three basic varieties.

Pinnate

(once compound)

UNDERSTANDING COMPOUND LEAVES

A leaf comes out of a bud. Realizing this helped me understand compound leaves, which at first seem like a bunch of simple leaves on a stem! Actually, the entire leaf came out of one single bud, and what appear to be regular leaves all along the midrib are actually called leaflets.

Bi-pinnate

(twice compound)

Palmate

LEAF EDGES (MARGINS)

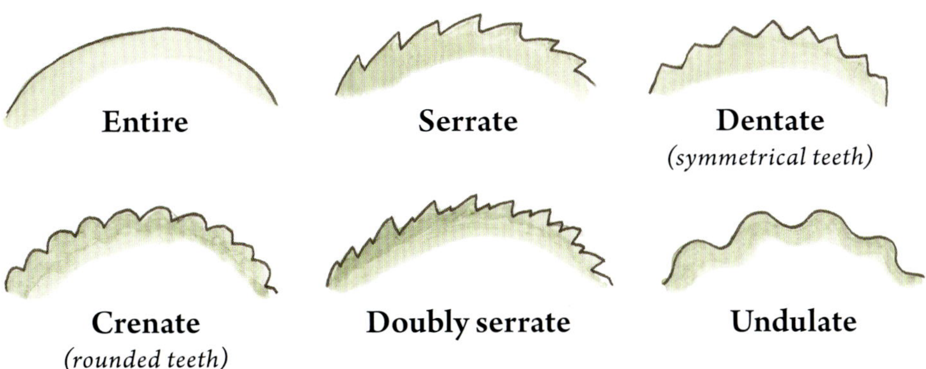

Entire

Serrate

Dentate

(symmetrical teeth)

Crenate

(rounded teeth)

Doubly serrate

Undulate

flower characteristics

There is a huge variety of flower types, shapes, arrangements of flowers on the stem, and arrangements of petals within the flower. When identifying basketry plants that are in flower, note the color and general shape and then refer to field guides for that type of plant. Below are a few common types you may encounter.

other characteristics

There are many other characteristics that can be helpful for identifying plants, including fruits, nuts, seeds, and bark. The bark is important for identifying trees and shrubs during winter, and, yes, there are dedicated field guides just for bark! When observing a new plant, take plenty of notes and photos or make drawings so you can reference a field guide later.

FLOWER SHAPES AND ARRANGEMENTS

Catkin
Elongated cluster of flowers, forming a downy, pendulous spike

Capitulum
Dense flat cluster of small flowers

Raceme
Cluster of separate flowers attached to the stem by short equal stalks at equal distances

Panicle
Loose branching cluster of flowers

Corymb
Flower cluster whose lower stalks are proportionally longer so the head is flat or convex

Umbel
Flower cluster whose stalks are equal in length and spring from a common center

Invasive Plants

Many excellent basketry plants are considered invasive, meaning they are not native to the country, state, or ecosystem in which they are growing, and they spread so zealously that they displace native plants in the process. Removing invasives can be a win-win for the basket maker and the environment. Visit your state's department of environmental protection website to find a list of invasive species in your area and consult regional field guides and online resources for identification.

Take great care not to spread the seeds. Either cut the plant before it goes to seed or remove the seeds judiciously and dispose of them in a tightly tied garbage bag. Beware that some invasive grasses, such as Japanese stiltgrass, have thousands of tiny seeds tangled in their roots and these seeds remain viable for years, which means new grass is likely to grow wherever you take them. I would only make a basket from this type of plant if I intended to keep it on-site.

Dry the plants thoroughly. When foraging for invasive vines, including kudzu or wisteria, bring them inside to dry out. Pieces you leave behind easily root in place.

Do not grow your own. Find a place where they are already growing and ask for permission to pick. If you must plant them, do so only in pots—never directly in the earth. I know it is tempting to start your own wisteria patch, intending to keep it under control, but the reality is that you won't always be there to tend to it. Safeguard the ecosystem for future generations!

Treat invasives with kindness and respect even as you remove them. Remember: They are simply taking advantage of the opportunity to do what all plants do—grow, reproduce, and thrive—often in the disturbed ecosystems that are a by-product of human interventions.

COMMON INVASIVE PLANTS FOR BASKETMAKING

The following plants are considered invasive in much of the United States. For specific information about your location, consult your state's department of natural resources, the names of which vary. In New York, where I live, I consult the Department of Environmental Conservation (DEC).

- Akebia (*Akebia quinata*)
- Bittersweet (*Celastrus orbiculatus*)
- English ivy (*Hedera helix*)
- Himalayan blackberry (*Rubus armeniacus*)
- Japanese honeysuckle (*Lonicera japonica*)
- Japanese stiltgrass (*Microstegium vimineum*)
- Japanese wisteria (*Wisteria floribunda*)
- Kudzu (*Pueraria montana*)
- Mimosa tree (*Albizia julibrissin*)
- Multiflora rose (*Rosa multiflora*)
- Phragmites (*Phragmites* species)
- Porcelain berry (*Ampelopsis brevipedunculata*)
- Privet (*Ligustrum* species)
- Rose of Sharon (*Hibiscus syriacus*)
- Yellow flag iris (*Iris pseudacorus*)
- Any type of long invasive grass (consult a field guide to identify exact species)

Planting a Basketry Garden

One way to positively identify a plant is to grow it yourself! You may even have some basketry materials growing on your property already. When choosing plants, be sure to consider the USDA Plant Hardiness Zone Map—a guideline for determining which perennial plants are most likely to thrive in a particular location. Here are some of my favorites for cultivation.

- Akebia (*Akebia quinata*; in pots only, to prevent spread)
- Crocosmia (*Crocosmia* species)
- Daffodils (*Narcissus* species)
- Daylilies (*Hemerocallis* species; varieties with long leaves)
- Grapevine (*Vitis* species)
- Little bluestem grass (*Schizachyrium scoparium*)
- Northern sweetgrass (*Anthoxanthum nitens*)
- Red hot poker (*Kniphofia uvaria*)
- Red osier dogwood (*Cornus sericea*; also known as red twig dogwood)
- Shrub willow (*Salix* species)
- Siberian iris (*Iris siberica*)
- Soft rush (*Juncus effusus*)
- Southern sweetgrass (*Muhlenbergia sericea*)
- Yucca (*Yucca* species)
- Zebra grass and other ornamental grasses (without serrated edges)

Hazardous Plants

Becoming familiar with the hazardous plants in your region as you begin foraging is important. Get a field guide, research online, or ask around. The most common in my area is poison ivy (*Toxicodendron radicans*).

"Leaves of three, let it be" is the common mantra regarding poison ivy, which grows as a vine or a small shrub and is often found alongside other desirable vines, such as Virginia creeper and grapevine. If you see any sign of poison ivy, don't harvest in that area. Even if you are not particularly allergic, repeated exposures will increase your sensitivity, and it's not worth it. I have yet to see someone make a basket out of poison ivy, either on purpose or by accident, and let's keep it that way!

Poison ivy has compound leaves consisting of three leaflets borne alternately on the vine with the middle leaflet having a longer petiole. They vary in shades of green and have irregular, large, jagged teeth. Sometimes there is just one tooth on the outside, resembling a thumb on a mitten. The petioles at the center of the leaflets are often reddish. When just emerging, the tiny leaves are typically red and shiny. Older vines are covered in fine hairs. In fall the vines bear white berries, which birds love.

Poison ivy

EXCEPTIONS TO THE RULE

Not all plants with three leaves are poison ivy, and some are great for basketmaking. By familiarizing yourself with a few key field marks, it is not difficult to tell them apart.

- **Clematis:** Leaves are opposite.
- **Strawberry vine:** Leaves have evenly serrated edges.
- **Brambles:** Stems have thorns, and leaves have serrated edges.
- **Virginia creeper:** Vines have thick tendril-like hairs and blue berries, and leaflets are borne directly from the vine with no long petiole. Though there are typically five leaflets, some may have three, especially when they're young.

CHAPTER 3

LEAVES, GRASSES, AND SOFT STEMS

These plants are my favorites to recommend to new basket makers because of their abundance and accessibility. You can make a basket from anything that is somewhat soft, flexible, long, and strong—from dandelion flower stems and daffodil leaves to grasses growing in an abandoned lot. The options are everywhere! This group is particularly easy to forage, process, and rehydrate for baskets. All it requires is a pair of scissors, and even a small bundle of material is useful.

PROJECTS THAT USE LEAVES AND GRASSES

Cordage (page 128)

Multistrand Braiding (page 132)

Coiled Bowl (page 145)

Twined Treasure Basket (page 173)

Diagonal-Plaited Cattail Basket (page 213)

HARVEST SEASON

Leaves and grasses: Late summer and early fall

Soft stems: Spring–late summer

The Plants

All the plants I've included in this book are what I consider basketry superstars. I've chosen them because they have some combination of a large geographic range, varied uses, or unique characteristics, or I have a particular love for them! I have tried to include those that grow in many different locations, although there is a bias toward North America, specifically the Northeast.

Cattail

Typha species

All cattail species are excellent for making baskets. In some places they behave invasively, and in others they're a critical component of a healthy ecosystem. If the plants are thriving or even aggressively covering an area, I'll harvest more; if there are only a few, I might harvest little to none.

- **Parts used:** Leaves.
- **Uses:** Cordage; multistrand braiding; core in coiled baskets; twined baskets; woven baskets; diagonal plaiting; twisted as weavers in ribbed baskets.
- **Qualities:** Long leaves; abundant; large range; many uses.
- **Range:** Worldwide in appropriate habitat.
- **Habitat:** Marshes; lakesides; ponds; some estuaries; other wet areas.
- **Identification features:** Long, linear leaves with smooth edges; female flower in summer is brown and resembles a hot dog on a stick; fluffy seedhead in winter is distinctive above dried dead leaves.
- **Harvest:** Harvest at the end of summer just when the tips of the leaves are beginning to turn brown, earlier than most other leafy plants. Avoid stands where invasive plants are encroaching. (Common reed, for example, will outcompete cattail.) Either cut only a few leaves per shoot or 1 entire shoot out of every 15 or 20 and don't cut flowering stems. Change this ratio depending on the health of the patch and whether it is invasive in your area. Only harvest plants without a seedhead on them.
- **Preparation:** Cattail leaves take 7 days or more to dry and are prone to molding, so turn them often. Use the mellowing method (page 49) to rehydrate. They are prone to kinking and oversoaking otherwise. Cattail leaves tend to be brittle when dry—the recommended uses require layering, twisting, or compressing the leaves, which helps mitigate their weakness.

Narrowleaf cattail

Iris

Iris species

Siberian iris (*Iris sibirica*) is my favorite iris to use for its narrow, strong, linear, long leaves. The invasive yellow flag iris (*I. pseudacorus*) is a close second.

Siberian iris

Any type of iris can be used, but bearded iris (*I.* × *germanica*), a common garden plant, has rather short leaves that do not split easily.

- **Parts used:** Leaves.
- **Uses:** As cordage; multistrand braiding; core in coiled baskets; sewing strands in closed coiled baskets; twining strands in twined baskets; stakes in miniature twined baskets; twisted as weavers in ribbed baskets.
- **Qualities:** Long; very flexible; strong.
- **Range:** Siberian iris is commonly cultivated as a garden and landscaping plant in the United States, but is native from Europe to Central Asia; yellow flag iris is invasive in the United States and native to Europe and the Middle East.
- **Habitat:** Siberian iris is cultivated, and yellow flag iris grows in wetlands.
- **Identification features:** Siberian iris has clumps of leaves up to 18 inches tall with 2-inch-wide blue flowers. Yellow flag iris has flat, swordlike leaves up to 3 feet tall and large, showy yellow flowers.
- **Harvest:** Cut at the base at the beginning of fall; harvesting all the leaves is okay, but let a patch rest every couple of years.
- **Preparation:** Follow general guidelines for preparing leaves and grasses.

Ornamental Grasses

Many species of ornamental grass are planted commonly in landscaping and cut down every fall. What a great resource! There are hundreds, but a few of my favorites are listed here.

- **Parts used:** Leaves, flower stalks.
- **Uses:** Leafy grasses can be split and twisted into cordage; core in coiled baskets; twining strands. Stiffer varieties are best as core in coiled baskets.
- **Qualities:** Long; varied colors and varieties; abundant.
- **Harvest:** Cut any amount of the plant at the base during early to late fall. I find these grasses persist later in the season than other leafy plants. Before harvesting, feel the edge of the leaf—some have serrated edges that can be irritating to work with, and drying and resoaking only helps a little.
- **Preparation:** Follow general guidelines for preparing leaves and grasses.

FAVORITE BASKETRY SPECIES

- Zebra grass (*Miscanthus* species): Very common and one of my favorites.
- New Zealand flax (*Phormium tenax*): Flat leaves that are great for many applications.
- Fountain grass (*Pennisetum alopecuroides*): Tons of variety and very pretty.
- Little bluestem (*Schizachyrium scoparium*): Native species growing both wild and in cultivation throughout almost the entire United States except the West Coast (see photo on page 48).
- Muhly grass (*Muhlenbergia capillaris* and other species): Native species with beautiful colors. Note that southern sweetgrass—ubiquitous in the Gullah basket tradition of South Carolina—is *M. filipes*, and it is threatened or endangered in many locations. *M. rigens* is known as deergrass and is used by California Indigenous groups.

Zebra grass

Palms

Arecaceae family

There are an incredible 2,500 species of palm in the world! I imagine most species can be used for basketry, but some well-known ones are definite candidates: coconut palm (*Cocos nucifera*), cabbage palm (*Sabal palmetto*), and saw palmetto (*Serenoa repens*).

- **Parts used:** Leaflets from fronds on small to large trees—either from huge pinnately compound leaves (fronds) in some species or fan-shaped palmate leaves in other species.
- **Uses:** Multistrand braiding; core in coiled baskets; woven baskets; diagonal plaiting.
- **Qualities:** Leaflets are shiny and fast to work with; abundant in some locations; not all are particularly long.
- **Range:** Tropical regions of the United States and worldwide.
- **Habitat:** Lowlands to higher elevation.
- **Harvest:** Available any time of year. Young plants, especially palmettos, are low to the ground and easiest to access. Look for fronds that have already fallen (both green and brown can be used, although green is stronger) or remove one frond per plant by cutting with a handsaw or pruning shears. Some palms have spiky trunks, so take care when harvesting or avoid harvesting from these types.
- **Preparation:** Remove individual leaflets from the frond. Use fresh for quick baskets or dry and rehydrate.

Coconut palm

Soft Rush

Juncus effusus

This unassuming plant has a very wide range and interesting uses in many cultures, including tatami mats in Japan and rope in Great Britain.

- **Parts used:** Soft, strawlike stems.
- **Uses:** Fibers can be extracted for cordage. Stems used whole in multistrand braiding; core in coiled baskets; twined baskets; twisted as weavers in ribbed baskets.
- **Qualities:** Thin; flexible; relatively strong; a bit short.
- **Range:** Native in temperate northern hemisphere; also parts of South America, Africa, India, and southern Asia.
- **Habitat:** Wetlands; riverbanks; marshes; fields.
- **Identification features:** Upright clumps 12–36 inches high; thin, smooth, squishy stems that are round in cross section. Flowers are inconspicuous brown clusters emerging from the side of the stem near the top.

Soft rush

- **Harvest:** Cut at the base with scissors; only take a small portion of what is present.
- **Preparation:** Use the mellowing method (page 49) to rehydrate. To extract fibers for cordage, pound the freshly harvested stems with a wooden mallet until flattened and coming apart. Then scrape or comb out the piths and let the fiber bundles dry.

Softstem Bulrush

(Also known as rush or tule)

Schoenoplectus tabernaemontani

This is one of the strongest yet most supple basketry materials out there. Bulrush, or rush, is a complicated category because the name refers to a variety of different marshland plants depending on the location. Plants in the sedge family (Cyperaceae), the rush relatives (*Juncus* species), and the bulrush, or cattail, family (Typhaceae) are all referred to at times as rushes, and many are good for basketmaking. Softstem bulrush is most common in the United States. Hardstem rush (*Schoenoplectus acutus*) and common club rush (*S. lacustris*) are used the same way.

- **Parts used:** Soft stems.
- **Uses:** As cordage; multistrand braiding; core in coiled baskets; twined baskets; stakes and weavers in woven baskets; twisted as weavers in ribbed baskets.
- **Qualities:** Flexible; strong, supple; many uses.
- **Range:** Worldwide in appropriate temperate habitat; some parts of South America, Africa, and Australia.

Softstem bulrush

- **Habitat:** Slow-moving streams; lakes; marshes.
- **Identification features:** Looks like giant green drinking straws sticking up out of the water; 3–6 (up to 9) feet high; soft; tubular; thickness varies, but in my area it is no more than ½ inch.
- **Harvest:** Cut at the base with scissors; only take a small portion of what is present.
- **Preparation:** Can break easily when dry, so be careful to store properly. Use the mellowing method (page 49) to rehydrate.

OTHER LEAVES, GRASSES, AND SOFT STEMS FOR BASKETRY

- Common reed (*Phragmites australis*)
- Daylily (*Hemerocallis* species)
- Daffodil flower stems (*Narcissus* species)
- Longleaf pine needles (*Pinus palustris*)
- Crocosmia (*Crocosmia* species)
- Red hot poker (*Kniphofia uvaria*)
- Northern sweetgrass (*Hierochloe odorata*, syn. *Anthoxanthum nitens*)
- Dandelion stem (*Taraxacum officinale*)
- Lavender (*Lavandula angustifolia*)
- Maidenhair fern stems (*Adiantum pedatum*)
- Wheat (*Triticum* species)
- Rye (*Secale cereale*)
- American beachgrass (*Ammophila breviligulata*)
- Corn leaves and husks (*Zea mays*)

1. *Diagonal-plaited basket with cattails*
2. *Twined basket from iris, daffodil flower stems, and corn husks*
3. *Multistrand braid from cattails*
4. *Multistrand braid from soft rush*
5. *Coiled tray from wild and cultivated grasses*
6. *Iris cordage*

How to Forage Leaves, Grasses, and Soft Stems

Late summer through fall is the season for foraging leaves, grasses, and soft stems, since the plants have mostly finished growing for the year but have not yet begun to decompose. The perfect moment is right before the material starts to turn yellow and die back. Some species, such as cattails, begin to die back in late August, and others, such as many field grasses and ornamental grasses, are still going strong into October. While it is possible to use leaves and grasses that have turned brown, they will be weaker. The only exception to this timing is with the soft flower stalks of plants such as daffodils and dandelions. These should be cut after the plant has flowered in spring or summer.

To harvest you need a pair of pruning shears or scissors with long blades. Take a bunch of leaves in your hand and cut them approximately 1 inch from the ground. Be sure to keep all the cut ends aligned while gathering bunches of materials. Being organized and neat helps later with drying and storing. When foraging a leaf from a palm or similar plant that doesn't die back each year, cut one single frond from a tree and then remove the leaflets individually.

Remember to harvest ethically, with the health of the plant in mind. Many of these plants are perennials, with underground systems of rhizomes and roots that live year to year. Cutting foliage at the end of the season right before the plant dies back won't negatively affect them outright, but if you are harvesting the whole plant in the same spot every year, the plant could still become weaker over time. Let the plant rest every couple of years or harvest different areas of a patch.

Cut leaves at the base, approximately 1 inch from the ground.

Keep cut ends neatly aligned for ease in drying and storing.

Remove individual leaflets from a palm frond.

How to Prepare Leaves, Grasses, and Soft Stems for Basketmaking

Review the basic guidelines for drying, storing, and rehydrating plant materials on pages 21–24. To dry, keep the material organized with the cut ends facing the same direction. In good drying conditions, this type of material takes anywhere from 3 to 9 days to dry completely, depending on the environment.

Once dry, these materials are pretty forgiving about how you store them and are not terribly prone to mold unless they're kept in a damp environment. Loosely tie bundles at both ends to keep them organized. You can stand them upright in a cardboard box or a brown paper bag, stack them on shelves, or hang them from the ceiling.

The process for rehydrating depends on the plant you've harvested, though I recommend the mellowing method with most leaves, grasses, and soft stems. Start with the guidelines that follow and adjust as needed.

Thin leaves. (Examples: iris, daylily, corn husks, sweetgrass.) Mellow by running under warm water and wrapping in a warm, damp towel then a plastic sheet

The leaves, grasses, and soft stems shown below are (1) cattails; (2) lavender; (3) softstem bulrush; (4) little bluestem; (5) Siberian iris; (6) corn husks; and (7) daffodil flower stems.

until flexible—anywhere from 1 hour to overnight, though corn husks need as little as a few minutes. Alternatively, submerge in hot water for 1 to 3 minutes.

Thick leaves. (Example: cattails.) Mellow by pouring water over them and wrapping them in a damp towel then a plastic sheet until flexible. If you're using very hot water, they can be ready in as little as an hour. For cold water, leave overnight.

Stiff grasses. (Examples: little bluestem, rye straw, field grasses.) Mellow by pouring very hot water over the grasses and wrapping them, loosely spaced, in a warm, damp towel then a plastic sheet overnight. If they are still not flexible, apply hot water again. As an alternative to mellowing, place the grasses in a plastic bin and submerge in hot water. Let sit until they become flexible—anywhere from 30 minutes to a few hours.

Pine needles. Submerge in a pot of steaming water for 10 to 15 minutes or put in a baking dish and pour steaming water over them, then let sit for 10 to 20 minutes.

basic mellowing method for rehydration

Mellowing is my preferred method for rehydrating leaves, grasses, and soft stems as it allows them to evenly soak up just enough water to become flexible without becoming waterlogged. A bonus to the method is that it uses minimal water. Following is a basic method, but many variations are possible, depending on your materials and preferences. See the more finely tuned guidelines above for specific material types.

1. Get a towel wet and then wring it out. Lay a shower curtain or a piece of plastic on the ground with the damp towel on top.

2. Place the plant materials on the towel. Pour water over the materials until they are thoroughly wet. The water temperature can be very hot or cold, depending on how fast you want them to be ready and the qualities of the materials.

3. Roll the plastic up and hold it vertically to let excess water drain. Then let the materials sit.

4. If you're using hot water, check the bundle in 30 minutes to see if the materials are flexible. If not, leave them longer and keep checking back every 30 minutes or so until they're ready. If you're using cold water, they will likely take longer and can even be left overnight.

5. While making your basket, pull materials out as needed and leave the rest wrapped up so they don't dry out. Keep in a shady, cool place, where they will remain viable for up to 2 days. In hot, sunny weather they will quickly start to decompose and smell bad, making them unusable.

CHAPTER 4

VINES

All plants love to thrive, but especially vines, which tend to grow vigorously. Vines often engulf fences, trees, and even houses—an abundance that makes them a great resource for basket makers. Many of the most common vines in the United States are invasive species, and by foraging them, you allow native trees and shrubs a better chance of survival. There is something very rewarding about freeing a trapped tree from a tangle of vines and then giving the vines a new life by making a gorgeous basket.

PROJECTS THAT USE VINES

Two-Hoop Harvest Basket (page 259)

Tension Tray (page 271)

Grapevine Market Basket (page 279)

Random-Weave Bowl (page 285)

HARVEST SEASON

Late fall–winter

The Plants

I absolutely love learning about both the natural and cultural history of plants and discovering which ones grow around my home. When I travel, field guides are the first things that go in my suitcase, but having this level of excitement about plants is not a prerequisite for wild basketry. All you need is some curiosity about what is growing around you and a willingness to experiment. Vines are a great place to start with foraging due to their abundance in many locations. Invasive vines also have intriguing natural histories in both their native lands and those they have spread to.

Akebia

(Also known as chocolate vine)
Akebia quinata
Akebia's superpower is its small diameter and flexibility. Use it when you need a vine to get into small spaces or for fine work. The vine is planted in landscapes for its interesting fruit and brown flower, but it is very invasive and completely takes over. Do not plant akebia in the ground, though anyone who has woven with it will need to fight that urge.

- **Parts used:** Vines, particularly ground runners.
- **Uses:** Core in coiled baskets; twining strands; weavers and lashing in ribbed baskets; random weave.
- **Qualities:** Thin; strong; flexible; very long.
- **Range:** Invasive in eastern to midwestern North America; native to China and Japan.
- **Habitat:** Gardens; woodlands; open areas; edge areas.
- **Identification features:** Vine both climbs and has ground runners; stays green in winter in warmer climates; palmately compound leaf with five leaflets; total leaf is 3–5 inches wide; thin vines; covers invaded areas in a mat of vegetation.
- **Harvest:** Late fall to winter is best, but any time is technically possible. Focus on harvesting ground runners, which are long and straight. Climbing vines, which wind around whatever they are climbing, are time-consuming to harvest and are often shorter and twisted.
- **Preparation:** Submerge in steaming water for 15–30 minutes. Soak longer if you want to remove the outer bark and use the whitish inner vine.

Akebia

Bittersweet

Celastrus orbiculatus
Freeing a tree that is being strangled by Asian bittersweet and using the material for a beautiful basket is a great way to reduce the impact of invasive species. Be careful not to spread the berries when harvesting! There is also a native species, American bittersweet (*Celastrus scandens*), which doesn't grow aggressively. Its berries are borne at the tips of the vines and are orange instead of red.

- **Parts used:** Vines, particularly climbing vines.
- **Uses:** Hoops and ribs in ribbed baskets; random weave; weavers in tension trays; weavers in wickerwork baskets.

Bittersweet

- **Qualities:** Sturdy, but tends to crack easily when bent at sharp angles; best diameter for use is ⅜–¾ inch, since thinner vines crack more; abundant and common.
- **Range:** Invasive in eastern to midwestern North America and parts of Europe; native to eastern Russia, eastern China, and Japan.
- **Habitat:** Wood edges; fields; yards; forests; disturbed areas.
- **Identification features:** Large vines twisting around other vegetation; sharp bud scars along its length; younger vines tend to be darker gray with whitish raised pores that stand out; older vines tend to be light gray with darker pores that stand out; leaves vary a lot in shape from roundish to ovate with serrated edges; distinctive bright red berry clusters surrounded by yellow capsules.
- **Harvest:** Look for places where established patches have long lengths of vine climbing into trees and shrubs. Young bittersweet patches on the ground tend to be mostly leaves and have very short vines.
- **Preparation:** The vine shrinks when used fresh but takes up a lot of space in storage, so I often use it fresh and then weave in more vines later to tighten up the basket. If you do dry the vines, submerge the coils in simmering water for 1–3 hours to rehydrate. Drying and rehydrating makes it much more flexible.

Japanese Honeysuckle

Lonicera japonica

This species is a vine and is completely different from the several honeysuckle shrub species that are commonly found in similar environments. I love the smooth, light color of peeled honeysuckle vines and use them often.

- **Parts used:** Ground runners and climbing vines.
- **Uses:** Thin vines in coiled baskets; twining strands in twined baskets; weavers in ribbed baskets; random weave. Thicker vines (¼–½ inch) as hoops in ribbed baskets; random weave; weavers in wickerwork.
- **Qualities:** Long lengths; beautiful, shiny, whitish color on peeled vines; can be brittle and crack at sharp angles if not prepared properly.
- **Range:** Invasive from eastern to midwestern North America; native to China and eastern Asia.
- **Habitat:** Open woodlands; wood edges.
- **Identification features:** Thin (ground runners are ⅛ inch in diameter or less); young vines have reddish, sometimes hairy outer bark that comes off in shredded plates revealing a whitish vine beneath; older climbing vines have tighter, wheat-colored bark that doesn't flake off as much; leaves are opposite, simple, oval, and 1–3 inches long.
- **Harvest:** I prefer ground runners for their length and straightness. Look for straight climbing vines.
- **Preparation:** Honeysuckle is a bit brittle and requires a longer soaking time than other thin vines: 45 minutes to 2 hours in steaming to lightly simmering water. To remove the bark (either right after harvest or after drying and rehydrating), submerge the vine coil in steaming or lightly simmering water. Remove a coil to check after 45 minutes and let cool. Pull the vine over a piece of towel to strip off the bark. If it doesn't slough off easily, put it back to soak longer. If you want the bark to stay on, try soaking for as little time as possible while still achieving flexibility.

Japanese honeysuckle

Grapevine

Vitis species

This is one of the most abundant vines in my area. Porcelain berry (*Ampelopsis brevipedunculata*) is a very similar non-native look-alike to grapevine that can be used in the same way.

- **Parts used:** Climbing vines.
- **Uses:** All parts of tension trays; hoops and ribs in ribbed baskets; random-weave baskets; wickerwork.
- **Qualities:** Sturdy; abundant; cracks when bent at sharp angles.
- **Range:** Temperate northern hemisphere to tropical mountains.
- **Habitat:** Forests; fields; wood edges.
- **Identification features:** Woody climbing vine; brown bark that flakes off in plates; in some species or in poor growing conditions, bark adheres more tightly to the vine and is grayish brown; distinct curly, woody tendrils for climbing; bluish purple grapes in clusters; palmate leaves with lobes that vary in size and shape.
- **Harvest:** Look for places where established patches have long lengths of the vine climbing into trees and over shrubs. Some ground runners can get quite long, too. Be cautious about pulling large vines that are climbing high into trees, which could cause dead treetops or branches to come crashing down. Grapevines can be susceptible to insect infestations (see page 60). Look for the characteristics of a strong, healthy, flexible vine: bark exfoliating in long plates, reddish bark with greenish wood underneath, thick climbing tendrils, and species with large ½-inch grapes. Avoid vines with tight, shredding, plain brown bark that is difficult to peel off; insect damage; the presence of mold or lichen; weak and frail tendrils; and species with small grapes less than ½ inch in diameter.
- **Preparation:** Can be woven fresh with minimal shrinkage or dried and stored. To rehydrate, simmer in hot water for 1–3 hours to attain maximum flexibility. Out of all the basketry materials I work with, grapevine is the only one I will simmer at length, as it can stand up to the heat well.

Grapevine

Kudzu

Pueraria montana

This is one of the most invasive vines in the United States, particularly in the South. Luckily, it is an excellent basketry plant!

- **Parts used:** Ground runners; some climbing vines.
- **Uses:** Ground runners split in half as twining strands in twined baskets; woven baskets; lashing and weavers in ribbed baskets; random weave. Thicker climbing vines as hoops in ribbed baskets and tension trays. Bark retted into fiber for cordage; twining; weaving; sewing material.
- **Qualities:** Abundant; very flexible; incredibly long (can be more than 50 feet); molds easily if it gets damp; not the most durable.
- **Range:** Invasive in eastern North America; native to Asia.

Kudzu

- **Habitat:** Woods; wood edges; fields; roadsides.
- **Identification features:** Can completely cover trees, shrubs, and even buildings with layers of vines and foliage; alternate compound leaves with three leaflets; look for expansive mats of light brown, dead leaves in winter.
- **Harvest:** Concentrate on ground runners. Forage only in areas that you are sure have not been sprayed with herbicides. Forage in fall, winter, or early spring, before everything around it starts growing, as it's hard to extract and strip the leaves off in summer. To peel bark for fiber, harvest in summer.
- **Preparation:** Split in half lengthwise right after harvesting before it dries—ideally within a few days to a week. It kinks and does not weave nicely when used as a whole piece. After splitting, coil the two halves together so you have matching pieces. Store in a cool, dry place as it molds easily. To rehydrate, soak in hot tap water. Kudzu doesn't like to be cooked and will turn to a strange jelly if the water is too hot or it soaks for too long. After 10–15 minutes of soaking in hot water, check to see if it is flexible. If not, put it back and check on it every few minutes.

Virginia Creeper

Parthenocissus quinquefolia

This native species is common, so I like to use it even though it isn't the most durable or flexible.

- **Parts used:** Ground runners; climbing vines.
- **Uses:** Tension trays; weavers in ribbed baskets; random weave; weavers in wickerwork baskets.
- **Qualities:** Somewhat flexible; long; commonly available.
- **Range:** Eastern and midwestern North America, south to Central America; invasive in other parts of the world.
- **Habitat:** Woodlands; edge areas; open areas.
- **Identification features:** Palmately compound leaves with five leaflets; toothed margins; leaves turn red in fall; small, dark blue berries are in clusters.
- **Harvest:** The vine and young leaves bear some resemblance to poison ivy. See page 39 for how to tell the difference.
- **Preparation:** I prefer to use fresh, but it can be dried and rehydrated.

Virginia creeper

Wisteria

Wisteria species

Japanese wisteria (*Wisteria floribunda*) is one of the best vines out there for basketry due to its versatility. It can be used either whole or split in half and with the bark on or peeled off. It is planted for its purple flower clusters and then completely takes over an area with long and persistent ground runners. American wisteria (*W. frutescens*) can be used as well, although it should be harvested with more care since it does not have invasive tendencies.

- **Parts used:** Ground runners; climbing vines.
- **Uses:** Thin vines can be used whole or split as twining strands in twined baskets; lashing and weavers in ribbed baskets; random weave; weavers

Wisteria

in wickerwork. Thicker vines as hoops in ribbed baskets and tension trays; all parts of wickerwork. Bark retted into fiber for cordage; twining; weaving; sewing material.

- **Qualities:** Very flexible; versatile; incredibly long (can be more than 50 feet); wide range.
- **Range:** Invasive in North America; native to Japan.
- **Habitat:** Woods; wood edges; fields; roadsides.
- **Identification features:** Opposite, compound leaves with 13 to 17 leaflets. Very showy pealike purple flowers hanging in clusters.
- **Harvest:** Pick both ground runners and long, untwisted climbing vines. Harvest in late spring or summer to peel bark for fiber.
- **Preparation:** Can be split in half to obtain thinner, more flexible weaving material either immediately after harvest or after drying and rehydrating. Bark can be peeled most easily right after harvest in the summer season. To rehydrate whole vines, submerge in lightly steaming water for 15–45 minutes (less for thin vines, more for thicker). Split vines will take less time as well. To keep the bark on, rehydrate for the minimum amount of time while still achieving flexibility.

OTHER VINES FOR BASKETRY

- Bindweed (*Convolvulus arvensis*)
- Boston ivy (*Parthenocissus tricuspidata*)
- Clematis (*Clematis virginiana*)
- English ivy (*Hedera helix*)
- Jasmine (*Jasminum* species)
- Trumpet vine (*Campsis radicans*)
- Vinca (*Vinca minor*)

The vines shown below are (1) Japanese honeysuckle with bark on and off; (2) kudzu; (3) Asian bittersweet; (4) grapevine; (5) Japanese wisteria; and (6) akebia.

How to Forage Vines

Vines have two growth forms. Ground runners travel directly on the surface of the earth or just beneath the leaf litter and occasionally send roots belowground. They are usually very straight, very flexible, and very long—the holy grail for basket makers! Climbing vines, also known as aerial vines, attach themselves to trees and other vertical supports. Look for long, straight sections that are a minimum of 4 feet and avoid those that are branchy and twisted. The same plant may have both ground runners and aerial vines, depending on the growing conditions. If a vine is struggling to find places to grow upward, it will put more of its energy into ground runners.

Technically, the best time for harvesting vines is their dormant season in fall and winter, because you don't have to contend with foliage and the stems are less likely to break when the sap is not flowing. However, I have found that summer-harvested grapevine and bittersweet work fine for many of the projects in this book, and I'll often harvest any species of vine if the opportunity presents itself, no matter what the season. Searching for vines in summer when they are leafing also helps a beginning basket maker identify the plant species. Note that the bark of vines such as wisteria, kudzu, and akebia will slip off easily in summer, which can either be a positive or a negative, depending on how you intend to use the plant.

Use pruning shears for thicker vines, such as grapevine and bittersweet. Use sharp basketry shears for thin vines, including akebia.

Harvesting ground runners. To locate runners in summer, look for places where vine leaves are emerging from the leaf litter. In winter look for dead leaves or aboveground vines. Explore with your fingers until you get hold of a vine that is traveling along the top of the ground or just underneath the leaf litter. Begin pulling the runner up, moving along its length and yanking any places where it has rooted to the ground. Inevitably there will be places where it crosses other runners,

Within a network of vines, follow a single runner or excavate an entire area.

and soon you will unearth a whole network of vines. Trim all side branches and the tip of each length of vine, removing any leaves and large rootlets. Make each length of vine into a storage coil for easier transportation and drying (see page 58).

Harvesting climbing vines. Climbing vines attach themselves to trees and other vertical supports. Look for vines that are long and straight and have few branches or splits, carefully pulling them free from whatever they are growing over. With time you will develop vine vision: the ability to spot long, straight sections of vine even in tangled undergrowth. Follow each vine shoot back to where it connects to its source and cut it there. As with ground runners, trim each vine by cutting off side branches until it is one single unbranched piece and wrap them into storage coils.

harvesting safely

Vines are often found in overgrown areas, and harvesting can be a tangled, messy business. Center yourself and approach this task with a calm mind, staying organized and aware of your surroundings. Here are some best practices:

- Don't pull vines out of dead trees or dead branches, which could break and come crashing down. Look up to check before yanking on a vine.
- Don't harvest near poison ivy, which is common in many areas and grows alongside many basketry vines.
- Close and lock pruning shears between cuts. Don't walk around with them open, especially in an area with uneven ground.
- Harvest slowly and be patient. I can't tell you how many times I was lucky to be wearing glasses because I got impatient, yanked a vine, and whacked myself in the face. Now I approach vine harvesting as a meditation and pay extra attention to ethical harvesting practices (see page 19).

taming the harvest

I recommend tidying and organizing vines as soon as possible after foraging, which makes them much easier to use later. A pile of untamed vines is likely to go to waste. My method is to wrap them into what I call storage coils, which are quick to make but solid enough to store and rehydrate later. Think ahead and be sure your coils are small enough to fit in the pot you are going to use for rehydration. In fact, I recommend having the pot on hand to make sure they will fit.

First, cut off any side branches to ensure that you are using only one length of vine. Following steps 2 to 5 for making vine hoops on page 255, bend one end of the vine into a circle the desired size of your final coil.

Next, turn the circle counterclockwise 90 degrees and brace the vine against the front edge of the top arc of the circle.

Turn the circle counterclockwise another 90 degrees and brace the vine against the back edge. The tension of the vine pressing against the edges of the initial circle will hold it in place.

Continue rotating the coil and alternating placement of the vine in front and behind. When you have about 12 inches of vine left, pass the end through the middle of the circle once or twice to secure the coil.

How to Prepare Vines for Basketmaking

While all vines are flexible enough to weave when freshly harvested, they do shrink—sometimes significantly—resulting in loose baskets. Woodier vines, such as grapevine, porcelain berry, and bittersweet, are exceptions. (Bittersweet shrinks the most out of the three.) I often choose to use each of these vines fresh for several reasons. They are common, and it's a lot easier to harvest as needed instead of trying to build up a stash as you might with a less common vine. They are big and take up a lot of space if stored for later use. Also, you need a very large pot for rehydration due to their size.

Whether you place a higher value on the ease of fresh materials or the better performance of those that have been dried and rehydrated is a matter of personal choice. I usually keep a couple of dried coils of larger vines in my studio but not a huge stash. If you're working with fresh ones, add more vines to the basket after it dries to tighten it up.

peeling bark from vines

Some vines have bark that easily peels off, leaving whitish, smooth material that is lovely to work with. Whether to peel or not is primarily an aesthetic choice. If you do, you end up with another weaving material: the bark! The bark peels off easily during the growth season, which is late spring through summer. If harvested during the dormant season, the bark will probably not peel easily, but in some cases can still be removed by rehydrating the vine in hot water a little longer.

Freshly harvested vines. Make a cut in the end of the vine or pinch the end of the vine and pull at the bark until it starts to come off. Strip it down, separating the bark from the inner vine. You might need scissors to help it past nodes and rootlets. If the bark is sticking to the inner vine, it may be too dry to peel. On vines thicker than 1½ inches in diameter, a knife may be needed to score the bark along the length of the vine before you can peel it easily.

When peeling bark from vines, you end up with two weaving materials: the bark and the inner vine.

Rehydrated vines. Submerge vines in hot water for the higher range of the recommended rehydrating time. Take them out and let them cool. If you're peeling a thin vine like honeysuckle, pull it through a folded rough piece of fabric and the bark should easily slough off. If you're peeling a thicker vine like wisteria, follow the instructions for peeling a freshly harvested vine. If the bark isn't coming off, try leaving it in the water longer. If it was harvested in fall or winter, you may not be able to remove the bark.

splitting vines

Kudzu and wisteria split in half beautifully. Splitting not only doubles your harvest but also results in thinner, more flexible material. Kudzu actually needs to be split to avoid kinks while weaving. Use scissors to cut the vine directly in half on one end. Grab each half of the vine between your thumb and the side of your pointer finger. Lever each side apart while pressing the knuckles of both hands against each other to control the split.

Bark often sloughs off thin vines like honeysuckle easily.

Vines tend to split evenly, but if one side starts to thin out, it can be corrected. *See page 113 for instructions.*

GRAPEVINE INSECT INFESTATIONS

Sometimes grapevine harbors hidden insects, which will turn vines—and the baskets made from them—into sawdust over time. To eliminate insects, you can boil the coils for 5 to 15 minutes just after harvest before letting them dry for storage. In addition, don't harvest vines that are already dead or unhealthy as they are more likely to have insects. Vines in poor health have very little flexibility, gray bark, and possibly black or white mold spots.

drying and storing vines

If harvesting for later use, follow the basic guidelines for drying, storing, and rehydrating plant materials on pages 21–24. Lay the vine coils next to each other in a single layer and flip them twice a day. Alternatively, hang them from the ceiling in a well-ventilated area, or stack them into a short tower and put that tower in front of a fan for a couple of days.

Vines are excellent for all parts of ribbed and random-weave baskets.

To store, stack coils on shelves or tie a group of them together and hang them from the ceiling or a wall. Since vines are susceptible to mold, store them in a dry place with plenty of airflow. Sheds and covered porches will most likely result in moldy vines.

rehydrating vines

Dried vines need time in hot water to become flexible enough for weaving. Submerge vine coils in a pot of water on the stove and turn on the heat. (Luckily, they will fit because you carefully coiled them to the correct size before storage!) How hot the water needs to be and how long the coils need to soak is not an exact science, because the species, thickness, age, quality, and other unknown growing conditions of the vine are all determining factors. Peeling and splitting shorten soaking times. I provide estimated ranges below, but only with practice will you develop your ability to test materials in each unique circumstance and judge whether they are sufficiently rehydrated. Takes notes on your results to learn from your efforts. Vines can be dried and rehydrated twice and still work quite well. After the third rehydration, however, they begin to degrade in quality.

Thin vines. (Example: akebia.) Submerge in a pot of steaming water for 15 to 30 minutes, or longer if you want to remove the outer bark.

Medium, stiffer vines. (Examples: thin and thick honeysuckle, wisteria.) Submerge in a pot of steaming water for 30 minutes to 1½ hours or more, depending on the thickness.

Thick, woody vines. (Examples: grapevine, bittersweet.) Submerge in a pot of simmering water for 1 to 3 hours.

CHAPTER 5

WOODY STEMS

Beautiful antique willow baskets in a museum were an early inspiration for me to try foraging my own weaving material. I was hopeful I had wild willow shrubs growing near me, and it turned out that I did! Gathering enough flexible, first-year's growth to make an entire basket was a challenge, and the results were certainly rustic, but it lit a fire in me that is still going strong to this day.

Baskets made with woody stems are exceptionally sturdy and can last a lifetime. Making them requires patience and hand strength, but I've spent some of the best days of my life sitting alongside rivers weaving baskets with wild harvested material. And some of those first rustic baskets are the ones I treasure most, even today.

PROJECTS THAT USE WOODY STEMS

Two-Hoop Harvest Basket (page 259)

Tension Tray (page 271)

Wild Wickerwork Basket (page 295)

HARVEST SEASON

Early winter–late winter

The Plants

The plants featured here include those that are very well known or that I have extensive experience with, but there are many others out there. Besides willow, I enjoy using red osier dogwood shrubs, water sprouts from various tree species, and canes from brambles, such as blackberries. I also love to explore using nontraditional materials, including invasive species, such as the canes of multiflora rose—after stripping off the thorns, of course!

Brambles

The term *brambles* typically refers to thorny members of the genus *Rubus* that grow in a spreading, shrublike form consisting of canes. I extend this term to refer to multiflora rose, barberry, and other thorny shrubs. I don't tend to use plants that produce edible berries very often, and instead focus on multiflora rose and other invasives. There are *many* species of thorny friends in this category.

- **Parts used:** Canes; bark.
- **Uses:** Canes as weavers in tension trays; all parts of ribbed baskets; weavers in random-weave baskets; wickerwork. Inner bark as cordage; sewing material in coiled baskets. A few species have outer bark that can be split off and woven.
- **Range:** Widespread in temperate climates.
- **Habitat:** Edge areas; open woodlands; meadows; sunny spots.
- **Harvest:** Available any time of year, although canes crack more easily in summer. For inner bark, harvest in spring or summer.
- **Preparation:** See general guidelines for preparing woody stems.

EXCELLENT BRAMBLES FOR BASKETRY

- Japanese barberry (*Berberis thunbergii*): Very thorny. Shave off the outer bark and thorns with a knife to reveal the beautiful yellow inner bark color. Not very flexible. Good for weavers in wickerwork or in tension trays.
- Black raspberry (*Rubus occidentalis*): The only native species listed here. Has smaller thorns. Needs a combination of rubbing with a thick, rough cloth, scraping, and shaving to remove thorns. Canes are a beautiful reddish purple color when fresh. If dried and rehydrated, they fade to brown.
- European blackberry (*Rubus fruticosus*): Remove thorns with heavy gloves and thick cloth. For cordage, scrape off the very thin outer bark and split bark away from pith, gently pounding to separate fibers. Other *Rubus* species are similar.
- Himalayan blackberry (*Rubus armeniacus*): Push off large thorns using thick gloves. Not as flexible as multiflora rose for wickerwork. Bark can be split off from pith and woven.
- Multiflora rose (*Rosa multiflora*): Thicker diameters get very stiff. Can be many different colors. Look for canes in shady areas, which grow long with few thorns. Push off large thorns using thick gloves.

Red Osier Dogwood

Cornus sericea

Red osier is my favorite dogwood species due to its lovely color, but all other shrub dogwoods including gray dogwood (*Cornus racemosa*) and silky dogwood (*C. amomum*) work the same way.

- **Parts used:** First-year shoots.

Red osier dogwood

- **Uses:** All parts of tension trays; ribs in ribbed baskets; weavers and lashing in ribbed baskets when flexible enough; wickerwork.
- **Qualities:** Lovely red color; abundant.
- **Range:** There is at least one species of shrub dogwood present everywhere in North America and Europe.
- **Habitat:** Wet meadows; roadsides; thickets.
- **Identification features:** Spreads by runners; bright red branches; opposite buds and leaves; simple ovate leaves with smooth margins.
- **Harvest:** In late fall through winter (dormant season); look for dusty reddish gray shrubs in wetlands. Look at the bases of plants to find sporadically growing, slender, red or maroon first year's growth. Shrubs are most likely to send up growth shoots when they have been damaged by floods or otherwise disturbed.
- **Preparation:** Stems darken in color when dried and rehydrated. To maintain some red, weave fresh and add more material in later to account for shrinkage.

OTHER SHRUBS FOR BASKETRY

- Hazel (*Corylus* species)
- Forsythia (*Forsythia* species)
- Rose of Sharon (*Hibiscus syriacus*)

Water Sprouts

Water sprouts are the shoots of new woody growth that some tree species send out from their base or trunk when the plant is stressed or damaged. They are also called suckers.

- **Uses:** Weavers in tension trays; ribs in ribbed baskets; other parts of ribbed baskets if flexible enough; wickerwork.
- **Harvest:** Late fall through winter (dormant season).
- **Preparation:** See general guidelines for preparing woody stems.

EXCELLENT WATER SPROUTS FOR BASKETRY

- Apple (*Malus* species)
- Black cherry (*Prunus serotina*)
- Elm (*Ulmus* species)
- Maple (*Acer* species)
- Willow (*Salix* species)
- Most fruit trees

Willow

Salix species

With more than 470 species, willow is one of the most widely used basketry plants in the world. Even when a plant is completely cut down, the root system will send up shoots and get stronger every year, making it one of the few basketry plants that is farmed for its material. The ubiquitous weeping willow branches are unfortunately brittle, so they are not typically used for basketry.

- **Parts used:** Three distinct parts of willow are used for different types of baskets—first year's growth (woody stems), bark, and inner bark fiber.
- **Uses:** Woody stems for all parts of tension trays; ribbed baskets; and wickerwork. Bark and inner bark strips for stakes in twined baskets; all parts of woven baskets; diagonal plaiting; folded bark baskets; random weave. Inner bark fiber for cordage; multistrand braiding; sewing material.
- **Qualities:** Strong; durable; vigorous growth.
- **Range:** Worldwide except Antarctica, though most common in northern hemisphere.

Willow

- **Habitat:** Cooler climates; moist soil; near water; sunny spots.
- **Identification features:** Grows as shrubs and trees; long, slender first year's growth has alternate buds or leaves; leaves are typically narrow and elliptical, but leaf shape varies among species; often the first plant to flower in late winter.
- **Harvest:** Cut the first year's growth in winter during the dormant season for rods. Harvest trees or saplings in late spring to summer for bark peeling.
- **Preparation:** See page 69 for working with woody stems, page 115 for preparing bark for weaving, and page 90 for retting willow bark. Willow bark peeled from saplings typically rets in less than a week.

How to Forage Woody Stems

The list of plants on the previous pages only scratches the surface of what is possible. Becoming familiar with the qualities of woody stems that are desirable for basketry will help you identify suitable plants in your own local environment. With most species, only shoots in their first year of growth are generally good for weaving. Ideal woody stems or canes have the following qualities.

Branchless. This is the hallmark of a stem in its first year of growth. After year two it starts to develop side branches and is thicker and less flexible.

Thin. Anything from half of a pencil width to ⅜ inch in diameter is usable. Larger than that would be best for large projects, such as garden trellis supports, stakes in giant baskets, coracles, or sculptural work.

Flexible. Although these stems are woody, they are still quite pliable. To test flexibility, bend a stem over your finger slowly (not at a sharp angle). Extremely flexible plants like willow may be able to make a full circle! Others will not. How flexible it needs to be depends on the desired use. For example, in a ribbed basket the ribs only need to be a little flexible, while the weavers benefit from being very flexible.

Long. Two to 6 feet or more is considered long in this case. Again, the use matters. Ribs can be quite short.

Only woody stems in their first year of growth are generally good for weaving. The willow plants in the foreground of this photo have been coppiced; those in the back have not been cut.

finding woody stems for weaving

When foraging, look for spots where shrubs, trees, and brambles have been damaged by mowers, pruning, floods, storms, fires, beavers, or other similar activity. This stimulates the plant to send out new growth that is excellent for weaving. Foraging from healthy, mature wild plants is possible but will likely not yield as much material, since new growth is minimal. An exception to this is brambles, which produce new canes prolifically as they spread.

Cutting plants back to the ground on purpose to produce copious shoots of new growth is called coppicing—an ancient crop management practice that is used all over the world. Willow plants are typically cut every year in winter. In spring each plant produces as many new stems as possible to support the root system it has developed. Even a home gardener can have a small and productive willow plot. Note that only some plant species respond to coppicing well, and others will not: They simply die when cut back.

harvesting woody stems

Harvest stems during the plant's dormant season: late fall through late winter—any time after the plant has shed its leaves but before the buds have opened. This is when the stems are flexible and less likely to snap, because the sap is not flowing in the plant. Also, that timing is best for the health of the plant. In winter the leaves fall off and the plant stores energy in its roots. By cutting stems back in winter only, the plant can conserve its energy and send up even more stems in spring. When cut in the growing season, the plant will struggle more to recover.

When foraging invasive plants, including multiflora rose, I don't worry as much about the health of the plant and tend to forage any time of year, although the stems do tend to crack more easily in summer, requiring more care. Whether I choose to harvest during the growing season also depends on how flexible the pieces need to be for the basket I want to make.

Use pruning shears to cut each individual stem close to the ground but still above two or three buds. If you're cutting a side branch or a water sprout, cut close to the main trunk without cutting into it.

Cut a stem near the base while still leaving two or three buds below.

How to Prepare Woody Stems for Basketmaking

In addition to the general guidelines for drying, storing, and rehydrating on pages 21–24, there are some special considerations for woody stems, which contain a lot of moisture and shrink significantly. For best results, dry them fully over several months and then rehydrate before weaving.

I make an exception with brambles, which dry more quickly. I tend to let them dry for a few days before weaving so they shrink a bit but remain flexible. This is mainly because they tend to be brittle when fully dry and break easily, making it hard to store them. The colors are also brighter when freshly harvested and tend to darken when dried and rehydrated.

Stems can be stored for many years. Sort by size (thickness of the rod and length) and bundle neatly with two reusable zip ties or pieces of twine, one at each end. Store upright against the wall or stack on shelves.

The general rule for rehydrating woody stems is to soak for one day per foot of length followed by 12 to 24 hours of mellowing.

Soaking. Submerge stems in a large vessel filled with water, such as a livestock trough or a large, upright PVC pipe with an end cap glued on. Rivers and other bodies of water also work for soaking, although the stems will accumulate a slimy coating that needs to be washed off. Warm water is best; in cold water the stems will take longer to soak and may not reach their full flexibility. Test after the allotted soaking time, using the calculation at left. If the stems can't bend over your finger without cracking, including the bark, then soak them longer.

Mellowing. Remove the stems from the water and wrap them in a lightly dampened towel, wool blanket, or plastic sheet for 12 to 24 hours. Put in a cool, shady place. This step is very important for allowing the moisture in the outer layers to wick into the center of each stem, making it more flexible.

Woody stems result in some of the most sturdy baskets out there, making them ideal for creations that will last a lifetime.

CHAPTER 6

WILD FIBERS

Wild fibers—long, strong threads extracted from plants—have been used for tens of thousands of years to create nets, baskets, bags, snares, lashing, clothing and adornment, weavings, mats, and more. There are two basic categories of wild fiber: leaf fibers and bast fibers. Leaf fibers are strong, individual fibers that run the entire length of some particularly sturdy leaves, providing structure. Examples include yucca, agave, and snake plant. Bast fibers are strong, flexible fibers in the inner bark layer of certain trees, herbaceous plant stalks, and vines. Examples include basswood (also known as linden), nettle, and wisteria.

Working with wild fibers embodies the transformational aspects of basketry more than any other material process. To me, it holds deep meaning to take a plant in its raw form, break it down into individual fibers through a labor of love, and then twist those fibers into something stronger, all by hand.

PROJECTS THAT USE WILD FIBERS

Looped Cordage Pouch (page 155)

Wild Fibers Twined Bag (page 183)

Woven Berry Basket (page 199)

Bark Necklace Pouch (page 239)

HARVEST SEASON

Varies by species

Basswood
inner bark
Yucca
Wisteria
vine bark
Elm inner bark
Nettle

Milkweed
Western red
cedar bark
Dogbane

The Plants

The number of plants from which you can extract basketry fiber is almost limitless. Pretty much anything threadlike can be twisted into a durable material. Following are a few of my favorite plants to use for fiber, all of which are particularly soft and flexible, making them great for many soft basketry projects.

LEAF FIBERS

Banana Plant

Musa species

The banana plant, which looks like a 10- to 12-foot tree, is in fact herbaceous! What looks like a trunk—called a pseudostem—has a soft core encased in leaf sheaths. Each pseudostem grows to maturity in under 15 months, producing bananas. Just after the bananas ripen, the entire stem can be cut down and processed into fiber. Some species, such as *Musa textilis*, produce better fiber than others. While not technically a leaf fiber, it is most similar to them in processing, so it is included in this section.

- **Parts used:** Fiber from leaf sheaths in the pseudostem.
- **Uses:** As cordage; multistrand braiding; sewing strands in coiled baskets; looping; twined bags; twined baskets; as thin weavers, rim filler, lashing material in woven baskets; necklace strands; sewing strands; any kind of lashing. Loose fiber for twining strands in twined bags and baskets; weaving; looping.
- **Qualities:** Long, strong, white fibers; high yield relative to the amount of harvesting labor.
- **Range:** Native to India, South China, and Southeast Asia; introduced all over the world in tropical climates; some varieties grow in the southern United States.
- **Identification features:** Single large stalk; long, oblong leaves; bananas are a dead giveaway!
- **Harvest:** Any time of year. After bananas ripen, cut the whole pseudostem at its base with a handsaw.
- **Preparation:** Cut the psuedostem lengthwise from end to end in one spot. It will start to come apart in layers naturally. Split out 3- to 6-inch-wide pieces with a knife. Each piece is composed of several layers. The inner (concave) side is soft, disposable tissue. The middle is open material with many chambers, and the outer layer contains the strong, long fibers that run lengthwise. Lay a section flat on a worktable with the outer, or good, side touching the table and use a kitchen knife to carefully slice off the top and middle sections and put them aside. Place the knife perpendicular to the table on the remaining material and scrape the fibers to remove extra tissue on and between the fibers. Flip over and scrape some of the waxy cuticle off. Hang and dry in the sun.

Banana plant

Snake Plant

Dracaena trifasciata

I fell in love with this plant in Costa Rica, where it is often planted in landscaping. Many are familiar with it as it is a common houseplant that is easy to care for.

- **Parts used:** Leaves.
- **Uses:** As cordage; multistrand braiding; sewing strands in coiled baskets; looping; twined bags; twined baskets; as thin weavers, rim filler, lashing material in woven baskets; necklace strands; sewing strands; any kind of lashing. Untwisted fiber for twining strands in twined bags and baskets.
- **Qualities:** Very strong; lovely white fiber.

Snake plant

- **Range/habitat:** Common houseplant; native to Africa; used widely as a landscaping plant in tropical climates.
- **Identification features:** Sword-shaped leaves standing 2–4 feet tall in varied patterns of light and dark green, often with yellow edges.
- **Harvest:** Cut sparingly from houseplants at the base. Outdoors take only a leaf or two per plant.
- **Preparation:** Follow detailed instructions for processing leaf fibers on pages 80–81.

Yucca

Yucca species

Many species are suitable for baskets, but some notable ones are Adam's needle (*Yucca filmentosa*), Spanish bayonet (*Y. faxoniana*), banana yucca (*Y. baccata*), and soapweed (*Y. glauca*).

- **Parts used:** Leaves.
- **Uses:** As cordage; multistrand braiding; sewing strands in coiled baskets; looping; twined bags; twined baskets; as thin weavers, rim filler, lashing material in woven baskets; necklace strands; sewing strands; any kind of lashing. Untwisted fiber for twining strands in twined bags and baskets. The thin, narrow leaves of some species can be used in weaving; diagonal plaiting; sewing material in coiled baskets.
- **Qualities:** Very strong, durable fiber; can be a bit coarse.

Yucca

- **Range:** North and Central America.
- **Habitat:** Arid or semi-arid climates; deserts at all elevations; scrubland; prairie; northern plains in rocky or sandy soils; *Y. filamentosa* is native to the southeastern United States and grows in sandy coastal soils; many species are common in landscaping.
- **Identification features:** Evergreen perennial; usually stemless and growing in clumps; long, sword-shaped leaves with pointed tips; green to bluish green; some are fleshy and stiff (*Y. baccata*, *Y. faxoniana*) while others are more floppy (*Y. filamentosa*); widths vary; lengths over 30 inches; many have filaments of fiber curling at their edges.
- **Harvest:** Any time of year. Cut only a few leaves from each plant at the base.
- **Preparation:** Follow instructions on how to prepare leaf fibers for basketmaking on pages 80–81.

OTHER LEAF FIBERS FOR BASKETRY

- Agave (over 250 species): Process fibers much like yucca, although the leaves are succulent and thick, requiring much more pounding or retting. Also note that some people are allergic to the sap in agave leaves, which can cause red, itchy skin. I recommend wearing gloves when processing.
- Pineapple plant (*Ananas comosus*): Use the leaves of the actual plant, not those found on the fruit.
- Sotol (*Dasylirion wheeleri*): Process fibers in the same way as yucca; alternatively, the leaves can be stripped of the edge spines and woven.

BAST FIBERS FROM PLANT STALKS

Dogbane

Apocynum cannabinum

Dogbane is one of the strongest fibers out there. Every year I look forward to visiting my favorite dogbane patches and shaking the fluffy seeds loose to spread them out as I forage.

- **Parts used:** Bast fiber in the stalk.
- **Uses:** As cordage; multistrand braiding; sewing strands in coiled baskets; looping; twined bags; twined baskets; as thin weavers, rim filler, lashing material in woven baskets; necklace strands; sewing strands; any kind of lashing. Untwisted fiber for twining strands in twined bags and baskets.
- **Qualities:** Fiber is very strong; beautiful range of honey and amber colors.
- **Range:** United States, Canada, and northwestern Mexico.
- **Habitat:** Fields; roadsides; along creeks and rivers.

Dogbane

- **Identification features:** Stalks are 2–5 feet tall; in fall, oblong opposite leaves turn yellow; in winter, stalks are reddish; 3-inch seedpods are narrow and legumelike with fluffy wind-dispersed seeds; resembles milkweed during the growing season.
- **Harvest:** Late fall and early winter. My preferred time is mid-November to early December after there have been a couple of frosts, a good rain, and a few days to dry off. Many factors contribute to the quality of a dogbane patch and how easily the outer bark comes off the fiber, including microclimates, rainfall amounts, presence of disease, and genetics. Sometimes it sloughs off at the touch, but most of the time it sticks and is difficult to remove. Foragers try to time their harvest so that the bark is most likely to separate easily from the fibers. Visit a patch throughout the season, testing the stalks, and take detailed notes year after year.
- **Preparation:** All parts of living dogbane are poisonous, particularly to livestock. When dry, it does not pose a threat to humans, although you should avoid breathing in dogbane bark dust. Dry next to a woodstove or heater for a few days before processing. Can also be stored for long periods before processing. Use instructions on pages 82–85 for either the scraping or breaking and scutching method to remove fiber from the stalks.

Milkweed

Asclepias syriaca

My favorite part about milkweed is the beautiful, shiny white fiber. It's also quite soft, making it great for necklace cordage in addition to baskets.

- **Parts used:** Bast fiber in the stalk.
- **Uses:** As cordage; multistrand braiding; sewing strands in coiled baskets; looping; twined bags; twined baskets; as thin weavers, rim filler, lashing material in woven baskets; necklace strands; sewing strands; any kind of lashing. Untwisted fiber for twining strands in twined bags and baskets.

Milkweed

- **Qualities:** Strong; white-colored fibers; common in some locations.
- **Range:** Central and eastern Canada south to central and eastern United States; introduced in Europe.
- **Habitat:** Fields; roadsides; pastures; open sunny areas.
- **Identification features:** Unique, inflated-looking green seedpods that turn gray in fall and release fluffy, white, wind-dispersed seeds. Stalks are 3–5 feet tall, unbranched with oblong, smooth-edged leaves.
- **Harvest:** I typically wait until the plant has gone to seed and the pods have opened and begun to disperse. Fibers can also be peeled from the green stalk. Timing the milkweed harvest can be a bit finicky. The fibers tend to degrade and turn into slime on the stalk, so be sure to test a few out before foraging a lot of stalks from one place.
- **Preparation:** Prepare using the breaking and scutching method found on pages 82–84.

Nettle

Nettle

Urtica dioica

Some folks dislike nettle for its stinging hairs, but I admire its many uses—including for food, medicine, and, of course, basketry material. In its native lands, it plays a role in many myths, legends, and fairy tales.

- **Parts used:** Bast fiber in the stalk.
- **Uses:** As cordage; multistrand braiding; sewing strands in coiled baskets; looping; twined bags; twined baskets; as thin weavers, rim filler, lashing material in woven baskets; necklace strands; sewing strands; any kind of lashing. Untwisted fiber for twining strands in twined bags and baskets.
- **Qualities:** Lovely light-colored fiber; strong; abundant.
- **Range:** Invasive in the United States; native from Europe to Siberia and western China.
- **Habitat:** Disturbed areas with nutrient-rich soil; floodplains; farms; along rivers and other edge areas.
- **Identification features:** Stalks are 4–8 feet tall; opposite leaves, coarsely serrated; covered in tiny stinging hairs; inconspicuous flowers and clusters of tiny green or brown seeds.
- **Harvest:** I harvest at the end of summer around mid-September when the seeds have ripened and started to turn gray. Wear gloves and cut at the base. Run your glove or a piece of fabric back and forth along the length of the stalk to remove the stinging hairs and leaves, using medium pressure so as not to

rip the fibers. When any leftover hairs dry out they no longer sting.

- **Preparation:** See processing plant stalk fibers on pages 82–86.

OTHER PLANT STALKS FOR BASKETRY

- Flax (*Linum usitatissimum*)
- Hemp (*Cannabis sativa*)
- Rosebay willow herb (*Chamaenerion angustifolium*)
- Thistle (*Cirsium* genus and others)
- Velvetleaf (*Abutilon theophrasti*)
- Wood nettle (*Laportea canadensis*)

BAST FIBERS FROM TREES

Basswood

Tilia americana

Wherever trees in the genus *Tilia* grow, local inhabitants have been processing the inner bark for thousands of years. The trees are also appreciated for their generous shade, medicinal tea made from the flowers, and flavorful honey. This section focuses on basswood, but most other *Tilia* species can be used in the same way, and their identification is quite similar, especially *T. cordata* and *T. platyphyllos* (see photo on page 31).

- **Parts used:** Outer bark; inner bark.
- **Uses:** Inner bark fiber as cordage; multistrand braiding; twined bags and baskets; sewing strands for coiled baskets and folded bark baskets. Bark for stakes in twined baskets; all parts of woven baskets; diagonal plaiting; weavers and lashing in ribbed baskets; random weave. Bark sheets for folded baskets.
- **Qualities:** Long, high-quality fiber that takes dye well; high yield relative to the amount of harvesting labor.
- **Range:** Eastern United States and Canada to the Rockies; Mexico; Europe; Japan; China.
- **Habitat:** Rivers; lakes; areas with rich soil; woodlands; European varieties planted in landscaping and as street trees.
- **Identification features:** Small to large tree; heart-shaped leaves with uneven bases and serrated edges; you will often find clumps of various-size trunks that all belong to the same tree.
- **Harvest:** Summer. If using for bark, follow instructions for harvesting inner bark (see pages 108–111). If using for fiber, begin the retting process immediately.
- **Preparation:** See pages 88–90 for retting basswood bark. For bark strips the inner bark strips tend to split lengthwise, making it difficult to cut and weave them without them splitting further (it just wants to become fiber!). To mitigate this, I use it for larger baskets, which don't require as much splitting.

Elm

Ulmus species

See complete entry on page 98.

Western Red Cedar

Thuja plicata

See complete entry on page 101.

Willow

Salix species

See complete entry on page 65.

How to Forage Leaves for Fiber

Cut leaves at the base and harvest only a few from a single plant. Pictured here is Adam's needle yucca.

Plant species that offer leaf fibers for basketmaking belong to a group called monocots. Monocot plants have large, somewhat stiff leaves with parallel veins running lengthwise. The leaves can be harvested any time of year since they are perennial plants. Take only a few leaves from each plant to allow the plant to continue to grow. One at a time, cut the leaves with scissors or pruning shears near the base. If harvesting from a plant with pointed ends, such as some species of yucca, cut off the point first to avoid poking yourself.

ANATOMY OF A MONOCOT LEAF

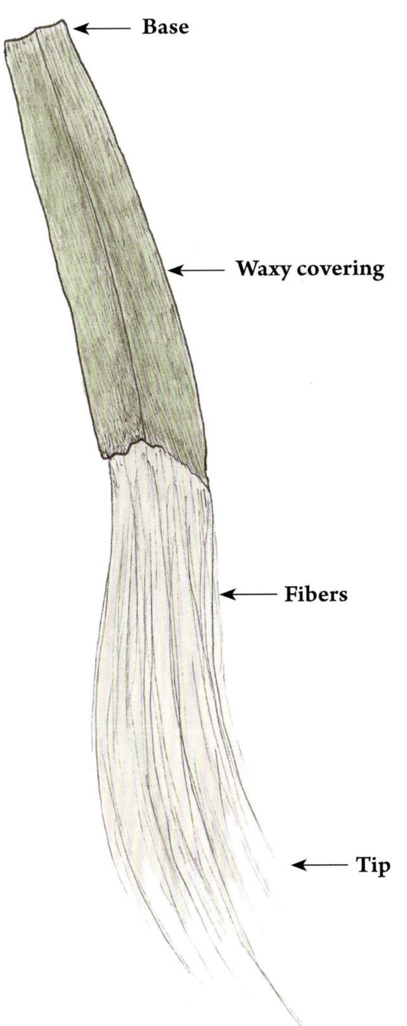

How to Prepare Leaf Fibers for Basketmaking

Adam's needle yucca (*Yucca filamentosa*), snake plant, and other similar species with relatively thin leaves (approximately ⅛ inch) can be scraped when dry to harvest the fibers. For plant species with thicker leaves, such as agave, use the retting method to dissolve the pectin and other matter before scraping and rinsing them to reveal the fibers.

scraping

To scrape leaves, you need a tool with a hard edge that isn't sharp. Try a spoon, a smooth-edged seashell, or any other similar implement. The goal is to scrape away the soft material without cutting through the fibers.

1. Find or prepare a flat surface that can withstand staining from plant juices. Hold a leaf securely against the surface and scrape from the base of the leaf toward the tip, applying pressure. Press hard enough to scrape away the top layers without severing the fibers beneath. Scraping is best done in one direction to avoid tangling. Scrape until the top layer of green, soft plant material is fully removed.

2. Flip the leaf over and scrape the other side from the base to the tip.

3. Once the outer, waxy layer of the leaf on both sides is removed, there is still plenty of squishy material between the fibers to scrape away. Keep scraping to clean as much as possible without destroying the fibers, though it's normal for some of the weaker fibers to rip away. Some material will still cling to the fibers when you're finished. You remove them either by rinsing or by rubbing dried fibers between your hands to agitate the excess material off.

The final bundle of fibers will probably be smaller than you imagined, compared to the size of the original leaf. However, if you end up with almost nothing left, then you may be scraping too vigorously and can go lighter. Experiment with multiple leaves until you find a balance.

retting

Retting is a process that exposes plant material to water over time to break down pectins and other cellular matter, leaving behind the strong and resilient fibers. For thicker leaves—some yucca species, pineapple plants, and agave, for example—ret before scraping.

In either a bucket, stream, lake, or other source of water, submerge the leaves and soak them anywhere from a couple of days to several weeks to help loosen and dissolve the nonfibrous tissue. How many days of soaking is needed varies tremendously. One to 4 days begins the dissolving process, making it a little more efficient to scrape. If left submerged long enough, the leaf will only need a light scraping and rinsing, but if left too long the fibers may weaken.

Check the leaves after 2 to 4 days to see if the outer layers and softer inner tissues have begun to soften. When soft enough, follow instructions on the facing page for scraping.

drying, storing, and rehydrating leaf fibers

Allow scraped fibers to dry either in the sun or in a well-ventilated room. Once completely dry, store in bundles in open plastic bags, on a shelf, or hanging from the wall. The material will last a very long time. To prepare them for basketmaking, spritz lightly with a water bottle.

How to Forage Plant Stalks for Fiber

Herbaceous plants are those whose stems are not woody and that die back to the roots every winter, sending up new growth in spring. Some herbaceous plants grow with somewhat stiff stalks that happen to have particularly strong inner bark, or bast fibers. Bast fibers from plants such as nettle have been used traditionally around the world for thousands of years because they are especially strong and flexible. Others have become commercially important, due to their ability to be processed into fine threads and woven into fabric, including flax and hemp.

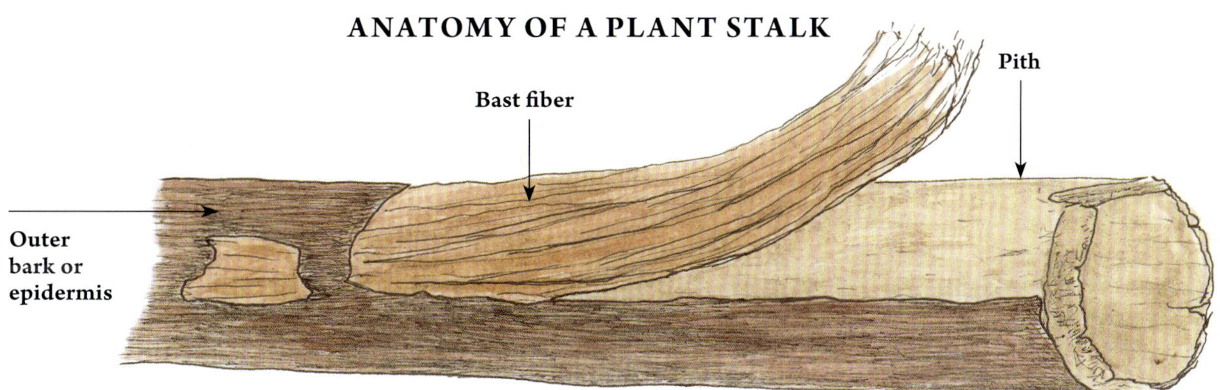

understanding plant stalks

Understanding the anatomy of herbaceous plant stalks will help you understand what is happening when processing the stalks for bast fiber as well as the qualities to look for when harvesting.

Stem or stalk. *Stalk* is an alternative term for *stem*, especially when the stem is stiff and supportive. This main upright portion of the plant is attached to the roots, bears leaves and flowers, and contains the transport system for water and nutrients.

Pith. This soft, spongy tissue in the center of a plant stalk can be solid or chambered. The pith dries out at the end of the season, when harvesting occurs, so it will feel dry, and the center often disintegrates, making it hollow.

Phloem. The inner bark of a plant stem, phloem serves as a transport system, allowing food produced by the leaves to move throughout the plant. It contains several kinds of cells and tissues, including bast fibers.

Bast. The fibers obtained from the phloem provide structure to the plant stem, but still retain flexibility. The term *bast* is typically used to refer to phloem fibers that are strong and therefore useful commercially.

Outer bark. The outer layer of an herbaceous plant stem is very thin and often covered in a waxy coating.

harvesting plant stalks

Use pruning shears to cut the stalk near the ground after it has gone to seed, but before it decomposes over winter. Each plant species has its own specifications for when to harvest. (See plant listings for wild fibers on pages 74–78.)

By harvesting at the end of the season, theoretically no damage is done to the roots and rhizomes of these plants. However, we can't entirely know how our harvesting affects an ecosystem. What insects overwinter in the stems? Does cutting too many stems invite pathogens into the root system? I prefer to make my footprint light and harvest conservatively.

How to Prepare Plant Stalk Fiber for Basketmaking

Every plant stalk has its own unique needs for processing. We'll focus on specifics for three of my favorites—dogbane, nettle, and milkweed—but there is a list of other plant stalks suitable for basketry on page 78. Be prepared to adjust the following methods when you try preparing different plant species for basketmaking.

breaking and scutching

Dogbane, nettle, and milkweed require you to separate the bast fibers from both the pith and the outer bark. You can process all three, and most other herbaceous plant stalks, using the breaking and scutching method. *Scutching* is a term used in processing flax to separate the fiber from the woody material, which essentially involves agitating it between your hands until the outer bark pieces all flake off.

Breaking

1. Flatten the stalk by either gently stepping on it or putting a cloth over it and pounding it with a mallet.

2. The flattened stalk will naturally start to separate lengthwise into four sections, which will be held together by bast fiber and bark. Slide your finger between only two of the pieces, separating them while making sure the rest stay connected.

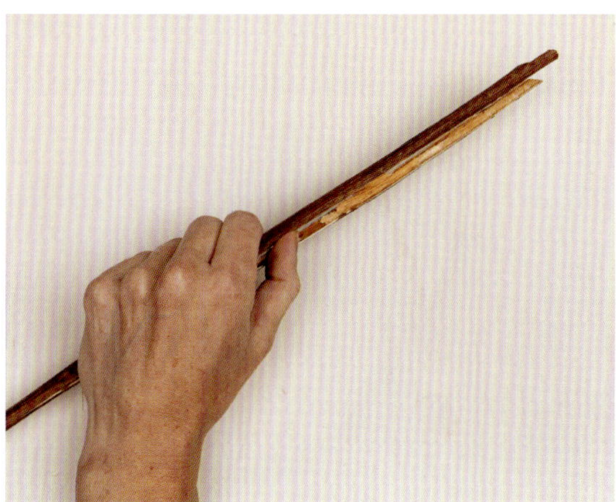

3. Open the four sections like a book along the side that you split so they lie flat in your hand and the remaining sections are still loosely connected with fiber. Be sure to open it flat along the entire length.

Removing the Pith Layer

The goal is to peel off the pith, piece by piece, and avoid tearing the fibers.

1. Start with the thicker end of the stalk. Lay the four pieces, still connected, pith side up, over the edge of your index finger so that they stick out about 3 inches.

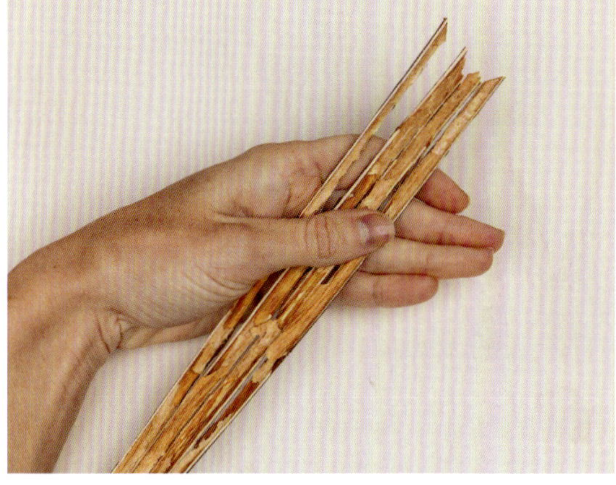

2. With your other hand, push the pieces over the edge of your hand so the pith cracks.

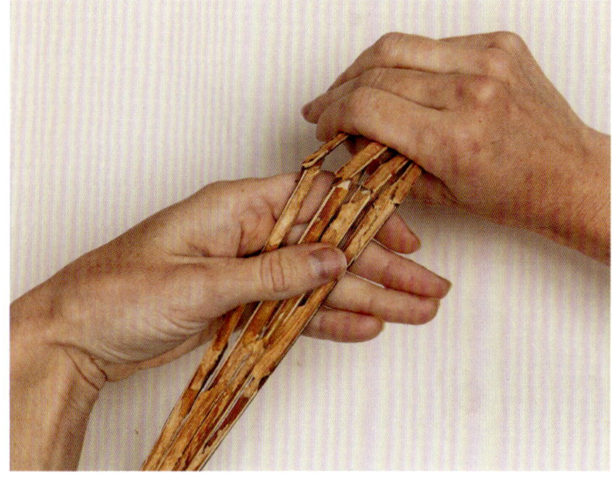

Continued on next page

3. Gently peel the pith from the bast fibers. Peeling away all four pieces with one motion, instead of doing each one individually, is more efficient and results in fewer torn fibers. Work your way up to this with practice.

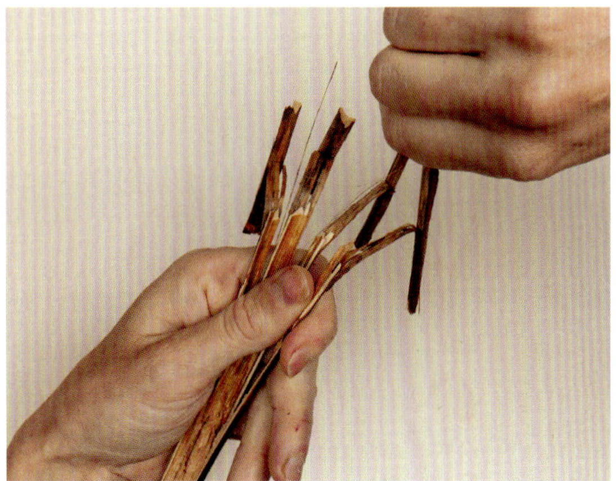

4. Slide the pieces up so another 2 to 4 inches stick over the edge of your hand. Again, crack the pith against your hand and peel it away. Keep working your way along the stalk until all the pith is removed.

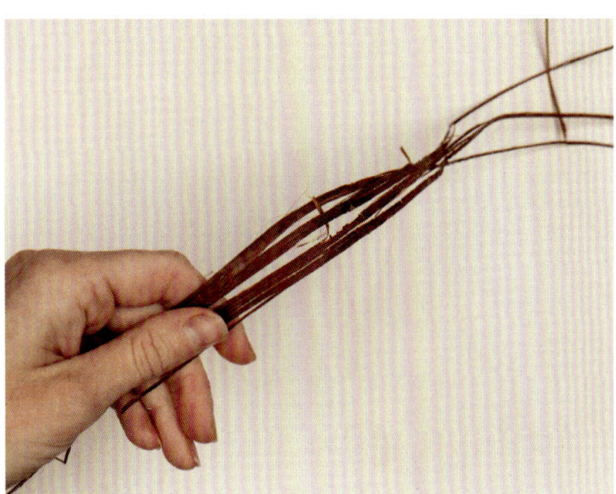

Removing the Outer Bark Layer

This is the scutching part of the process, where you agitate the fibers until the outer bark comes off. The goal is to remove as much bark as possible, or as much as you can manage. The work can be tedious, and sometimes the outer bark sticks and is difficult to completely remove. If the outer bark is sticking a lot on your stalks, try retting the stalks in water for several days to loosen the outer bark, let them dry again, and then process. If retting doesn't help, keep agitating the stalks. Sometimes time and patience are all that are needed. Also keep in mind that you can use the fibers for cordage even when they aren't totally clean.

1. Grasp two points on the bundle of fibers about 2 inches apart. Scrunch up and agitate the fibers so that the outer bark starts to flake off and the fibers are revealed.

2. Repeat until the whole bundle is clean.

preparing dogbane

Dogbane has slightly thick outer bark. Removing the outer bark layer first by scraping it off, rather than last, quickly and efficiently results in the cleanest fiber. However, I recommend using the standard breaking and scutching method on a few practice stalks to develop a feel for the depth of the outer bark so you don't damage dogbane's delicate fibers when you follow the scraping process below. After trying both you can decide which you prefer. Note that scraping doesn't work for milkweed and nettle.

1. Place a piece of leather or a towel on your knee to protect it and catch dust if you like. Place the stalk so the thick end is hanging off your knee by 4 to 5 inches.

2. Using a dull edge, such as the back of a butter knife, push the edge against the dogbane stalk and scrape away from your body to remove the outer bark. If it is a cooperative piece, with loosely attached outer bark, it will come off easily in big chunks. More often, this process takes some time. This image shows using a butter knife to scrape.

3. Continue to rotate and scrape until all the outer bark is removed.

4. Follow instructions for breaking and removing the pith on page 83. Take extra care because the fibers are delicate. If there are very few fibers left once the pith is removed, that means you scraped too aggressively. Just scrape more gently next time!

preparing nettle stalks

Unlike the short, soft fibers that textile artists extract from nettle for spinning, our goal as basket makers is to extract long fibers for making cordage or twining. The challenge in processing nettle is that white slivers of pith tend to stick to the fibers, and they can be very time-consuming to remove. My preferred method is to dry nettle stalks indoors for several days to weeks before breaking and scutching. You can also process the plants fresh, but expect the pith to stick more. You must allow the fiber to completely dry before attempting to remove the outer bark either way.

Dew retting—exposing the stalks to dew and ambient moisture—is a great option for preparing the fibers to separate from the pith and outer bark more easily. Some folks also wait to harvest until fall or winter, allowing nettle to ret on the stalk. Depending on the climate and how much rain you get in your location, this may or may not be successful.

1. Lay the stalks on the ground in a shady, grassy area. Turn them over every day. If it is dry and no dew is gathering on the stalks, spray them with water once a day.

2. Check after a week to see if the fibers separate from the pith more easily. Continue turning, spraying with water if needed, and testing the stalks. If they dry out or you ret the stalks too long, the fibers will degrade.

preparing milkweed stalks

I appreciate milkweed for its common availability, though it can be somewhat fickle to work with. The fiber tends to get slimy and rot on the stem, so I often harvest milkweed at the end of summer, before the stalks turn completely black, instead of waiting until fall. Other times I find perfect, dry stalks with beautiful fiber late into winter. Experiment with the milkweed you have in your area and take notes on what you find. Process using the standard instructions for breaking and scutching on pages 83–84.

drying, storing, and rehydrating

Herbaceous plant stalks can be stored in three states: as unprocessed stalks, as bundles of fiber with the outer bark still attached, and as finished bundles of fiber with all the outer bark removed. If kept dry, all states are resistant to mold and pests. I've always processed stalks within 2 years of harvest and drying, but they probably would remain viable for longer. Fiber on its own, after being separated from pith and outer bark, will last for many, many years. As always, store in a dry, cool place, referring to the directions for drying and storing on pages 21–22. Fibers do not need to be rehydrated, but they do benefit from being lightly spritzed with water while working with them.

The fibers in this basket, from top to bottom, are nettle, milkweed, western red cedar, milkweed, and nettle.

How to Forage Tree and Vine Bast for Fiber

While the term *bast* is used commercially to refer to herbaceous plant stalks, it can also refer to fibers in the inner bark of some trees and vines. Much like in plant stalks, it is the fibers present in the inner bark, or phloem, that you extract. However, there are some differences. The inner bark layer in trees is much thicker than in herbaceous plants and takes more effort to extract, but the yield is also much larger. The inner bark of vines is relatively simple to remove and process in comparison to trees, but does not have as large a yield.

For trees that are more than 5 inches in diameter, I typically remove the outer bark with a drawknife and ret only the inner bark to extract bast fibers. For those that are smaller, and therefore have thinner outer bark, I peel and submerge the bark in its entirety without removing the outer bark first. Follow the instructions in Chapter 7, Bark, for understanding bark, choosing and reading a tree, removing the outer bark with a drawknife, and peeling the inner bark (pages 104–111).

Vines such as wisteria, kudzu, and bittersweet also offer excellent fiber, and you can peel and process the entirety of the bark for fiber without removing the outer bark first. In late spring to late summer, look for straight, thick vines anywhere from 1 to 4 inches in diameter. Those that twist or spiral will have twisted fibers that are difficult to work with. Even a straight section of 2½ or 3 feet yields plenty of useful material. Follow the instructions in Chapter 4, Vines, for finding, foraging, and peeling vines (pages 57–60).

This basswood tree is an excellent size to harvest for bast fiber.

How to Prepare Tree and Vine Bast Fibers for Basketmaking

Once a tree or vine's bark is peeled, it must be processed from stiff, solid strips into layers of soft, flexible fibers. There are two methods for doing this: water retting and cooking in wood ash. Each has its own advantages. Water retting is gentler and results in lighter-colored fiber since you aren't introducing heat and ash, but the process takes longer, and if left soaking in the water too long the quality will degrade. Cooking in wood ash is faster and yields a reddish-colored fiber, but it is somewhat caustic and messy, and it requires more equipment. The resulting fiber also tends to be stiffer. I generally prefer water retting but know others who prefer wood ash.

Basswood fiber bundles

water retting

To ret material from trees, submerge long, unsplit lengths of inner bark in water for several weeks until the weaker tissues melt away, leaving the strong, flexible bast fibers. Basswood, linden, elm, and willow can all be retted this way. Retting in rivers and creeks is my preferred method since the water is alive and full of movement, which will aid in the process. The moving water is also convenient for rinsing the slimy fiber as you extract it. Lakes, ponds, and plastic bins or cattle troughs filled with water from a hose will also do. Be warned, however: Wherever you ret it, the bark will be slimy and wonderfully stinky by the end!

Water Retting Basswood Bark

Basswood and linden (both species in the *Tilia* genus) are my favorite tree bark fibers to work with. The retted bark splits naturally into even, paperlike sheets and has a retting process all its own. I find that the following process takes an average of 4 weeks, more or less. Water temperature, the thickness of the bark, and many other factors will affect the required retting time.

1. Submerge the lengths of inner bark completely under the water without bending them. The fibers can easily crack if stuffed into a bucket or bent too aggressively, and even a tiny crack will sever that layer of fiber. Do not allow even an inch to stick up above the water. I typically ret in a creek and use heavy rocks to weigh the bark down in several spots.

2. Leave for 2 weeks and check back a couple of times a week to be sure the water is covering the bark. If the bark dries out, that section won't be able to water ret.

3. After 2 weeks, pull a length of bark out. At this point the bark may not be completely retted, but I prefer to remove the layers as they are ready to ensure that the surface layers, which are the best quality, do not over-ret and become weak. Squeeze, massage, and bend one end of the bark until a few layers start to separate. These will probably be the layers on the smooth side that touched the wood of the log.

4. Slide your hand between each surface layer, or a group of several layers, and the rest of the bark. If the layer easily separates, it is ready to be peeled off completely. If it sticks and is stiff, allow more time for retting. At 2 weeks, expect to only have a few layers peel off.

5. Once a fiber sheet has been removed, it will still be filled with pectin and other slimy material that needs to be rinsed out. Squeeze the sheet gently and rinse it in running water, such as in a river or from a hose, to remove as much slime as you can. Be warned that it will be stinky! The odor will fade as the material dries. Try to keep it from splitting too much lengthwise during the process to ensure that you have the most whole material to work with later.

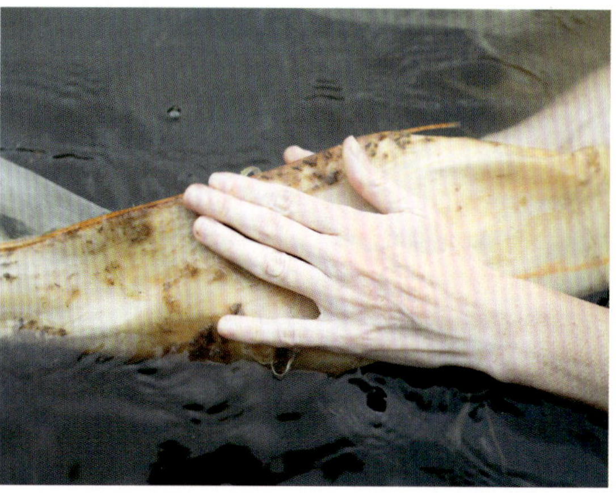

6. Dry the rinsed layers fully in the sun or hang in a well-ventilated room.

7. Put the rest of the length of bark back in the water to continue retting and check on it every week until the rest of it is ready to separate and rinse. As you get closer to the side that touched the outer bark of the tree (the rougher side), the fiber quality degrades and the bast fibers are more intertwined with each other, as opposed to staying in even, paperlike sheets. The pieces you pull off will be shorter and not as wide but are still of good quality. Separate as much as you can before discarding the stiff, rough outer layer or saving it for sculptural use. I manage to find a purpose for almost every piece of material!

Water Retting Other Types of Tree Bark

Other types of inner bark, such as elm or willow, do not behave in the same way as basswood when retting. The fibers are more interlaced and tangled and do not come apart in layers. They end up being a bit stiffer and may need to be agitated between your hands to soften them before use.

1. Completely submerge the bark lengths in water.

2. Check back once a week to squeeze, massage, and check if the fibers are soft enough to be considered finished. Depending on the thickness of the bark, this might take anywhere from a few days for very thin willow to more than 4 weeks for thicker bark.

3. Rinse completely to remove all slimy layers and grainy remainders of the nonfibrous components of the inner bark that have melted away.

4. Dry the finished bark in the sun or hang in a well-ventilated room.

Water Retting Vines

Without removing the outer bark, follow the instructions above for other types of bark. The bark from thinner vines will need as little as 2 to 3 days in the water, but most pieces take more time, even up to a month to achieve soft fiber.

cooking in wood ash

Wood ash from hardwood trees, combined with water, creates lye, a caustic substance that will ret inner bark in only a day and vine bark in as little as an hour. The goal is to cook the bark in a slurry of wood ash that completely covers all its surfaces. I've seen it done with a relatively light covering of ash or as a thick slurry. I typically go somewhere in between. This process tends to darken the bark or turn it a reddish color.

Use a large pot made of nonreactive metal, such as stainless steel or enamel. Wood ash will eat away at aluminum. Be warned that this process can be messy and will burn your skin on contact. Don't use your best pot, be sure to work outside on a cookstove or fire, and take safety precautions. It is important to wear heavy-duty waterproof gloves, goggles, and a mask.

1. Add 1½ inches of wood ash to the bottom of the pot. Coil a piece of bark into the pot, taking care not to crack it. Make sure the layers are not sandwiched too tightly against one another so that ash can contact every surface. Generously add more ash until the bark is mostly covered but there is still about 3 inches of space at the top of the pot to keep it from boiling over. You do not need solid ash all the way to the top—just a good heaping amount!

2. Very slowly and carefully add water by making a divot in the center of the ash and pouring water in until the bark is covered by a slurry of wood ash and water with 3 inches of space still remaining before the top of the pot. If you go too fast, it will send up a cloud of ash. If necessary, place a weight on top of the bark to hold it down to make sure every inch is below the surface of the water.

3. Cook the mixture for 3 to 8 hours over low to medium heat so it's bubbling but not boiling over. Thicker bark typically needs the higher time in this range. Monitor carefully, especially at the beginning when you are finding the best temperature to keep it from boiling over. Top off with water as needed to keep the bark completely covered.

4. After 3 hours turn the stove off and use tongs to pull out part of the bark. Let it cool for a moment, then squeeze and massage it. If it's not very soft and flexible, it needs to cook longer. Keep cooking and checking on it until the bark is soft and separates into layers or fibers. When done, turn off the stove and let the bark cool.

5. Remove the bark and rinse it thoroughly outside. Remember that you are rinsing off a caustic substance, so continue to wear gloves. Let the fibers dry completely in the sun. Dilute the remaining solution with water and spread outdoors or contact the department of environmental conservation in your state for guidelines on disposing of wood ash water.

CHAPTER 7

BARK

Everything from seeking out a tree to that magic moment when a gorgeous strip of bark slips off the log fills me with a deep sense of gratitude and celebration for the life of the tree. Bark is a unique material, providing either long strips for weaving or sheets for making durable folded containers. Luckily for beginners, getting started with bark harvesting does not require cutting down a tree. All you need is a freshly fallen or pruned branch.

PROJECTS THAT USE BARK

HARVEST SEASON

Late spring–summer

Shrub willow
Tulip poplar
Black walnut
Basswood

White ash
Hickory
American elm

1
2
10
9

1. White pine and birch bark
2. Black walnut and tulip poplar bark
3. Elm inner bark, western red cedar bark, and kudzu vine
4. Black walnut bark, birch bark, and sweetgrass
5. Black ash and willow bark
6. Tulip poplar and willow bark
7. White pine and birch bark
8. White pine and birch bark
9. Tulip poplar outer bark and hickory inner bark with elm bark cordage
10. White pine bark, paper birch bark, red osier dogwood, and basswood fiber

The Plants

I love experimenting with barks from different trees and shrubs. Each type provides a different texture, color, and flexibility. While classics such as willow and tulip poplar have been used throughout history due to their strength and reliability, there are many more to discover. Use whichever species are locally abundant to you and enjoy the process of discovery. When testing bark from a tree species not listed here, be sure that it peels from the wood easily and is somewhat strong. Once you have a peeled piece, twist it and try to tear it. Bark that breaks very easily is best for decoration only or not worth using.

Basswood

Tilia americana

See complete entry on page 78.

Black Walnut

Juglans nigra

This tree is cut down often in my area, and it's one of my favorites for the beautiful dark inner bark color, which is only revealed after it has been dried and resoaked. When first peeled from the log, it is white to pale yellow.

- **Parts used:** Inner bark.
- **Uses:** Stakes in twined baskets; stakes and weavers in small- or medium-size baskets; rims on folded bark baskets; weavers in ribbed baskets; random weave.
- **Qualities:** Beautiful dark brown color; peels easily; a bit weak and brittle.
- **Range:** Southeast Canada to central and eastern United States.
- **Habitat:** Fields; yards; open areas; riverbanks.
- **Identification features:** Medium to large deciduous tree; fruits are conspicuous green balls 2½ inches in diameter that turn brown as they rot; alternate pinnately compound leaves 12–24 inches long.
- **Harvest:** Late spring through summer.
- **Preparation:** Bark shrinks a lot, so cut it a little wide and don't split very thinly.

Black walnut

Elm

Ulmus species

Many species are good candidates for basketry, including American (*Ulmus americana*), slippery (*U. rubra*), winged (*U. alata*), and field (*U. minor*). American elm is threatened by Dutch elm disease, so only use it if the tree is already being cut for another reason.

- **Parts used:** Outer bark; inner bark strips; inner bark fiber; water sprouts.
- **Uses:** Bark sheets for folded bark baskets. Inner bark strips as stakes in twined baskets; woven baskets; diagonal plaiting; rims in folded bark baskets; weavers and lashing in ribbed baskets; random weave. Inner bark–retted fiber for cordage; sewing strands. Water sprouts as weavers in tension trays; ribs in ribbed baskets; wickerwork.

Slippery elm

- **Qualities:** Strong; excellent flexibility; splits well; beautiful color.
- **Range:** North and Central America; Eurasia; North Africa.
- **Habitat:** Temperate forests and moist bottomlands.
- **Identification features:** Medium to large deciduous tree; simple alternate leaf, ovate to oblong with double serrated teeth and an uneven base; seed is a nut surrounded by a papery winged casing.
- **Harvest:** Late spring through summer. Do not harvest bark if the tree shows signs of decline, even if already cut down. Bark beetles are attracted to cut elms, so harvest bark right away from cut trees and boil the bark immediately after harvest to kill them if you notice any tiny holes and sawdust on the bark.
- **Preparation:** Follow general instructions for working with inner bark. The inner bark of slippery elms is good, but it can produce enough mucilage to be prohibitive. Using the bark fresh is best since the application of water during rehydration draws out the mucus.

Hickory

Carya species

This is one of my favorite trees to work with because of the incredible strength of the inner bark, as evidenced by its traditional use as woven chair seating. All species are good for basketry, including shagbark (*Carya ovata*), pignut (*C. glabra*), and mockernut (*C. tomentosa*).

Shagbark hickory

- **Parts used:** Inner bark.
- **Uses:** Woven baskets; rims on folded bark baskets; lashing and weavers in ribbed baskets; random weave.
- **Qualities:** Extremely strong and durable—difficult to process because of this, but worth it.
- **Range:** Eastern and midwestern North America; parts of China and Southeast Asia.
- **Habitat:** Wide range of temperate forests.
- **Identification features:** Medium to large deciduous tree; pinnately compound leaves are 8–11 inches; younger trees have very hard, smooth outer bark divided by interconnected fissures; hard green nuts that split into several parts.
- **Harvest:** Late spring through summer.
- **Preparation:** Remove every bit of the outer bark to make it easier to cut to width and split later. Consider using smaller trees where the inner bark isn't thick enough to require splitting. To cut to width, lay flat on a table, clamp, and score using a sharp utility knife. There is no need to cut all the way through. You can fold and crack the bark at the score marks, cutting any parts that stick out with scissors. To rehydrate, it needs more time or hotter water than other barks. Submerge in steaming or lightly simmering water for 30–75 minutes. Alternatively, submerge it in steaming water for 30 minutes, turn off the heat, and let it sit overnight.

Paper Birch

Betula papyrifera

You can't miss the beautiful white sheets of paper birch bark in a northern forest. It is one of the few barks that can be harvested from a live tree without killing it, although the tree is permanently scarred. It is a material of choice across its range due to its myriad wonderful qualities. There are similar species in Europe, Russia, and northern Japan that are used in the same way.

- **Parts used:** Outer bark.

Paper birch

Spruce

- **Uses:** Sheets of bark as folded bark baskets; rims on woven and folded bark baskets. Strips of bark as woven baskets; diagonal plaiting; random weave.
- **Qualities:** Strong; flexible; antimicrobial; waterproof; splits easily.
- **Range:** Subarctic North America to Canada; northern United States south to Virginia.
- **Habitat:** Mixed hardwood and conifer forests.
- **Identification features:** Small to medium deciduous tree; smooth, white, paperlike bark, peeling in sheets on older trees; has sporadic black branch scars that resemble eyes; long, thin horizontal pores; leaves are 2–4 inches, ovate to triangular, with serrated edges.
- **Harvest:** Peel bark from live trees in early summer. Forage from dead or fallen trees anytime.
- **Preparation:** See detailed instructions for preparing birch bark on pages 118–120. The longer the bark has been sitting on the ground, the less flexible and harder it is to work with. Use stiff material for rims.

Spruce

Picea species

Harvesting spruce roots is a very rewarding experience. Just be sure to follow the guidelines for ethical harvesting when digging roots, as it is important to care for the tree. While all conifer roots can be used to some degree in basketry, spruce (particularly white spruce) roots are very high quality.

- **Parts used:** Roots; bark.
- **Uses:** Roots for coiling; twining; weavers in ribbed baskets; any kind of sewing or lashing. Bark sheets for folded bark baskets. Inner bark strips for woven baskets.
- **Qualities:** Roots are incredibly strong, smooth, and grow very long in some conditions.
- **Range:** Temperate northern hemisphere.
- **Habitat:** Forests; mountains; in northern climates, mixed woods; some species in swampy areas.
- **Identification features:** Conifer with single, short, prickly needles (usually less than 1 inch) that leave a raised bud scar when removed from twigs; cones hang down from branches; trees are conical and narrow.
- **Harvest:** Late spring through summer.
- **Preparation:** I have a hard time finding long pieces of bark for weaving and tend to favor it for folded bark containers. See general guidelines for preparing inner bark and roots (pages 110 and 121).

Tulip poplar

Western red cedar

Tulip Poplar

Tulipifera liriodendron

This is one of my favorite trees for foraging inner bark. My only regret is that it does not grow more abundantly in my area. In the North this tree is called tulip tree, and in the South it's known as poplar or tulip poplar.

- **Parts used:** Bark.
- **Uses:** Bark sheets for folded bark baskets. Bark strips as stakes in twined baskets; woven baskets; diagonal plaiting; rims in folded bark baskets; weavers and lashing in ribbed baskets; random weave. Inner bark–retted fiber for cordage; sewing strands.
- **Qualities:** Strong, even when split thinly; splits easily; lovely light color; tree tends to grow straight, so you can get long strips.
- **Range:** South Ontario to north-central and eastern United States.
- **Habitat:** Wide range of temperate forests.
- **Identification features:** Medium to large deciduous tree; tends to grow straight and tall; tulip-shaped leaves; flower resembles a tulip; lemony smell.
- **Harvest:** Late spring through summer.
- **Preparation:** See general guidelines for preparing inner bark (page 110).

Western Red Cedar

Thuja plicata

What an incredible material with a rich history of use! Despite its shredded appearance, the bark is very strong. Northern white cedar (*Thuja occidentalis*) can be used in the same way, although I typically use the entire trunk of trees already being cut and am not sure if strips can be peeled from live trees.

- **Parts used:** Bark; roots.
- **Uses:** Bark sheets for folded bark baskets. Bark as cordage; multistrand braiding; all parts of twined and woven baskets; diagonal plaiting; weavers in ribbed baskets; random weave. Roots for coiling; twining strands; sewing strands; folded bark baskets; any kind of lashing.
- **Qualities:** Very strong; flexible; can be harvested in strips from live trees without killing them.
- **Range:** Southeast Alaska to northern California, including the Pacific Northwest.
- **Habitat:** Moist shaded forests.
- **Identification features:** Conifer; medium to large tree; grayish red outer bark; leaves are flat and scalelike, pressed closely to twigs with a fanlike appearance.
- **Harvest:** Spring and summer. Make a horizontal cut several inches wide and tear upward to remove bark from live, standing trees without killing them.
- **Preparation:** Cut into strips, split into thinner pieces.

White Pine

Pinus strobus

In my area, multitudes of white pines grow densely packed together and sprout up quickly in abandoned fields. Some think of white pine as a weed tree, but I love them. They are stately, graceful, and excellent for basketry.

- **Parts used:** Bark; roots.
- **Uses:** Bark sheets for folded bark baskets; rims in woven and folded bark baskets. Inner bark for thick cordage or cut into strips for woven baskets. Roots for coiling; twining strands; sewing folded bark baskets; any kind of lashing.
- **Qualities:** Thin outer bark allows for great flexibility in folded bark baskets; roots are not as strong as spruce but still usable.
- **Range:** Eastern North America from Canada to North Carolina.
- **Habitat:** Widespread habitats, including mixed forests; old fields.
- **Identification features:** Small to large conifer; needles are five to a bundle and notably thinner and softer than other pines, having a feathery appearance from a distance; can grow in dense stands.
- **Harvest:** March to September, depending on the dryness of the climate. White pine can be quite sappy. Either wear gloves or remove sap from hands by vigorously rubbing them in coconut oil until the sap evaporates, then washing in hot water. To get the biggest, best material possible, look for white pines with smooth bark, a large trunk circumference, and long spaces between branch whorls. If you harvest during the winter season, putting a log next to a fire and heating up the sap makes it possible to peel. Bark beetles are attracted to cut white pines in some locations. If you notice any tiny holes and sawdust on the bark, boil the bark immediately after

White pine

harvest to kill any beetles that may be present. If left untreated the beetles will continue to eat through dried bark in storage, ruining it.

- **Preparation:** Prepare according to instructions for folded bark sheets on pages 116–118. Soak in hot water for 10–30 minutes or until flexible.

Willow

Salix species

See complete entry on page 65.

OTHER TREE BARKS FOR BASKETRY

The best way to figure out if the bark of a tree can be peeled is to do a test (see Making a Test Peel on page 105). I have successfully peeled bark from the trees listed below and found it to be strong enough to use extensively.

- Eastern hemlock (*Tsuga canadensis*)
- Mimosa (*Albizia mimosa*)
- Paper mulberry (*Broussonetia papyrifera*)
- Royal paulownia (*Paulownia tomentosa*)
- Staghorn sumac (*Rhus typhina*)
- White ash (*Fraxinus americana*)

Trees that others have used but that I have not personally tried:

- Box elder (*Acer negundo*)
- Lilac (*Syringa* species)
- Poplar (*Populus* species)
- Privet (*Ligustrum vulgare*)
- Red maple (*Acer rubrum*)
- Sweet chestnut (*Castanea sativa*)

FIELD NOTES OF UNSUCCESSFUL TESTS

These trees have bark that either wouldn't peel off the log or tore so easily it wasn't worth using. If you have them nearby, it may still be worth experimentation, but start on a small section.

- American sycamore (*Platanus occidentalis*)
- Norway maple (*Acer platanoides*)
- Red oak (*Quercus rubra*)
- Silver maple (*Acer saccharinum*)
- Sugar maple (*Acer saccharum*)
- Witch hazel (*Hamamelis virginiana*)

How to Forage Bark

Fortunately, there are many ways to obtain bark for basketmaking that don't require processing a large tree, which for many people is intimidating or unrealistic. Pruning a branch off a healthy tree requires a small folding saw or a pair of loppers. Cutting a small sapling or a shoot from a multistemmed shrub or tree requires a folding saw and perhaps a friend to hold the sapling while you cut it.

understanding bark

At its simplest a tree trunk or branch consists of three elements: wood, inner bark, and outer bark. For basketry, we make use of both types of bark by peeling them away from the solid wood center. If the bark is thin and flexible, the inner and outer layers can be left together, harvesting and using them as is for folded or woven baskets. If the bark is thick and too inflexible for weaving, the outer bark is first removed. Then the inner bark can be used in strips to make many types of woven baskets.

ANATOMY OF A TREE TRUNK

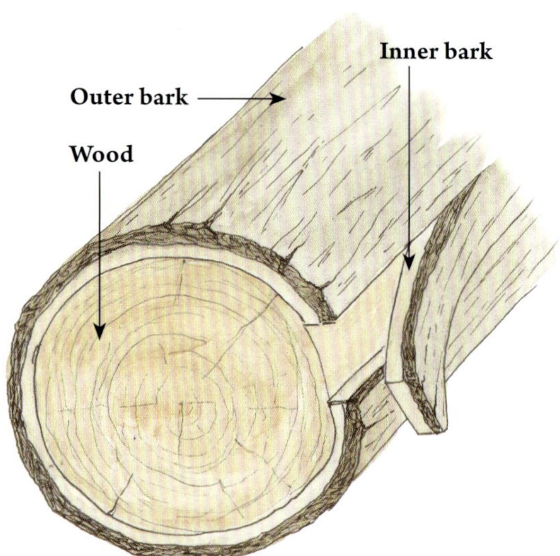

choosing a tree

All trees have bark, but only some species have bark that both peels easily and is strong and flexible enough for basketry. Once you know a tree is a contender, consider the following additional criteria.

Harvest from live, healthy trees. Trees that fall due to storms or human interventions are great opportunities for basket makers. However, there is only a brief window during which the bark will slip, since fallen trees dry out within a few days to 2 weeks, depending on the environment. The wetter the air, the more time you have. Alternatively, look for a tree in a forest or grove that would benefit from thinning, meaning that by removing one tree the others around it will have more space to thrive. If you can't find a suitable whole tree or don't want to tackle a project of that scale, prune a branch from a healthy tree. Trees that are sick or dying will likely have inner bark that is dry or damaged by insects.

Harvest in late spring to summer. This is the time during which the sap is flowing, and bark will slip off the wood. Depending on how dry the year is, the season may be shorter or longer. June is generally the golden time for harvesting bark where I live in the northeastern United States. Conifers such as white pine are an exception. These trees have an extended growing season, and the bark reliably slips off earlier in the year.

The trunk diameter should be under 14 inches. This is a manageable size, and it's a clue that the tree isn't too old. Larger is possible, but peeling will be much more difficult and yield inner bark of lesser quality.

The tree should have smooth or light- to medium-textured outer bark. This indicates that it will be easier to remove the outer bark and that the tree isn't too old. Older trees have inner bark that is thicker but weak and prone to tearing.

The tree should be as straight, tall, and branchless as possible. This quality is most important for woven bark basketry, where long strips are desirable. (However, folded bark can be done with pieces as short as 10 inches for small baskets.) Also, inner bark has a grain to it. If a section of the tree is leaning or crooked, the grain of the inner bark will be diagonal, making it more difficult to split later.

Making a Test Peel

Before cutting a tree or removing the outer bark, do a test peel to see if the bark slips and will be good for basketmaking. This is especially worthwhile if it is early or late in the season, or you are working with a species of tree that is new to you. Use a straight-bladed knife to shave the outer bark from a 3 × 5-inch area in an inconspicuous spot. If the outer bark is thin and smooth, as in the white pine in the photo at right, proceed without shaving off the outer bark.

Make a 1-inch horizontal cut and two vertical cuts, one on each side. Use a packing tool to pry up the piece of bark and peel it downward. If the inner bark is not easily and cleanly separating from the wood, it may be too early or too late in the season, the tree might be the wrong species, or the tree may be unhealthy. It is a good sign if the bark is very flexible and there is a lot of moisture as the bark slips away from the wood.

Make a 1-inch horizontal cut and a vertical cut on each side.

cutting branches and saplings

Harvesting small trees and pruning branches with confidence is empowering. You don't need a chain saw or any special skills to get started—just a folding saw and good safety technique. Follow the knife safety rules on page 18 and learn how your saw unfolds and locks in place before using it. Beginners should not attempt to cut anything that is larger than 1½ inches in diameter or particularly tall or heavy. Also avoid scenarios that force you into awkward positions while working. For challenging jobs, consider finding a professional or taking a course in pruning.

BE OPEN TO POSSIBILITY

I made my first bark basket from a short, crooked linden branch that fell on the sidewalk near my home. Even though the branch wasn't ideal, I cut the inner bark into strips and wove a lopsided basket that I treasure to this day. As you embark (pun intended) on this journey, embrace the material that comes into your life with a spirit of curiosity and possibility.

How to Use a Saw

If you are new to saws, be aware that they are designed for the teeth to cut on either the pull or the push stroke. I prefer pull saws because they afford more control than push saws. Most folding saws are pull saws. Also know that saws are difficult to sharpen. Keep them clean and avoid cutting into dirt, which quickly dulls them. Pine sap is very difficult to remove, so I have a cheaper saw for cutting pine and a higher-quality one for everything else.

To begin a cut, rest the saw on the bark and pull it toward you lightly but firmly. Repeat this until there is enough of a trough for the saw to rest inside. Begin sawing back and forth with long strokes that utilize the full length of the blade, putting more emphasis on the direction cut for your saw (typically on the pull for folding saws). It is better to go slow and steady than to rush and put on a lot of downward pressure.

Pruning a Branch

When pruning a branch, consider the health and safety of both you and the tree. Only prune a couple of branches from any one tree, choose those you can comfortably cut from the ground, and only cut those that are short and light enough for you or a friend to support.

1. Position yourself so your dominant hand can hold the saw close to the tree trunk and your nondominant hand can support the branch.

2. The cut should be made just outside of the branch collar, which is where the wood of the branch begins to slope into the trunk of the tree. Do not cut flush to the trunk or far out on the branch, which allows for decay and damages the tree. Try to keep the cut straight and clean.

3. Make sure the branch is supported so it doesn't rip at the end of the cut. Note that cutting straight down will not work well on anything thicker than 1½ inches or particularly heavy.

Cutting Saplings and Small Trees

For beginners I would not recommend cutting anything larger than 1½ inches in diameter and taller than 5 or 6 feet without professional help. Something this size will be light and easy to handle. Choose a sapling with enough space around it for the tree to fall without getting caught in anything.

1. Kneel next to the sapling and position yourself so your dominant hand can cut near the base. Your other hand should support the rest of the sapling to keep it from falling on you. Even better, bring a friend along to help.

2. Position the saw 2 inches above the ground to cut through the sapling's base horizontally. If you need to cut higher to be comfortable, make a second cut later to leave a stump behind that's closer to the ground.

3. As you get close to the end of the cut, the sapling may begin to lean. You can let it fall, but be sure to push it gently away from you, and when it is steady, finish the cut. If it rips or is uneven, make a second, cleaner cut straight across after moving the sapling away.

reading a tree

Whether you can harvest bark strips for woven baskets or sheets for folded baskets will depend on how the tree grew, including how thick the bark is and how many branches the tree has. One section of a tree might be straight and branchless, yielding long strips of bark well suited for weaving. (Longer pieces are harder to come by, so I tend to save them for weaving material, although they could just as easily be cut into sheets.) Another section might have many branches, lending itself to shorter rectangular sheets for folded baskets. Another tree might be suited to each type.

Here are a few case studies to help you learn how to read a tree and assess how its bark might be used for basketmaking.

A sapling with thin, flexible bark. You harvest a 1½-inch-diameter willow sapling from a cluster of several saplings. Its outer bark is so thin that it would be unnecessary to shave it off. Plus the smooth outer bark is a beautiful color. A good decision here is to peel the bark off in one or two pieces and cut it into long, fine strips for weaving.

A tall, straight tree trunk with thick bark. A 16-inch-diameter black walnut tree with deeply furrowed outer bark falls in your neighbor's yard. The 20-foot-long trunk is perfect for weaving strips, but first you must remove the thick, inflexible outer bark with a drawknife and then peel off the inner bark.

A branched trunk with mixed types of bark. You find an 8-inch-diameter tulip poplar with lightly furrowed bark and some straight sections interrupted by branches, as seen in the illustration below. In this case you can partition the tree into different sections. Shave the outer bark from the long spans between and around branches to harvest inner bark strips for weaving. For the shorter sections between branches, peel the bark off in sheets with the outer bark intact to use for folded baskets. There is also a pile of branches with smooth bark, which you can peel as is to use for twining and for weavers in ribbed baskets.

Sections A, B, C, and D are short, so leave the outer bark intact for use in folded baskets.

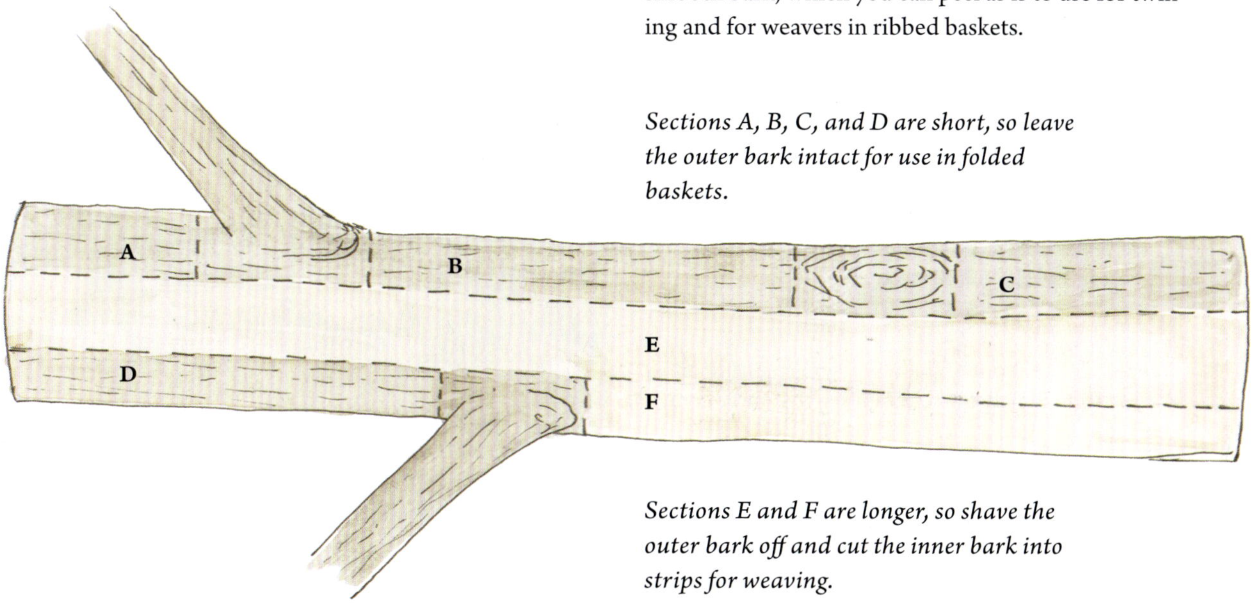

Sections E and F are longer, so shave the outer bark off and cut the inner bark into strips for weaving.

How to Prepare Bark Strips for Woven Baskets

Harvesting bark from trees can be broken down into four steps.

1. Remove the outer bark with a drawknife.

2. Peel off sections of inner bark.

3. Cut lengths of bark to the desired width.

4. Split lengths of bark to a weaveable thickness.

At any point after you've peeled the bark, you can dry and store it to work with later. In some cases removing the outer layer isn't necessary because the bark is thin, smooth, and flexible enough to use as is. (See Harvesting Bark Strips from Saplings or Branches on page 115.)

removing outer bark

After acquiring a log, the first step is to shave the outer bark off with a sharp drawknife. The goal is to remove all the outer bark without cutting too far into the inner bark, which is precious basketmaking material and, on younger trees, might be less than ¼ inch thick. Since you are working with a blade, take some precautions:

- Position yourself comfortably.
- Never grab the drawknife by the blade.
- Keep your knees out of the way if you're sitting on the log from which you're removing the outer bark.

1. Set a log on a sawhorse or sit on top of the log if it is too big to lift. Using a folding saw, remove side branches so you don't have any obstacles in the way while working.

2. Extend your arms as far as they will go in front of you and place the drawknife blade on the surface of the log with the flat part touching the log.

3. Bend your elbows and pull the drawknife toward your body in a long stroke. The blade should shave off a layer of outer bark. You may have to put some muscle into this, depending on the thickness of the material. Repeat until you have removed as much of the outer bark as possible, following the tips below as needed. It's important to get most of the outer bark off, so the inner bark will be easier to split and weave later.

4. After you have cleared an area of outer bark in a continuous strip at least 5 or 6 inches wide all the way down the length of the log, you can begin to peel off the inner bark. Alternatively, continue to remove outer bark and do all the peeling later.

Tips for Removing Outer Bark

On one end of the log, experiment with shaving all the way through to the wood so you can clearly see how thick the inner bark is. You'll know you are at the wood when you reach a shiny, wet, hard layer although the color of the inner bark and wood may be very similar. This will help you find the balance of taking off enough outer bark without going too deep.

- Shaving off all the outer bark takes many passes. Long strokes will take off bulk; smaller movements are good for detail work. Some dark streaks may remain where the outer bark goes more deeply into the inner bark.
- For detail work, try angling one side of the drawknife to bite into the outer bark and slide the drawknife toward you at an angle with more of a slicing than a pulling motion.
- Look for places where the outer bark comes to a peak or a triangle. Place the drawknife at the tip of the triangle and draw it toward you.
- Trim as much outer bark as possible closely around any knots. Even an inch of outer bark left on will make peeling very difficult.
- As you practice, you will begin to intuit how gentle or aggressive you need to be with your drawknife to remove outer bark from different areas of a log. Use your best judgment as you learn, always being careful with your knife.

The color of the wood is only subtly different from the surrounding inner bark.

peeling inner bark

Harvesting strips of inner bark for weaving is a labor of love, worth every second of effort and ounce of sweat. After acquiring a log, removing the outer bark, peeling the inner bark, cutting it to size, and splitting it, each piece of weaving material is something to be treasured. The basket you make from it becomes priceless. Even if your first attempts yield only scraps of bark, make a miniature basket with them and keep going! Becoming proficient at bark processing takes time.

1. Using a long ruler and a crayon or water-soluble pencil, draw two straight lines all the way down the length of the log 2 to 4 inches apart. I usually aim for 3 inches. The edges of the strip will almost always be uneven and need to be trimmed to straightness, so strips narrower than 2 inches are more wasteful than wider ones. Strips wider than 4 inches are usable but tend to be cumbersome when processing later.

2. Using a utility knife and positioning your body so that it is not in the knife's path, cut into each of the predrawn lines. Press down with enough force to completely sever the inner bark down to the wood. If you don't cut deeply enough, the edges of the bark can stick and tear when peeling.

3. Starting at the end of the log, use a strong, bent-tip packing tool or a butter knife to lever up the end of the strip of inner bark.

4. Get your fingers under the edge of the inner bark and pull up gently—it should slip off easily. Enjoy how it feels to peel! I think this is the most satisfying part of working with bark.

5. Keep a very close eye on the edges of the strip. If an edge is sticking, you didn't cut deeply enough. Stop peeling immediately and use your knife to cut more deeply into the spot where it's sticking. If your cuts are deep enough and the bark still won't peel off the wood, then it may be too early or late in the season, or the tree is not in good health—just do your best to remove what you can.

6. Repeat steps 1 to 5 to remove all the inner bark from the log. If you want to cut the lengths of inner bark to your desired width right away, proceed, following the instructions below. To dry and store them for later, refer to directions for drying and storing inner bark strips on page 114.

cutting bark strips

You can cut a bark strip to width using a leather strap cutter, a tabletop leather lace cutter, or, in a pinch, very sharp scissors.

If you dried the bark for storage, rehydrate it before cutting by heating a pot of water to a low steam, then submerging the strips in the water to soften them until they're workable. This process might take as little as 5 minutes or as long as an hour, depending on the thickness of the material. (Notable outliers are hickory bark, which sometimes needs to soak overnight, and the bark of young saplings and branches, which rehydrate in moments.) To test the readiness of the strips, remove the bark from the water using tongs, cool briefly, then proceed to cutting. If you are not able to cut or split the bark easily, then put it back in the water a little while longer.

If you are cutting your strips fresh, without having dried them first, cut them 1/16 inch wider than you want them to be since they will shrink a bit.

Method 1: Leather Strap Cutter

This relatively inexpensive leatherwork tool cuts bark into strips one at a time and works well for thinner bark. The width of the strips can be as small as 1/4 inch and as wide as 3 or 4 inches.

1. Hook the strap cutter's blade on one edge of the bark.

2. Press the flat of the handle firmly against the edge of the bark. It is essential to push the handle and the bark against each other so there is no space between them—otherwise, the strip of bark being cut will vary in width. Pull the strap cutter toward you while pushing the bark through with the other hand. If the movement feels difficult, clamp the end of the bark to the edge of a table to hold it steady while cutting.

Method 2: Leather Lace Cutter

This leather cutting tool needs to be solidly attached to a strong table. One advantage over the strap cutter is that it creates multiple strips at the same time.

1. Firmly attach the lace cutter to the edge of a sturdy table. Lift the guard on the top and press one end of the bark into the blade about 1½ inches from the edge.

2. Use one hand to hold the bark flat and straight against the blade and use the other hand to pull the bark toward you. Pay close attention to keeping the bark straight.

Method 3: Basketry Scissors

If you don't have other tools, you can use very sharp scissors to cut thinner bark into strips, but it will take longer and be difficult to cut evenly.

When you're finished cutting, proceed to splitting the strips or dry and store them for later, following the directions on page 114.

splitting bark strips

Unless your inner bark strips are already 1⁄16 inch or less in thickness, you need to split them in half or sometimes into three pieces to achieve a workable depth. Bark strips that are too thick don't weave well. Splitting requires a lot of practice, so just be patient and expect to have some scraps with the first couple of pieces. First review the knife safety guidelines on page 18, then practice on scrap strips.

If you dried and stored cut strips at an earlier time, rehydrate by submerging them in a pot of steaming water for 5 to 10 minutes (possibly longer) until they are flexible but not oversoaked. (They're oversoaked if you squeeze them and a lot of water comes out.) If you soak them too little or too much, they will not split as nicely. In general, bark is relatively forgiving when it comes to drying and rehydrating and can go through this process several times without the quality of the weaving material degrading.

Continued on next page

GETTING AN EVEN SPLIT

When splitting bark strips, the goal is to keep both sides even, but inevitably one side will start to thin and the other will get thicker. Pay close attention so you remedy this unevenness as soon as it starts. To reestablish an even divide, bend and pull harder on the thicker side. (My mantra: Bend the bigger side.)

If you are unable to even it out with your hands or there is a hole or some other imperfection in the bark, use a utility knife to carefully slice into the thicker side to reestablish an even divide. Always go slowly and angle the knife away from your fingers.

In general, it is much better to correct an uneven divide with your hands instead of the utility knife. Even so, sometimes the knife is necessary.

1. Lay one end of the strip on a flat surface that is safe for cutting. Use a utility knife to carefully cut halfway through the thickness of the bark about ¾ inch from the end.

2. Pick up the strip and bend it in half at the cut to begin splitting the two halves apart.

3. Grasp the two halves with your thumb and the side of your pointer finger. Pull the two sides apart, rolling and leveraging your knuckles against each other to control the splitting. Work slowly and carefully.

drying, storing, and rehydrating bark strips

Roll long strips of bark in individual coils so the inner part is facing out, then secure each coil with a spring clamp or string. See general guidelines for drying and storing on pages 21–22. Once dry, remove the clamp. Short pieces can be tied in bundles with two ties—one at each end.

Inner bark is highly susceptible to mold, so take care to dry and store it properly. Hang coils on the wall, stack them on shelves, or keep them in a bin or box with the top open. Store shorter pieces in a box or stacked on a shelf.

To rehydrate thinly split inner tree bark, submerge it in a pot of steaming water for 2 to 10 minutes. For unsplit coils of inner bark (approximately 3 inches wide), submerge in a pot of steaming water for 15 to 60 minutes.

HARVESTING BARK STRIPS FROM SAPLINGS OR BRANCHES

When a tree or branch is very young and has thin, smooth, flexible outer bark, you can peel it without removing the outer bark first. Willow coppices (see page 66)—or other places where many similar-size stems are growing from one root system—are common for this technique.

1. Choose a sapling or branch that is as straight and branchless as possible and cut it off at the base. Using a sturdy utility knife, make a long cut along the length of the sapling or branch below where it starts to split and branch further. Turn it over and make a second cut down the opposite side. The more careful you are to keep the cuts straight, the more usable bark you will have later. (On pieces with a larger diameter, a third lengthwise cut may be needed to peel strips without cracking them. Saplings with very thin and flexible bark may only need a single lengthwise cut—the final piece of bark will look like a tube with a cut down one side.) Follow the knife safety guidelines on page 18 and be very cautious while cutting saplings and branches as the knife can easily slip.

2. Peel the bark starting at one end. If you are unable to get the peel started with your fingers, use a packing tool to help separate it from the wood.

3. Before using, cut and split the bark strips to your desired width and thickness, following the directions on pages 111–114. Often the bark is already thin enough to weave and won't need splitting. To store the bark for later use, roll pieces into a loose coil with the inner side facing out. With such thin bark, rehydration only requires a few moments in steaming water.

How to Prepare Bark Sheets for Folded Baskets

Harvesting sheets of bark for folded baskets is very similar to harvesting inner bark strips for woven baskets except that it doesn't require removing the outer bark. Folding bark is best for trees with a lot of branches where you can't harvest longer strips. Because this technique doesn't require the material to be very flexible, and in fact benefits from the sturdiness of the outer bark, the bark can be somewhat furrowed and textured.

I used smooth to lightly textured white pine outer bark for the folded White Pine Bark Catch-All on page 245. The inner and outer bark of deciduous trees is not as flexible as in white pine and other conifers, so their bark sheets lend themselves to the simple fold or cat's-eye baskets on pages 235 and 250 rather than those that require more cutting and folding.

As you plan the size and placement of the sheet to cut, note that the height of the basket should run along the length of the log, because that is the direction of the bark's grain. Also consider that you'll fold the sheet in half to form the basket height, so the length you cut must be double the height of the final basket.

harvesting bark sheets

The following instructions are shown using white pine, which grows prolifically in my area. The outer bark of white pine is thin yet strong, ideal for folded bark projects. Because white pine branches always grow in whorls, the sheets can only be as long as the space between the whorls. When choosing a tree, I look for those that have the longest spaces between the whorls.

Other conifers, such as spruce and hemlocks, have the same whorl pattern in their branches and can be peeled the same way. The difference is that the outer bark is much more textured than white pine and the bark will take more time and patience to peel off.

On deciduous trees, branches don't grow in whorls, so there is more freedom in the size and area from which you cut and peel sheets. However, you still have to "read the tree" and work around what branches and knots are present, planning how to divide the cuts to get the most usable bark. The thicker the outer bark, the more times you will need to score a cut line to get through completely, and peeling will take more effort.

1. Set a log on two sawhorses or sit on top of the log if it is too big to lift. Using a folding saw, remove side branches so the work area is free of obstacles. Be sure not to cut into the bark you want to harvest when removing the side branches.

2. Using the folding saw, make cuts around the entire circumference of the log just below and above each of the branch whorls. Make sure you cut all the way through the bark to the wood and that the two ends of each cut match up.

3. Using a sharp utility knife, make a lengthwise cut between the two circumference cuts. If the log is damaged anywhere, make the lengthwise cut in that spot, so the damage will be less conspicuous on your basket.

4. Using a packing tool, a butter knife, or a stick whittled to a flat edge, peel the bark from the wood. Bark sheets are ready to use right away. They will shrink a bit, but in my experience, the shrinkage doesn't affect the final basket. Alternatively, dry, store, and rehydrate following the directions for bark sheets at right and on page 118.

drying and storing bark sheets

Bark sheets are flexible when they are peeled off the log, then harden as they dry. For drying and storing you can fold the sheets, leave them flat, or roll them into a tube. No matter how you choose to dry the bark, do not allow the inner sides of the bark to touch; if they do, they will mold. You will need to immerse the bark in a pot of hot water when you rehydrate, so make sure the size at which you dry the bark will fit into the pot you'll use. If the pieces are too large—even folded—and won't fit any pot you have, flip the bark over halfway through the rehydrating process. Store in a cool, dry place in a bin, box, paper bag, or large clear plastic bag with the top open.

Folding Bark Sheets

I find that bark sheets that I've folded before drying and storing fit most easily into a pot of water later.

1. Loosely fold each piece in half (so there is a bit of space between the sides) and hold in position with a 2-inch spring clamp.

2. Lay the pieces on a table and run a strong fan on them until they are completely dry. This process takes from a few days to over a week, depending on air circulation and humidity. If you don't have a fan, place them on a table in an area that is cool and dry and has good air circulation.

rehydrating bark sheets

Bring a large pot of water to a light simmer. Submerge the bark and leave it in the water for 5 to 30 minutes or more, depending on the thickness, until it is flexible. To check your bark, try bending it with tongs. If it feels pliant, take it out and start working with it. If it cracks when you start to work with it, then put it back in the pot for a bit longer.

preparing paper birch bark sheets

While there are many species of birch, paper birch (*Betula papyrifera*) is best for basketry in North America. In Europe and Russia there are four similar species that have the same properties and are used in the same way. Although we don't have to fell (and, in the process, kill) the tree to access this material, the tree is permanently scarred once we peel the bark, which is undoubtedly a stressor. I harvest conservatively, with permission, in areas with abundant birch. Processing paper birch bark for basketry is unique because you only use the outer bark, which you can peel from live, standing trees in early summer. Birch bark doesn't hold any moisture so it can be used fresh or stored for later use.

Peeling Outer Bark from Birch

Choose a tree whose trunk has large, smooth white areas mostly free from branches or branch scars (which appear like black eyes on the trunk). If you try to remove bark at the wrong time of year, the outer and inner bark will not separate. In the Northeast, where I live, early summer is the right time.

Using a utility knife, make a long, shallow cut down the trunk, being careful to cut through the outer bark only. You'll know you're at the correct depth when you feel the white outer bark naturally separating from the brown inner bark. If your shallow cut isn't deep enough, repeat, going very slightly deeper. The depth of the cut on a live tree is very important. If you cut into the inner bark, you will damage the tree.

At the top and the bottom of the vertical cut, make two shallow cuts around the circumference of the tree, again just through the outer bark. Severing the inner bark around the entire circumference of a tree is called girdling and will kill the tree.

Only the outer bark has been removed from the center of this birch tree. It will continue living since the inner bark is left intact.

Breaking

When first peeled off the tree, the sheets are usually quite thick and difficult to cut. I recommend processing the sheets into more manageable pieces. First, plan how you will divide up the sheets to get the most usable bark. Any place with rough spots—which are most visible on the back of the bark—won't split well later, but areas between the rough spots will yield long strips. Save areas with rough spots for basket rims.

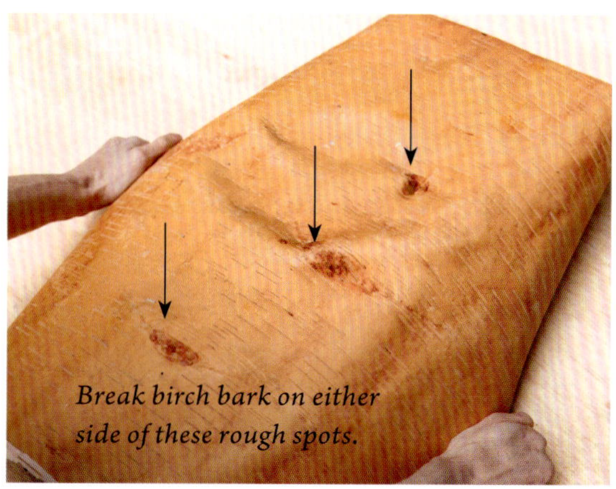

Break birch bark on either side of these rough spots.

Birch bark easily snaps, or breaks, along the grain. Find the grain by bending a corner of the bark and seeing which way it naturally splits. (The grain runs in the direction of the long, narrow pores covering the bark.) In the direction of the grain, score the bark lightly into sections with a utility knife, working around the rough patches. Snap the sections apart with your hands to separate them completely. If there are no rough patches to work around, divide the bark into pieces about 15 inches wide, which is a manageable size to work with.

First Splitting

To process the bark into strips for weaving, begin by splitting the thickness in half. If your bark is flexible and you are planning to fold it rather than weave it, splitting may not be necessary.

Split the bark in half using a utility knife or your fingernails. Start at a corner and follow the material's lead on how it wants to split. Birch bark separates very cleanly and does not require much manipulation to keep the split even. If you reach a rough spot and the bark is sticking, proceed slowly, using a utility knife to help if needed.

Cutting

Using a utility knife and ruler on a cutting mat or other appropriate flat surface, divide the strips to the desired width for your project. Alternatively, use scissors to cut strips freehand, though they won't be as straight.

Second Splitting

For a woven project, I recommend a thickness of two or three sheets of copy paper, but experiment with your own preference. You may need to split the strips again to reach your desired thickness.

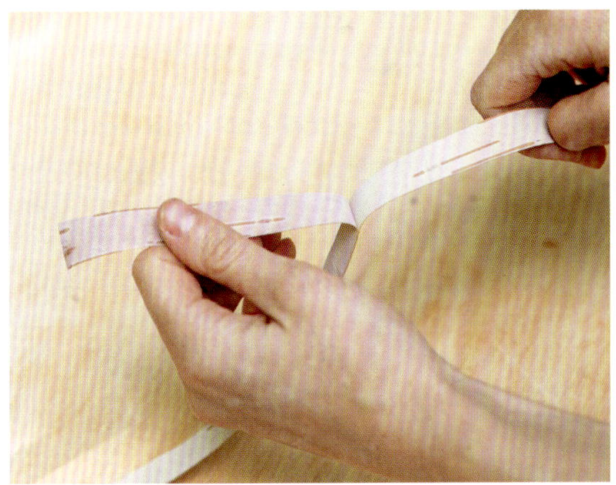

Continued on next page

Oiling

To prepare the bark for final use, rub a tiny bit of any kind of oil—coconut, sesame, or olive oil, for example—into both sides of the birch bark with your fingers. Make sure each piece is completely covered but not greasy to the touch. Unlike other kinds of bark, birch does not need to be rehydrated in hot water. In fact, hot water will cause it to curl up. The only exception is very old pieces that you are planning to use for rims or decorative elements, which may be too stiff to use without submerging them in very hot water for a few moments.

USING FALLEN BIRCH BARK

When choosing a birch, you can also look for standing dead trees and fallen logs that are propped up off the ground. Even after a birch tree dies, the bark often remains viable for over a year, especially if it isn't touching the ground. (Bark from all other types of trees must be harvested promptly after the tree falls.) To determine if the bark is still viable for basketmaking, use a utility knife to cut a square out of the bark and then try to peel it off. Look for pieces that remain a bit flexible. Any samples that crack very easily, are full of holes, or fall apart indicate that the bark has degraded. Fresher bark is best for weaving and folded containers, though some older pieces that are not quite as flexible and have a few holes are still viable for rims or decorative elements.

The bark at right is too stiff and holey to split and use for weaving, but it has character and would be great for a decorative rim.

MAKING BASKETS WITH ROOTS

Roots tend to go unnoticed because they are not easily visible, but they are long, incredibly strong, resilient, flexible, and have a lovely coloration. Use them for sewing folded bark baskets and coiled baskets, twining, or in small ribbed baskets.

How to Forage Roots

Fallen trees with exposed rootballs are great sources. Otherwise, you can dig them from the soil, but take care not to injure the tree by harvesting too much. In sandy soils and areas without a lot of underbrush, roots tend to grow longer and straighter in addition to being easier to dig up. In my neck of the woods, I look for open forests, higher-elevation forests, or colonies of spruce or pine. You can harvest at any time of year when the ground is not frozen.

To dig, clear the layers of forest floor and soil a couple of inches deep about 3 feet away from the tree trunk. As you unearth the network of intersecting roots, look for one that is about pencil width or a little bigger and follow it gently and patiently—without tugging—clearing the area as you go. Cut where it connects to a larger root. Coil up each length that you harvest and re-cover the remaining roots.

How to Prepare Roots for Basketmaking

First remove the outer bark layer and then split the roots in half lengthwise, preferably right after harvest before they dry out. If you don't have time, you can dry them and then rehydrate them in hot water later for processing.

To remove the bark, create a tight notch either with two nails hammered into a table in the shape of a V or cut into a sturdy stick. Pull the root through the tightest space of the notch with force and agitation until an area of the skin loosens. Once the white inner root is revealed, peel the outer bark off.

To split, refer to the instructions for vines on page 60. Roots very naturally split in half along the edge, which makes the process relatively easy. After splitting, coil the root to store. Rehydrate before using by soaking in hot water.

Removing the bark

Splitting the root

PART TWO

MAKING WILD BASKETS

Making a basket with wild foraged plants is a conversation between the maker and the materials. Would that twisty vine in the front yard make a good handle? Can I coil the leaves sitting on top of the compost pile?

The answer to these questions is often yes, and the engaging part is figuring out how. Let go of making the "perfect" basket. Create space to explore freely, even when results go in an unexpected direction. I put a strong emphasis on creativity and experimentation as an invitation to develop your skills through trial and error. Open your heart; you have permission to get it wrong and try again! Just make sure you are having fun in the process.

The basket forms and techniques featured here have rich, wide-ranging histories and can be made from myriad materials. While they are all baskets, many are wildly different from each other. A folded pine bark vessel and a ribbed basket have little overlap in technique. Others, like woven and twined baskets, are more closely related. I find that each of us tends to have an affinity for particular techniques and styles. There's a good chance you'll love the first basket you make, but if you don't, keep trying and find out which styles make your heart sing.

I've organized this section of the book by technique. For each technique, I designed one or two projects that build on each other. Completing the first project will give you valuable skills for the second. While I show the projects with plant material that is available over a fairly large range, I also suggest substitutions and describe the qualities of the material you need so no matter where you live you can find something that works.

A NOTE FOR LEFT-HANDED FOLKS

Most of the techniques featured here are worked ambidextrously, not from left to right or vice versa. For the few that are done with one hand dominant—twining, weaving, and coiling—I demonstrate the techniques right-handed. Left-handed readers may prefer to reverse the directions, though many of my left-handed students have been content to follow the right-handed directions as is. The truth is that both hands are always busy.

Getting Started

The following information will help you choose a project, make sure you are set up to start on it, and understand how to care for your basket both during its creation and after it's done.

choosing a project

Cordage and multistrand braiding are perfect ways to begin working with natural materials without the pressure of completing a project. If you do want to start with a project, the following provide a good introduction with materials that are often readily accessible. However, if you are inspired by a different one, I say go for it.

- Coiled Bowl (page 145)
- Looped Cordage Pouch (page 155)
- Bark Necklace Pouch (page 239)
- Tension Tray (page 271)
- Grapevine Market Basket (page 279)

preparing materials

As exciting as it can be to jump into a project, wild basketry usually requires a little advance planning to harvest and, in most cases, to dry and rehydrate the material. When choosing a project, start by reading the section on what materials are needed and how to prepare them. Take lots of notes as you are learning, and soon all of the prep will feel natural.

planning your time

Some projects might only take a couple of hours, but most require a full day or more. I've included a time estimate for each project, but keep in mind that everyone works at a different pace and most things take longer than we expect, especially on the first try.

Fortunately most of the projects in this book can be paused at certain points if you want to take a break. If you'll be back at it within 24 hours, wrap the basket loosely in a lightly dampened cloth and place it in a slightly opened plastic bag in a cool place to keep it from drying out. If you are putting your project aside for longer, let it dry completely and rehydrate it when you're ready to continue. For each project I've provided notes on the best timing for pauses.

embracing variability

I've included an approximate size for each project, but each person's will vary, even when using the exact same materials and instructions.

caring for finished baskets

When you have completed a basket, dry it thoroughly to avoid mold. Put it in front of a fan or near a heater for a couple of days, check on it regularly, and turn it so different sides are facing up during drying time. If you don't have access to a fan or a heater, prop up the basket in a dry place with good circulation and turn it frequently. Once it's completely dry, the basket will resist mold unless it gets damp or is subjected to high humidity. Avoid leaving your basket outside where it can absorb moisture again.

CHAPTER 8

CORDAGE AND MULTISTRAND BRAIDING

Cordage and multistrand braiding are excellent introductions to the world of wild basketry. You likely have a suitable plant for these techniques growing near you in any season, and you'll get a feel for handling natural materials without the pressure of completing a bigger project. I encourage my students to always keep a pocketful of plant material for making cordage: It's the perfect thing to pull out and work on for a few moments here and there! Many projects in this book require cordage and multistrand braids to complete.

PROJECTS THAT USE CORDAGE

Multistrand Braiding (page 132)

Looped Cordage Pouch (page 155)

Wild Fibers Twined Bag (page 183)

Woven Berry Basket (page 199)

Bark Necklace Pouch (page 239)

PROJECTS THAT USE MULTISTRAND BRAIDING

Twined Treasure Basket (page 173)

White Pine Bark Catch-All (page 245)

Cordage

Have you ever picked up a blade of grass or the wrapper from a drinking straw and absentmindedly twisted it between your fingers? You are repeating an ancient practice. Essentially, cordage is cord, or twine, in which two individual strands of material twist around each other to add strength. Think of it like rope on a smaller scale or two-ply yarn. Our ancestors used cordage for everything from nets and snares to clothing and shoes, plus fishing and sailing lines, and, of course, baskets. You can never have too much cordage—in fact, every basket maker should have a ball on hand. There are so many applications. Try different materials so you get a feel for how each one behaves.

Uses for Cordage

- Multistrand braiding
- Looping
- Filling rims
- Sewing
- Lashing
- Weaving
- Twining
- Necklace strands

choosing plants for cordage

You can make cordage from any plant material that is a little soft, twistable, and at least 5 or 6 inches long. The longer the material, the better. Bast fibers—particularly long, strong, flexible fibers from the inner bark of some trees, vines, and plant stalks—are ideal for cordage. Leaf fibers from a few specific monocot plants are also excellent. You can use the entire leaves from some plants that are very flexible and long, though the cordage will be stiffer and not as strong.

The following plants are great choices. See Chapter 6, Wild Fibers, for how to forage and process many of them.

Bast fiber from plant stalks, such as milkweed, dogbane, nettle, velvetleaf, rosebay willow herb (fireweed), evening primrose, flax, hemp, and jute.

Bast fiber from retted bark, such as basswood, western red cedar, willow, elm, wisteria, and tulip poplar.

Strong leaf fibers from some monocots, such as yucca, agave, and snake plant.

Leafy material, such as cattail, iris, daylily, crocosmia, corn husks, and dandelion stems.

preparing plants for cordage

If you are using processed bast fibers or leaf fibers, make sure they are relatively soft. If the material is stiff, soften the fibers a bit by peeling, splitting, or agitating them.

Cordage made from fresh leafy material will lose moisture and loosen as it dries. One solution is to let the material dry completely before using it, then rehydrate it by running it under warm water, wrapping it in a warm damp towel, and leaving it for several hours or overnight. Alternatively, let fresh material sit for a few days until it's lost enough moisture to twist into cordage without shrinkage. Most leaves twist into cordage more easily if they are split lengthwise into several narrower pieces and bundled together rather than using one wide piece.

With any of these plants, keep your material slightly damp while you work. If necessary, spray with or dip in water as you go.

basic cordage technique

These basic instructions work well and are easy to learn. I'm demonstrating with Siberian iris leaves that I split into several narrow pieces. The final cordage is about ⅛ inch in diameter, but the more material you start with, the thicker the cordage will be.

1. Using a spray bottle of water, lightly spritz a bundle of plant material that is about 1⁄16 inch in diameter when twisted (in this case four lengths of split iris leaves). Arrange it so that all the ends are at different lengths. Fold the bundle in half. With your left hand, pinch at the fold and hold the bundle in front of you with both halves hanging.

2. Pinch the right half of the folded plant material between the thumb and pointer finger of your right hand and roll it between your fingers away from you, using a snapping motion and a gentle turn of the wrist. Twisting in the correct direction is important.

3. While holding the twist, cross the right strand over the top of the untwisted plant material on the left. The untwisted material is now on the right. Pinch the overlap in place with your left fingers.

4. Repeat steps 2 and 3 over and over—twisting the right strand away from you and bringing it over to the left. After a few moves, you won't need to pinch the overlaps in place, and you can hold the work quite loosely without it unraveling. Lightly dampen the plant material as you go.

5. Once an individual piece of the plant material begins to taper off and run out, splice in a new piece (see Splicing Cordage on page 130). When you are finished with the length of cordage you want to make, secure the end with a knot or a clip.

SPLICING CORDAGE

To make long lengths of cordage, you need to continually add, or splice in, new material. Keep a close eye on the bulk of the plant material as you work and splice while there is still existing material to grab onto. Following are three different methods.

Method 1: Splicing in the Middle

Use this technique to add material on both sides of the cordage at the same time because both are thinning out. To splice, fold a new piece of lightly dampened material roughly in half so that the ends are uneven. Place the fold of the new material directly in the center of the cordage where the two sides separate. Continue making the cordage while holding the spliced piece in place. After two twists it will be snugly integrated.

You often end up with a nubbin at the point where you started the splice. If you don't like how that looks, try one of the other methods.

Method 2: Splicing on One Side

Use this technique when only one side of the cordage is thinning. To splice, place a new piece of damp material alongside the strand that is thinning, allowing the tip to stick out under the other strand. Continue making the cordage and trim the end later.

Method 3: Invisible Splicing

Also used when only one side is thinning, this technique makes the splice nearly invisible. To splice, choose a new piece of material with a tapered tip. Insert as shown for Method 2, then fold the tapered tip down so that it joins the existing strand on the side that is not being spliced onto. Continue making cordage.

thigh-roll cordage technique

This technique makes cordage more quickly but takes some time to get the hang of. You twist the plant material on your thigh, which works best if your legs are bare. If that's not practical, wear tight pants made of a nonslippery fabric such as denim. Here are some additional tips for success:

- Keep both your leg and the cordage strands lightly dampened, helping them grip against each other and build up twist.
- Keep everything neat and organized; don't allow the ends of the fiber to tangle.
- Make sure there is a wide angle between the two fiber strands by constantly separating them and using the index finger of the nonrolling hand to keep them apart.
- Take breaks as needed, so your skin doesn't get irritated.

1. Have a bowl of water at your side to dampen the fiber and your leg. Follow the basic cordage technique on page 129 to create about 1½ inches of cordage. Lay the cordage on your right thigh. Lightly dampen the plant material.

2. Position your left index finger between the two strands to keep them separated at a wide angle. Press the flat of your right hand on one strand and add a twist to it by sliding your hand away from your body a couple of times. If your strand is not twisting, dampen it a bit more and keep rolling.

3. Repeat on the other strand, taking care not to tangle them.

4. Place the flat of your right hand over both sides of the cordage at the same time. Pressing down a bit more firmly than you did in steps 2 and 3, add a twist to both strands simultaneously by sliding your hand away from your body. Keep your left index finger in place between the two strands.

Continued on next page

5. While keeping your right hand in place, use your left fingers to spin the cordage away from your body, allowing the two sides to twist onto each other.

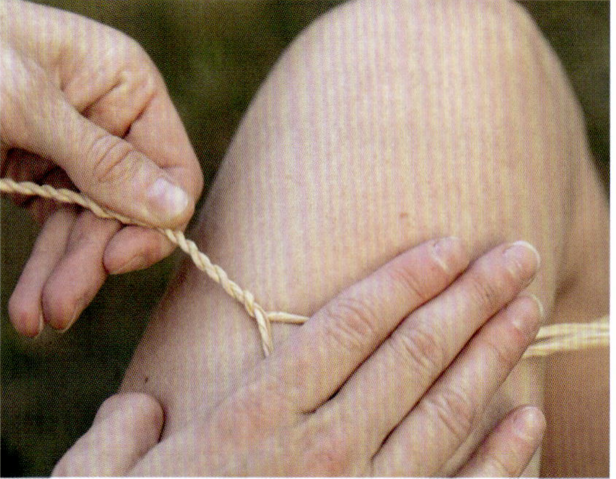

6. Secure the twist in place and keep the two strands separate with your left index finger. Repeat the sequence to continue twisting the cordage.

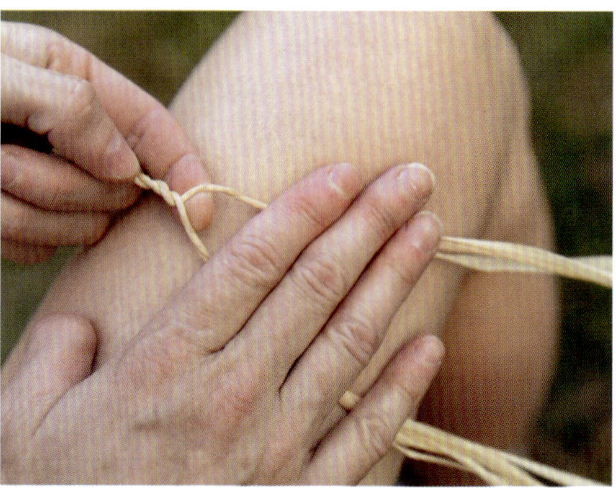

Multistrand Braiding

Multistrand braiding, also known as plaiting, is where three or more strands of material are woven over each other, creating a long length of material that has many uses in basketry. They also make lovely sculptural pieces or studies of new plant materials to hang on the wall. I find multistrand braiding to be one of the most meditative basketry techniques, and I love the methodical practice of watching a braid materialize inch by inch. You can braid with an odd or even number of strands and either round or flat materials.

Uses for Multistrand Braids

- Hangers for wall baskets
- Weaving strands in regular woven baskets
- Weaving strands in ribbed baskets
- Rim fillers
- Long strips as core material in coiled baskets
- Straps for bags
- Wall hangings

You can create multistrand braids with anything relatively soft and flexible, including leafy materials and inner bark. Rushes, cattails, iris leaves, yucca leaves, inner bark strips, cordage, basswood fiber, and straw are a handful of my favorites. Don't hesitate to research plants native to your area and experiment. Materials can either be flat, like cattail leaves, or round, like cordage. The technique is the same for both, although you'll fold flat materials at the edges as you braid them to keep the sides straight.

See Part One for details on harvesting, processing, and preparing individual types of material. Before braiding, rehydrate any dried materials or lightly dampen any fibers.

starting a multistrand braid

To start a braid, either tie the ends together in a knot or secure them with a clip. Clamp the end of the braid to the edge of a chair or table, which helps maintain tension while working. For those new to braiding, work loosely. Once you understand the structure, tighten your weaving up.

SPLICING A NEW STRAND

To make long braids, you need to add in new material. When a strand has 3 or 4 inches left, lay a new piece on top of it and they will weave as one until they turn around the edge one time. Ideally all your strands are different lengths so that you are splicing onto them at different points. If they all end at the same length, use scissors to trim some shorter.

1. Take a new piece and weave it backward along the same path as the one that is ending.

2. Slide the new piece underneath the ending one so that it is tucked up against the edge of the braid.

3. Continue braiding, keeping the old and new pieces together as one until they go around an edge. If there is still a lot left on the old piece, leave it hanging out of the back and trim it later.

odd-stranded braids

I prefer an odd number of strands because the resulting braids are symmetrical, making the process flow a bit more seamlessly for me. The left-side and right-side pieces take turns weaving into the center.

Basic (Three-Strand) Braid

The three-strand braid is the simplest. Practice it first to become familiar with tensioning natural materials while you work.

1. Secure three strands together at the end. Pick up the rightmost strand.

2. Fold the rightmost strand over the center piece, so it is now in the center.

3. Fold the leftmost strand over the center piece, so it is now in the center.

4. Repeat steps 2 and 3 as you continue to braid. Practice evenly tensioning the strands so that the braid is straight-sided and tight.

Five-Strand Braid

This is my favorite multistrand braid. It's complicated enough to have an attractive pattern but doesn't require as much adjustment as braids with more strands. Each edge piece weaves over, then under to the center.

1. Secure the ends of five strands together. Separate them so there are three on the right and two on the left. Pick up the rightmost strand.

Continued on next page

2. Weave the rightmost strand toward the left, over one strand then under the next, so it is now in the center and joins the two strands on the left. There are now three strands on the left.

3. Pick up the leftmost strand while holding the remaining strands in place with the other hand.

4. Weave toward the right, over one strand then under the next, so it is now in the center and joins the two strands on right. There are now three strands on the right.

5. Repeat steps 2 to 4 and alternate folding the leftmost and rightmost strands as you continue to braid. If you forget which one is next, remember that you always weave from the side that has the greater number of strands—in this case, the side with three strands.

BRAIDING WITH SEVEN OR MORE STRANDS

These follow the same pattern as the five-strand braid except that the leftmost and rightmost strands need to weave over and under additional strands to reach the center.

even-stranded braids

Using an even number of strands is a little different as the pattern is not symmetrical for each side. Take care to maintain tension so that the sides of the braid are straight.

Four-Strand Braid

1. Secure the ends of four strands together and divide them into two halves. Pick up the leftmost strand.

2. Fold the leftmost strand toward the center. There are now three strands on the right side and one on the left.

3. Weave the rightmost strand toward the center going under one strand, then over the next. There are now two strands on either side.

4. Repeat steps 2 and 3 and alternate folding the leftmost and rightmost strands. The leftmost strand will always fold over one strand. The rightmost strand will always weave under one strand then over the next. After every fold, pull tension on each half and cinch them upward at a wide angle to tighten.

BRAIDING WITH SIX OR MORE STRANDS

These begin with the same pattern as the four-strand braid, except each edge strand will have to weave over and under additional strands to reach the center. The left-side strand starts first with a weave over and then the right-side strand starts with a weave under.

BERKSHIRE & BECKET SILK CO'S
BOUNTIFUL & BETTER
COLOR

CHAPTER 9

COILED BASKETRY

Coiling is my favorite technique for beginners because you can make a basket with so many different plants that are easy to find and harvest. In fact, at least a few great coiling plants are probably growing in your backyard! Coiling begins with a tightly wrapped start of plant material that you build up in a spiral formation to create a basket, sewing the coils in place. We'll focus on open-stitch coiling, in which your stitches are far enough apart that the core plant material shows.

Anatomy of a Coiled Basket

The simple spiraling structure of coiled baskets is one of my favorites.

Coil. A bundle of plant material stitched together into rounds. The diameter of a coil can range from tiny (just a few leaves) to large (1½ inches or more). The size of the coils does not determine the size of the basket, but it does affect how long it will take to make the basket. Small coil diameters require more time. If you want to make a large basket quickly, use a thick coil size and space the stitches up to an inch apart.

Core/bundle. The plant material that makes up the coil and forms the body of the basket.

Start. The starting bundle of plant material into which you work the first row of stitching. A short start makes a round basket, and a long start makes an oval basket.

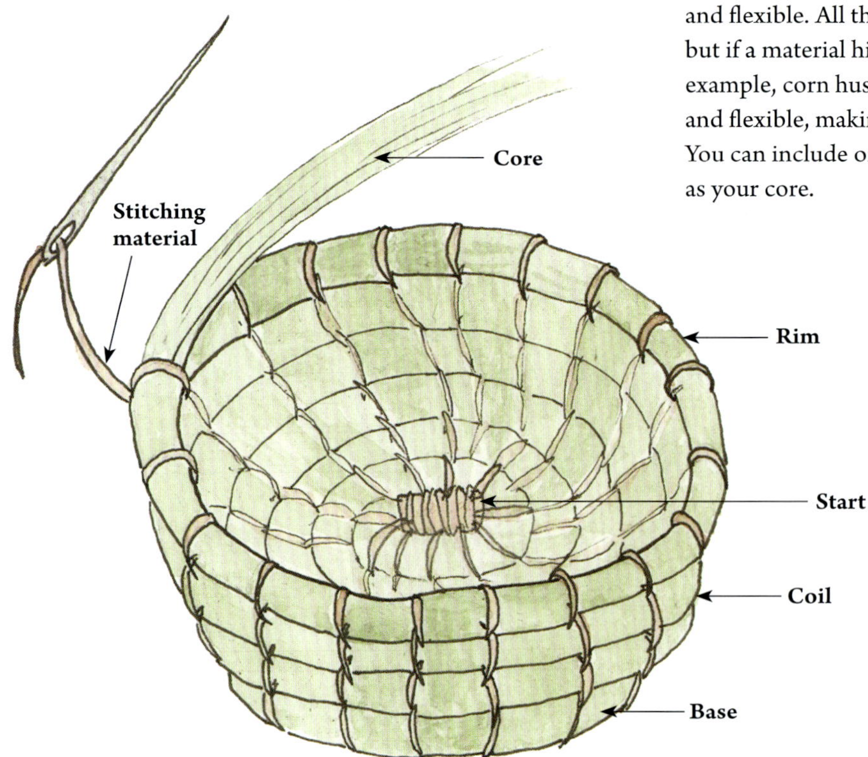

Stitching material. String, twine, or similar material used to sew a new round of coiling to the previous one. The closer you place your stitches, the more time it will take to make the basket.

Rim. The top edge of the basket, which tapers to create a flat top.

Base. The bottom part of the basket. The diameter of the base determines the size of the basket.

choosing plants for coiling

All the plants included in Chapter 3, Leaves, Grasses, and Soft Stems, are excellent candidates for coiling. Siberian iris, cattails, daylilies, and ornamental grasses are some of my favorites, but the possibilities are nearly endless. Look for materials that are long, strong, and flexible. All these qualities make coiling easier, but if a material hits two out of three, it's okay. For example, corn husks are short, but they are also strong and flexible, making them a wonderful coiling material. You can include one or many different types of plants as your core.

Stitching options include:

1. *Cordage*
2. *Retted elm inner bark*
3. *Spun basswood fiber*
4. *Plant-dyed yarn*
5. *Embroidery floss*
6. *Basswood fiber*
7. *Waxed linen*
8. *Narrow-cut inner bark strips*

choosing a stitching material

I suggest that you sew your first coiled basket with a strong material that is easy to stitch with, such as yarn, twine, jute, or any medium-weight string. Keep in mind that the color and thickness of the stitching material will be visible on the finished basket.

After you get the hang of coiling, try stitching with foraged materials, such as dogbane, nettle, basswood fiber, split yucca leaves, iris leaves, and inner bark strips, which are wonderful but more finicky. People all around the world have been sewing coiled baskets with material made from wild plants for tens of thousands of years. Processing this material requires more time, and it often relies on shorter pieces compared to store-bought string, but it is well worth the effort.

Some foraged stitching materials are very fibrous and might need to be made into cordage before sewing. Stiffer materials like inner bark need to be split into very thin strips. Many natural sewing materials are too thick to be threaded onto a needle, in which case you use an awl to pre-poke a hole in the previous coil and push the material through.

starting a coiled basket

In the project that follows, I demonstrate a wrapped start, but you have options. If you discover that you love to make coiled baskets, have fun experimenting with these other methods!

Wrapped start. This is my favorite method to teach because it creates a solid, clear foundation to sew the first round of coiling into. Wrap 1 inch of the bundle of core material and begin stitching and turning (see the Coiled Bowl project on page 145).

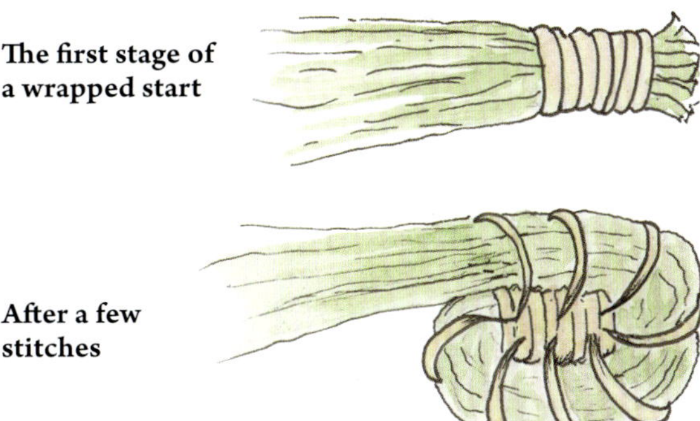

The first stage of a wrapped start

After a few stitches

Long wrapped start. This method is best for plant materials that are prone to cracking and breaking since the stitching material holds them together at the base. A caveat is that the technique uses a lot of stitching material, so begin with a very long length to avoid splicing in new material before completing at least a couple of rounds. Wrap the bundle of core material as instructed in the Coiled Bowl project (page 145) with one change: Wrap for 2 to 3 inches instead of ¾ inch. Continue to follow instructions as given, except you will stitch through or around the wrapped start for the first several rounds.

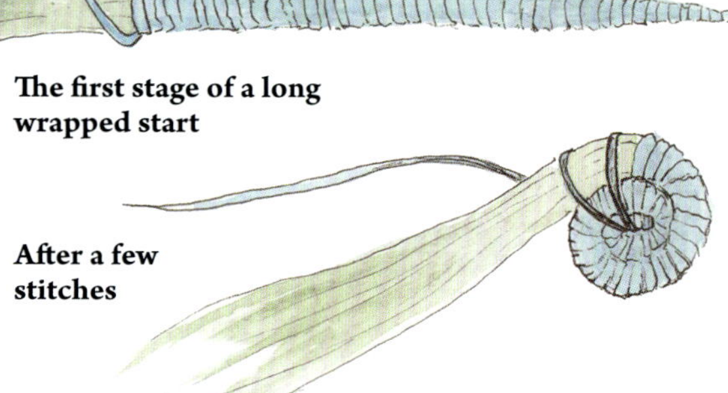

The first stage of a long wrapped start

After a few stitches

Knotted start. This technique requires a very flexible plant material and produces a very round, tight start, making it the best option for a round basket. The other starts are more oval. Tie the end of the bundle of core plant material in a knot, pull the tips down to integrate with the rest of the material, and begin stitching into the center of the knot, turning as you go until you have completed a round. Then start stitching into the previous round, not the knot.

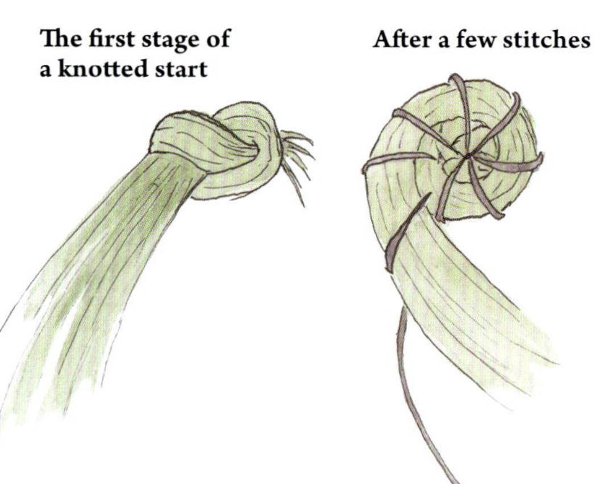

The first stage of a knotted start

After a few stitches

stitching a coiled basket

In coiled basketry, rows of coils are stitched together to build the basket. Besides being functional, the stitches are an aesthetic choice. You can even thread beads, shells, or feathers onto your needle in between stitches to add embellishments. This can be time-consuming, but the lovely result is satisfying. The Coiled Bowl project that follows demonstrates line stitching, but there are several stitching methods to choose from.

Line stitch. Each stitch goes around the newest coil and pierces the coil below it about a third of the way down. You can space each stitch randomly or interlock each new stitch with one on the coil below to create a pattern that spirals out from the base.

V-stitch. You begin with the line stitch, then add an extra stitch to make a V-shape.

Long stitch. Each stitch wraps completely around the previous coil and does not pierce any plant material. This method is good when your coiling material is too tough to sew through.

Figure-eight stitch. Each stitch wraps around the new coil *and* the previous coil, connecting the two without piercing any plant material. Unlike the long stitch, the twist in the center creates the appearance of single-coil stitch length.

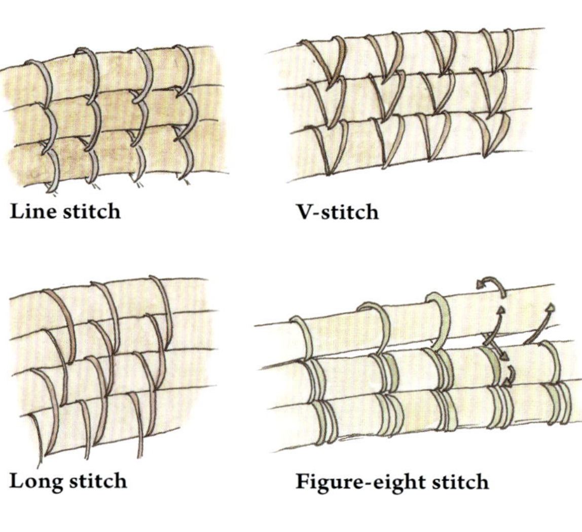

Line stitch

V-stitch

Long stitch

Figure-eight stitch

CLOSED COILING

In closed-coiled basketry, the core is covered completely with the sewing material—either with closely spaced stitching or a technique I call core wrapping. To core-wrap, do a regular stitch, then wrap your stitching material three to five times around the unstitched core material in the same direction that you have been sewing. Repeat this pattern—regular stitch, three to five wraps—for the entirety of the basket. Core wrapping is my preference because it goes much faster than doing many stitches right next to each other.

Closed coiling takes more time to complete but it creates a remarkably sturdy and resilient basket that invites you to embrace slow practice.

COILED BOWL

THERE IS A PLACE IN EVERY ROOM OF THE HOME for a coiled basket, whether you make it small to hold shells on the bathroom sink or larger for apples on the dining room table. To make a smaller or larger basket than the one shown here, adjust the quantity of plant material called for in the instructions accordingly. I love this project because just about any "kind of long, kind of strong, and kind of flexible" plant material can be added in. The instructions call for specific plants (and the photos show Siberian iris), but feel free to use whatever you have readily available. Any plants featured in Chapter 3, Leaves, Grasses, and Soft Stems will work. I've had students use materials as diverse as lavender stems, goldenrod, and corn husks.

BASKET SIZE

5½ inches wide × 4¾ inches deep × 2 inches high

TOOLS

- Small ball of medium-weight stitching material, such as cotton string, hemp, twine, or yarn
- Size 18–22 chenille needle or another large-eyed sharp needle
- Basketry scissors
- Needle-nose pliers

PLANT MATERIALS

Approximately 8-inch-diameter bundle of dried Siberian iris, yellow flag iris, daylily leaves, or any other very flexible leafy material or grass that is 17–22 inches long

PREPARING MATERIALS

See Chapter 3, Leaves, Grasses, and Soft Stems, for details on harvesting and processing. Plants used for coiling need to be dried and then rehydrated. If you try to make a coiled basket with fresh plants, the material will shrink as it dries, and the basket will be very loose. To rehydrate the leaves, run them under hot water, wrap in a damp towel, and leave for several hours, or overnight if they are particularly stiff. Alternatively, dip the plant material into a pot of hot water for a few minutes, then wrap in a damp towel for an hour or so.

TIME REQUIRED

The basket size in this project takes 4 to 6 hours to make. However, there's nothing limiting the size that a coiled basket can grow to; simply add new material for as long as you like. You can pause your work at any point, let it dry, and then continue later by rehydrating whatever materials on the basket are unstitched. Also, you can store the damp basket and materials in a plastic bag in a cool environment for a day or so.

prepare core and stitching material

1. Thread the needle with a piece of string about 7½ feet long. Leave a 10-inch tail and do not tie a knot.

2. Gather a handful of leaves and twist them tightly to reveal the actual size of the coil. Add or remove leaves until you get approximately ⅜ inch in diameter while twisting.

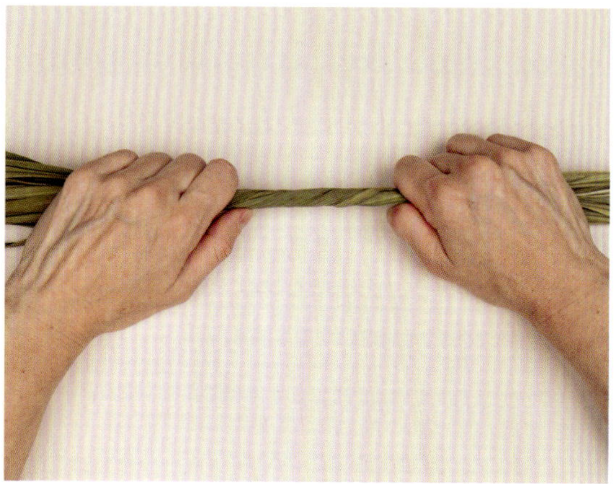

3. Align the leaves so that most of the thin ends are on the right side of the bundle. Don't worry if a few of the thicker ends point to the right if they are flexible and don't crack when bent. You will begin on the thin side because it is more flexible. Cut 2 to 6 inches off to remove the wispy ends.

4. Tie the long end of the string in a snug double knot around the bundle, about ¾ inch from the cut end.

wrap the start

1. Wrap the string under the bundle of leaves, then over the top toward you. This is important, so take a moment to make sure you are wrapping in the correct direction.

2. Wrap 1½ inches from right to left, making each wrap snug but not so tight that you dig into the leaves. Each wrap should be just next to its neighbor, not overlapping. Secure the wrapped section by inserting the needle through the middle of the bundle, just to the left of the last wrap. Pull tight.

3. Trim the leaves ⅛ inch from the right end of the wrapping. Be careful not to cut too close or the wrap will fall off.

STITCHING TIPS FOR COILED BASKETS

Occasionally check to make sure each stitch comes out the back of the project. If you make an error and the string is coming out the front, push the needle through to the back right next to where the string comes out. Pull tight. Now the string is in the correct position.

To keep the distance between stitches even, use your index finger to pinch the string and make sure the stitches stay where you want them while pulling tight; if you don't, they will slide close to each other.

As your basket grows, the stitches may spread too far apart, resulting in a loose basket. If necessary, add new stitch lines to remedy. Following are a couple of options.

- **Middle method.** Start a new stitch directly in the center of the two stitches that are too far apart. It will not be interlocked with anything in the back.
- **Branching-off method.** In this method the new stitch branches off a previous stich, making a V.

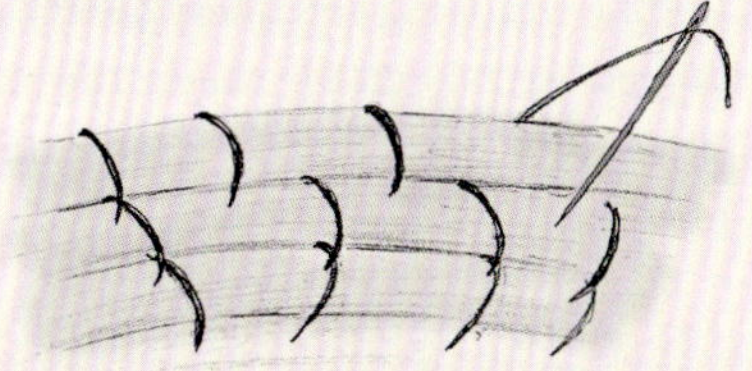

Middle method

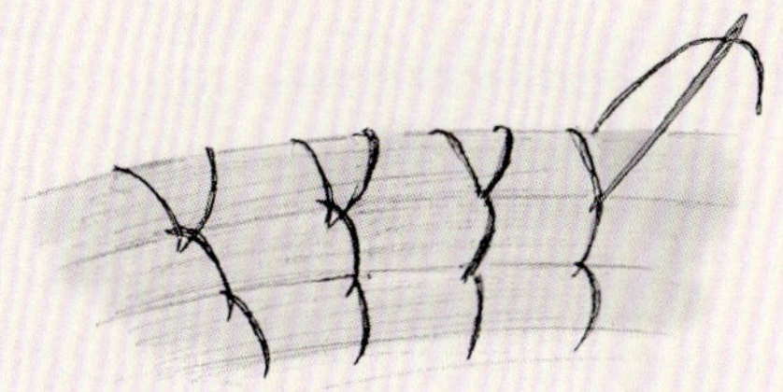

Branching-off method

stitch the base

1. To begin the first round of stitching, hold the bundle in front of you with the wrapped start on the right and the loose leaves on the left. Fold the wrapped start down to meet the loose leaves. The string should come out the back of the wrapped section; adjust, if necessary.

Tip: *Practice holding the project as shown. Grip the bundle so that you can lift your pointer finger up and down on top of the leaves. (I call this pinching the string.) You need to pinch the string to hold each stitch in position while pulling the string tight.*

2. To work the first stitch, pull the string over the top of the loose leaves toward you.

Continued on next page

3. Pinch the string. Insert the needle through the middle of the wrapped start below where you are pinching the string. Make sure the needle comes straight out the back of the wrapping and doesn't angle up through the unstitched leaves. Pull the needle through and tighten. If it is difficult to pull the needle through, use needle-nose pliers to help.

4. To work the second stitch, pull the string over the top toward you, angling it to the left to make a ½-inch space between this stitch and the previous one. Pinch the string while inserting the needle through the middle of the wrapped section. Pull the needle through and tighten.

Tips: *From this point forward, twist the bundle of leaves just before stitching them. Always twist in the same direction. Twisting makes the coil tighter and helps it stay round and tall. This can be challenging for those with wrist pain, so opt out if it doesn't feel good. Using a clip to secure the twisted section for a few inches while you work makes it easier.*

5. Keep stitching until you reach the end of the wrapped section.

6. Bend the wrapped start clockwise so a small section of loose leaves is on top of the short side. Make a single stitch on this short side, inserting the needle into the same hole as the previous stitch, pinching the string so it doesn't slide off the edge.

7. Turn the project clockwise again so that the loose leaves are still on top. Work another row of stitches from right to left. The first new stitch on this row goes into the same hole as the last two stitches. After that, match each stitch with the one across from it.

SPLICING STITCHING MATERIAL

When you can't make any more stitches because you've run out of stitching material, use this overlap method to add more.

1. Remove the needle and let the remaining short length of stitching material hang. Thread the needle with a new piece 4 to 6 feet long. If the length is too long, the material tends to tangle. If it's short, you'll need to splice frequently.

2. Count back three stitches and put the needle in the stitch hole at the base of the third stitch back in the same direction that you have been sewing. Pull through, leaving a 3-inch tail hanging from the front of the basket.

3. Loop the stitching material over the top of the basket and insert the needle into the bottom hole of the next stitch to the left. Repeat. The new material will cover the last two stitches.

You now have one short piece of new stitching material hanging out the front and another short piece of old material hanging out the back. Leave them for a couple of stitches, then trim flush with the surface of the basket. Be sure to keep stitching in the correct direction when you continue by inserting the needle in the front of the basket and bringing it out the back.

8. Turn the project clockwise and add one or two more stitches through the wrapped start. Then begin stitching into the unwrapped leaves in the coil of the previous row, rather than the wrapped start. This will continue for the entirety of the basket. Maintain a consistent distance between each stitch.

Continued on next page

9. Splice in new leaves and string as needed until the basket base is whatever size you like. (See Splicing Stitching Material on page 149 and Splicing Leaves on page 151.) For this project I worked four rows of coiling on all sides to achieve a base that measures 3½ × 4½ inches.

build the sides

1. For this bowl-shaped basket, turn up the sides by pulling the loose plant material upward and toward you so that instead of sitting on the outside like a disk, it is now resting either on top of or at a 45-degree angle to the previous row.

2. Hold the loose plant material in place while pulling the stitches tight or the coil will sink flat. It will take a few rows for you to clearly see the sides forming. Continue working until the basket is as tall as you like. This example is 2 inches high.

finish the rim

1. To finish, look at the basket in profile and find a spot where you can taper the leaves in neatly to make the top level.

2. Taper the leaves with scissors by trimming some shorter than others so the coil thins as it nears the end.

3. Keep stitching until the very tips of the leaves are covered. For the final stitch, insert the needle straight down through the top of the last coil and at an angle so it goes through three to four rows of coiling and out the side of the basket. It will be difficult to push through. If necessary, press the end of the needle against the table or use a thimble or needle-nose pliers. Pull tight. Trim the string flush with the basket wall.

4. Trim the loose leaf ends to a finish that is as neat or shaggy as you like. Dry the basket well to prevent mold. The color of the leaves will mellow to yellow over time, particularly when exposed to sunlight.

SPLICING LEAVES

No core material is long enough to make an entire basket, so as you continue, you will repeatedly add, or splice in, new leaves. Also, the goal is to keep the coil size consistent, so splice new leaves in as the material begins to thin. How much material you add at a time depends on how thick the material is and how fast it's running out. If you are using thick cattail leaves, add one leaf at a time. If you are using thin iris leaves, add three to six at the same time, or more if you've let the coil get too thin and are in an "emergency splice zone." Always pay attention to the coil size and the amount of material remaining by both looking at and feeling it as you pull the stitches tight.

1. Using scissors, trim the leaves to different lengths so that you won't have to splice all of them at the same time. Aim for a staggered look.

2. Tuck the new material between the previously coiled section and the loose leaves. (The new leaves are a lighter color in the photo.) Hold the new leaves in place for the next couple of stitches so they don't fall out.

CHAPTER 10

LOOPED BASKETRY

Looping, also known as knotless netting, is a soft basketry technique found all over the world. Cordage is sewn together in a loop pattern to create a flexible basket of any size. All kinds of cordage are suitable, and many artists even use human-made materials, such as wire or twine, to create gorgeous sculptural pieces. Knitters and crocheters will also love looped basketry. This ancient yet adaptable technique is open for experimentation.

Anatomy of a Looped Basket

There are only a few basic parts to a looped basket, and you create all of them using cordage.

Looping. The structure of the basket, in which you attach rows of loops to previous rows of loops.

Rim. The top strand of the basket, to which the first row of loops is attached.

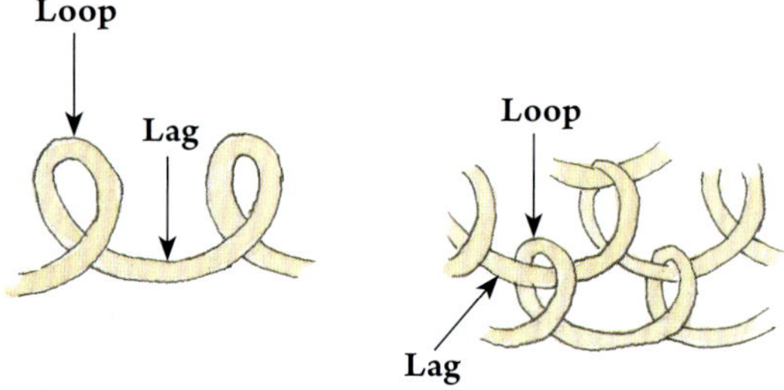

Drawstring. An optional strand added at the end to cinch the basket.

Loop. One of two basic elements in looping. Each individual loop attaches onto a lag in the previous row to create the bag's structure.

Lag. The short length of cordage between each loop. It looks like a valley, or a U-shape, and each new loop is made on a lag from the previous row.

choosing fiber and preparing cordage for looping

You can use any fiber to make the cordage, although I prefer soft, flexible materials, such as dogbane or nettle, over stiff ones, like corn husks. Softer fibers allow for a more flexible basket with tighter loops. Stiffer fibers require slightly larger loops, resulting in a basket with a more open mesh, which could be great for hanging plant holders, bowls, or other items that benefit from a stiffer form.

For instructions on making cordage, see pages 128–132. You don't need to complete all the cordage for the basket before you begin, so the end should be loose and tapered—not cut off abruptly—since you will splice in more material later. How much total cordage you'll need for making a looped basket is difficult to gauge precisely, so have some handfuls of prepared fibers on hand. Alternatively, if you want to make a quantity of cordage in advance or have a stash, see Splicing Cordage on page 130.

LOOPED CORDAGE POUCH

THIS PROJECT IS IDEAL FOR CARRYING AROUND WITH YOU to work on at odd times—it's small enough to fit in your pocket, and the materials don't require any rehydrating to use. It's also the perfect opportunity to practice making cordage. For color variation, use fiber from different plants. I used nettle, dogbane, and yucca fibers for this pouch. For different-size projects use a larger or smaller mold. Looping is one of the most ancient and widespread techniques in the book. I often feel connected to my ancestors when practicing this meditative method.

BASKET SIZE

3¼ inches wide × 2 inches deep × 4 inches high

TOOLS

- 4-ounce bottle (6½-inch circumference) to use as a mold. The mold only determines the diameter of the basket; it can be made to any height.
- Tape or masking tape
- Tapestry needle
- Safety pin

PLANT MATERIALS

- 7-foot-long piece of cordage to start, about ⅛ inch in diameter, with a loop on one end as directed in the cordage-making instructions on page 129; additional fibers for making more cordage as you go
- Alternatively, 40–60 feet of premade cordage, ⅛ inch in diameter

PREPARING MATERIALS

See Chapter 7, Wild Fibers, for details on harvesting and processing material. See pages 128–132 for details on making cordage.

TIME REQUIRED

Since you are making cordage as the project progresses, plan to work on it over the course of several days or weeks. (If you have ample cordage premade, you could complete this basket in a day.) You can pause your work at any point. Secure the working end of the cordage with a small clip so it doesn't come undone.

attach the rim

1. Untwist the end of the cordage so it makes an open circle. Place a piece of tape next to the starting end to secure it to the bottle, which serves as a mold. The rest of the cordage should circle to the left. If your cordage does not have a loop on the end, tie the cordage onto the mold using any knot and skip to Build the Sides.

2. Thread a tapestry needle onto the opposite end of the cordage. Put the needle through the open circle from back to front.

3. Pull tight. The cordage is now cinched around the diameter of the mold, creating a rim that attaches to the first row.

build the sides

1. Place your thumb over the rim and hold it in place for the next steps. Insert the needle behind the rim and cross it over the cordage that hangs from the starting end.

2. Pull down to make the first loop.

Tip: *How tight you cinch the loops and how closely you space them is a matter of personal preference. Snug loops that are tightly spaced create a fabric. Open loops that are farther apart create a mesh. For this project, I recommend leaving the loops loose enough that their structure is obvious and arranging them so they are just touching.*

Continued on next page

3. Place the tip of your thumb over the first loop to hold it in place. Again, pass the needle behind the rim and cross it over the length of cordage.

4. Pull tight and arrange the second loop so it lightly touches the edge of the first one.

5. Continue making loops until you get back to the beginning of the row. There is a U-shape of cordage, called a lag, between each loop. To start the second row, insert the needle under the first lag, over the working cordage, and pull tight to create the first loop on the second row. The first one may look a little strange because it occurs right where the top strand is cinched on.

6. Continue around, making each new loop by inserting the needle under the next lag, over the working cordage, and pulling tight. Stop when you have approximately 8 inches of cordage left.

Tip: *After four rows you can remove the project from the mold if you find it cumbersome. Keeping it on the mold will give the basket a very even shape; removing it helps you develop tensioning skills on your own. Both are good choices.*

add cordage and continue looping

When you run out of your first length of cordage, you can continuously make more right onto the project. (If using premade cordage, see Splicing Cordage on page 130.)

1. Untwist the last 8 inches of cordage.

2. Take the project off the mold to make it easier to hold. Add more plant fibers and continue making cordage until the strand is 7 feet long.

Tip: *To create a color pattern using different types of plant material, switch to a new fiber at any point you like. Sometimes I'll map out a basket's design in advance, and other times I work in the moment, splicing in whatever I am interested in using next.*

3. Keep looping until the pouch reaches approximately 4 inches tall.

decrease the rows

Reducing the number of loops in a row is called decreasing, which tapers the width of the pouch. To make a decrease, skip one lag and go under the next one. Be sure to pull the loop snug enough that there is no gap below the skipped lag. The following pattern gradually decreases the rows by 3 loops, which is good if your pouch has 25 or more loops per row—count them. If your pouch has less than 25 loops per row, decrease by 2 loops per row instead.

When decreasing loops in a row, skip one lag and go under the next one.

1. Put a safety pin into a loop to mark the beginning of a row.

Continued on next page

2. Do three decreases in each row until there are 12 loops remaining. Space the decreases out within a row and avoid decreasing at the same point from one row to the next. Otherwise, edges form in the pouch's bottom. Look for opportunities to decrease where the loops are naturally a bit closer together, making it less likely to leave a gap. For clarity, the image below shows the decrease before it is pulled tightly. When finished pulling tightly, there should be no gap.

3. When there are only 12 loops remaining, keep skipping loops to decrease, but the pattern is less defined. Some loops will naturally press together. Decrease those first and continue working your rows until the hole is as small as possible.

4. When the hole at the center is almost closed, the looping is complete, and you will weave in the tail to close the bottom.

Tip: *If your pouch has a more open looping structure than the one shown, you may want to unravel the two sides of the cordage and tie a square knot across the opening before weaving in the tail so that it does not come loose.*

TYING A SQUARE KNOT

The square knot is excellent for holding two ends together. The action is to pass right over left, then left over right. If you accidentally do right over left twice, you'll get a granny knot, which isn't as secure.

1. Lay the right end over the left end.

2. Wrap the right end around the left end and back up.

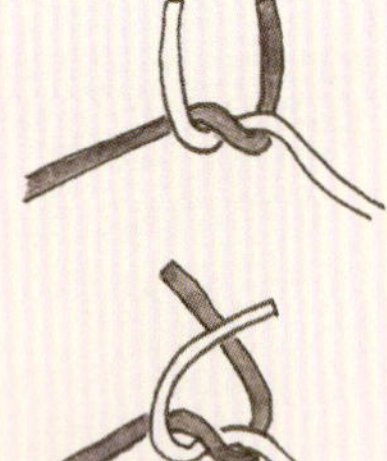

3. Now cross the left end over the right.

4. Wrap the left end around to finish the knot.

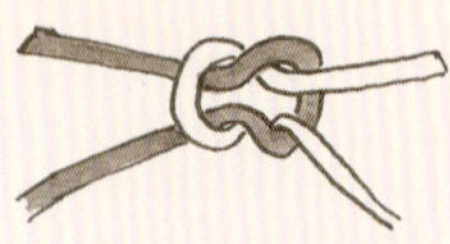

finish the pouch

1. Weave your needle under and over the cordage at the bottom of the pouch to secure the tail. Repeat once more, using the opportunity to fill in any gaps. Weave the tail at least 2 inches to secure it. Trim the tail and any other bits of fiber that are sticking out. Be careful not to cut a loop.

2. To add an optional drawstring, make a piece of cordage approximately 12 inches long. Sew it around the circumference of the top of the pouch just under the rim strand by weaving under two loops, then over two loops until you reach the start.

3. Tie a knot at each end of the drawstring. Optionally, thread a bead onto the strands before knotting to help keep the opening of the pouch cinched.

SPLICING TWO PIECES OF CORDAGE

When making a looped basket from pieces of premade cordage, rather than making the cordage as you go, there are a couple of methods for connecting the separate lengths.

Tie-Together Method

A large ball of cordage is a treasure, but you need to cut it into manageable lengths of 7-foot pieces. You splice them together by tying the new cordage onto the old piece after narrowing down the ends to make them less bulky. Try to arrange the knots so they end up on the inside of the basket. Weave in or trim the tails.

1. Start by thinning out the ends of both pieces of cordage as in step 1 of the End-Loop Method (at right) so the knot isn't bulky.

2. Use an overhand knot, square knot, or weaver's knot to tie them together.

End-Loop Method

This elegant method creates a seamless connection between the original and new cordage pieces, but calls for each piece of cordage to have a loop at one end. (Either technique for making cordage on pages 129–132 will create a loop at one end.) If you have one big ball of cordage, you will not be able to use this method. Use the Tie-Together Method instead.

1. As you are looping the rows, stop when you have approximately 8 inches of cordage left. Take the needle off and untwist about half the remaining cordage. Trim the plant material to different lengths, thinning the strands so that the end, and therefore the splice, is not too bulky. Retwist the cordage.

2. Thread the needle back onto the thinned end of the original cordage and insert it through the loop on the starting end of a new length of cordage. Pull approximately 3 inches through.

3. Remove the needle and insert the tip through the twist of the original cordage directly to the left of the connection point.

4. Thread the end of the original cordage back onto the needle.

5. Pull through.

6. Repeat steps 3 to 5: Remove the needle and insert the tip through the next twist to the left; rethread the needle and pull through. Essentially you are weaving the end of the cordage backward through itself. Because the tail end is so short, you need to remove and rethread the needle each time. Note that the needle will alternate going up and down as it weaves through the cordage.

7. After repeating four times, remove the needle and trim the end flush.

CHAPTER 11

TWINED BASKETRY

Twining is perhaps the most versatile and widely used technique in basketry and is not tied to any specific basket style or type of material. Twining with fiber results in a soft, flexible bag. Twining with willow results in a sturdy, large-scale basket. Twining with bark stakes or cattails each has its own characteristics. Exploring the creative potential of different materials within this technique is a richly rewarding path in your journey as a basket maker.

Anatomy of a Twined Basket

Since you can adapt twining to so many basket styles and materials, there isn't one common structure shared by all. The following anatomy relates to the Twined Treasure Basket project and depicts a variation with an attached rim.

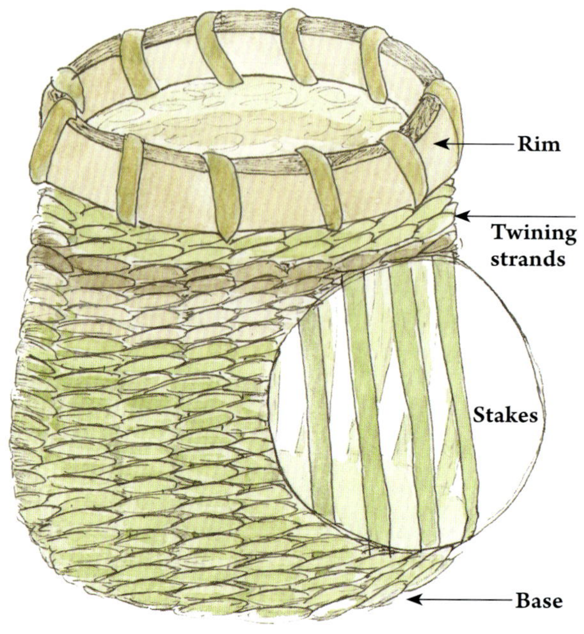

Rim. The top part of the basket, which finishes and secures the stakes as well as the last row of twining. The Twined Treasure Basket (page 173) has a braided rim that is made from the top few inches of the stakes themselves.

Stakes. The solid pieces around which you twine that become the vertical elements of the basket. Stakes must either be thicker or the same thickness as the twining strands. They should never be thinner.

Twining strands. Two individual strands of material that are worked at the same time, twisting around the stakes to create the fabric of the basket. The twining strands should be thinner or more pliable than the stakes so as not to overpower them.

Base. The bottom part of the basket.

base shapes

These two basic bases are options for both twined and woven baskets. When making a large basket I tend to prefer the square base because it creates a solid foundation, and no additional stakes need to be added later.

VARIATIONS FOR TWINED BASKETS

Even within this single construction method, there is a lot of room for variation in your choice of base shape, twining pattern, and rim style. I outline some options in the sections that follow, which can also be used to create variations on the Woven Berry Basket (page 199) since twined and woven baskets overlap in both structure and technique. Likewise, the various weaving patterns on page 197 in Chapter 12, Woven Basketry, can be used to add stripes of contrast to a twined basket. I recommend completing the projects as instructed before experimenting with variations.

Square Bases

Weave this base tightly or with open spaces, depending on the material and your goals for the design. When using inner bark strips or other sturdy materials, you need open space between the stakes so that the twining strands or weavers will have room on the walls of the basket. (Use instructions on pages 200–201 for the Woven Berry Basket to create a square base with spaces.) The more space between the stakes, the wider the footprint of the basket will be. If desired, you can weave in filler rows at the end to close the gaps. With soft, flexible twining materials, such as cattails and yucca, best practice is to space the stakes very tightly to mitigate shrinking as the materials dry. (Use instructions on pages 215–216 for the Diagonal-Plaited Cattail Basket to create a tightly woven square base.) Note that even though the baskets start out square, the walls and rim will naturally round out as you weave.

When building a square base, lay out the center pieces first. If there is an uneven number of stakes on a side, there are two center pieces. If there is an even number, there are four center pieces, and the true center point is the space between them.

You can turn a square base into a rectangle by adding more stakes to either the horizontals or the verticals. The stakes in whichever group has fewer will need to be a bit longer to end up with an even top.

Round Bases

Also known as a star base, you can work this style with either flat materials, such as inner bark strips, or softer materials, such as cattail or iris. (Use instructions on pages 174–175 for the Twined Treasure Basket to create a round base.) The more stakes you begin with, the bulkier the construction gets. To more easily increase the diameter of the basket, start with slightly wider stakes or use scissors to narrow the middle third of each stake so it gets thinner toward the center. Alternatively, add more stakes later.

Tight-weave base

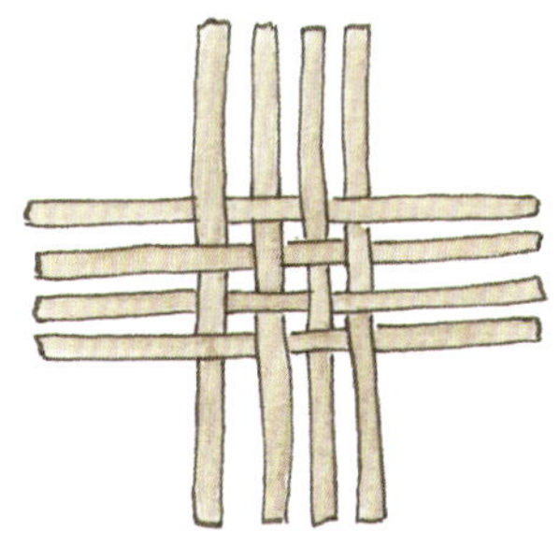

Open-weave base

When weaving with a larger number of stakes, narrow them in the center to reduce the bulk of the base.

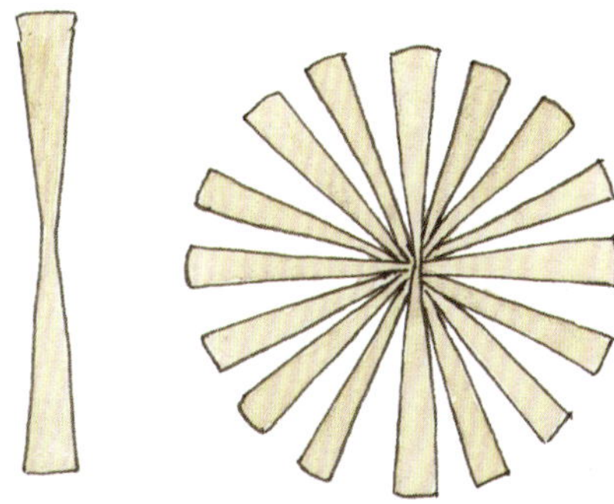

For clarity, the illustrations below show the center stakes shaded.

Odd number of stakes

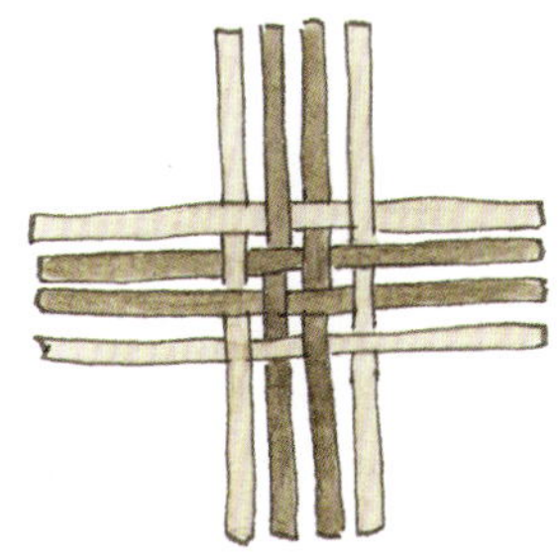

Even number of stakes

To add a new stake, either (1) narrow the center of a long strip and fold it in half over an existing stake; or (2) narrow a short strip on one side and insert between two existing stakes.

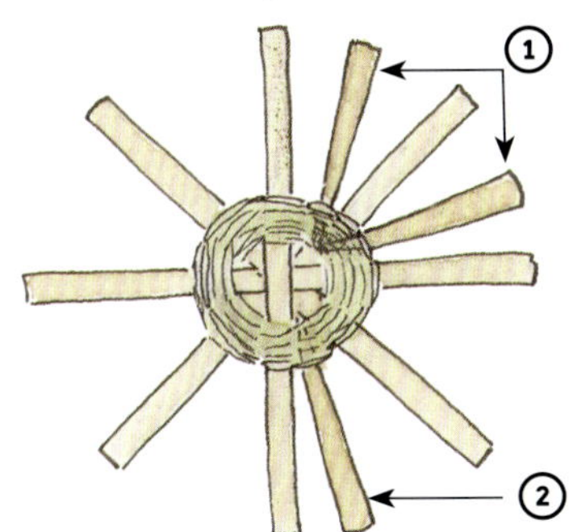

twining patterns

There are many twining patterns to choose from. Pick one or use more to create stripes of different textures and colors.

Regular twine. Twine over one stake. This is the most basic twining pattern and can be done with an odd or even number of stakes.

Diagonal twine. Twine over two stakes. There must be an odd number of stakes for the twines to create a diagonal pattern. If you have an even number, you can cheat by twining over just one stake at the beginning of each row to create the diagonal. There will be one visible spiraling line of single twines that travels up the basket if you do this, but I find it to be a lovely design element.

Arrow twine. One row of regular twine followed by a row in which you twist the twine in the opposite direction, creating the appearance of an arrow.

Color variation. Create stripes or a dotted pattern by using a different color for each twining strand.

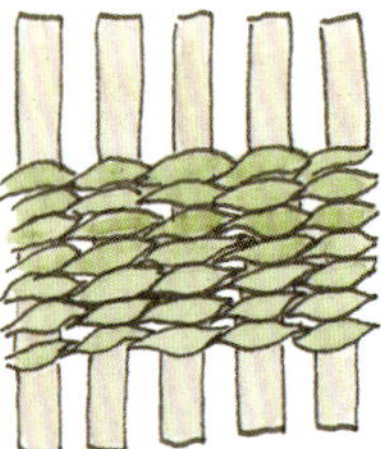

Regular twine

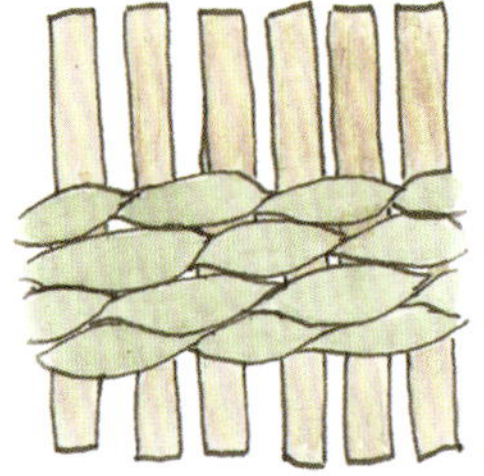

Diagonal twine

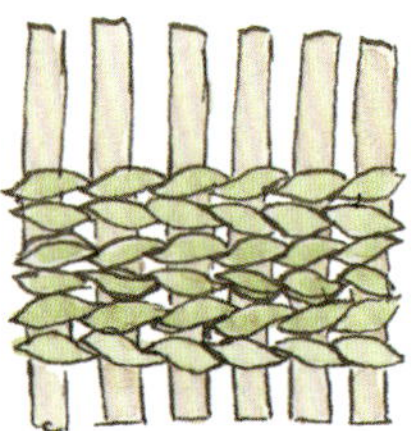

Arrow twine

rim styles

The rim creates the finishing touch on your basket, and each has its own look. The following three styles are some of the best to start with.

Attached rim. A classic rim in which a separate inner and outer rim are lashed onto the basket top to secure the stakes and create a sturdy finish. (See instructions in the Woven Berry Basket project on page 199.) To adapt it for twined baskets and achieve a solid finish, tuck all the stakes down beneath three rows of twining (as in the tucked-down rim described below) before you add the attached rim.

Braided rim. This pattern, which resembles a braid, involves weaving one stake in front of the next in line, then behind the next, and out again, resulting in a fringe of stakes as the rim of the basket. (See instructions in the Twined Treasure Basket project on page 173.) This is very similar to the trac border done in the Wild Wickerwork Basket (page 295) but has a different appearance and feel when done with soft materials. When applied to a woven basket with wider stakes, leave extra length on the stakes to complete it or cut each stake in half widthwise for a finer pattern.

Tucked-down rim. There are many variations of this style, but basically you fold each stake over and tuck it beneath the last several rows of twining. This style works best with stakes that are soft enough to thread on a needle and sew down. The construction will be most invisible when tucking stakes to the inside of the basket, although it is a tighter space to work in.

Attached rim

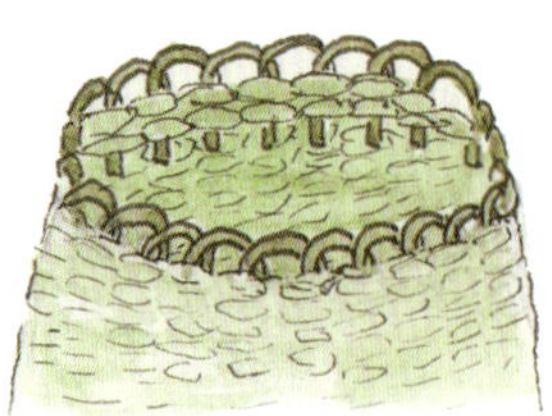

Braided rim

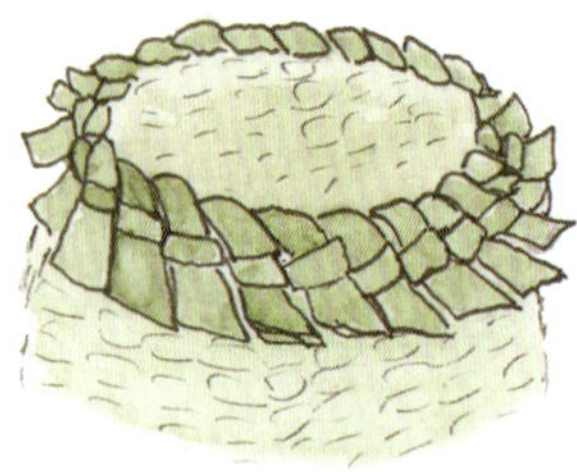

Tucked-down rim

Understanding Twining

Twining is unique because you work with two strands that cross over each other between each vertical element of a basket; this creates a very solid weave. Several projects in this book use twining, each with their own nuances that are noted in the directions. However, they all rely on understanding foundational twining techniques.

basic twining technique

I recommend practicing twining a couple of times before moving on to a project. The demonstration photos use two strands in different colors to clearly show how each one is moving.

1. Lay eight or more vertical elements (called stakes) flat on a table and place a weight over the bottom half.

2. Tie two twining strands together using any knot. (Note that some projects call for one long twining strand folded in half instead of two tied together.) Position the knot on the outer edge of the left-most stake. One twining strand should be over the first stake and the other should be under it. Comb the two twining strands to the right so they fan out in a <-shape, positioning the strand that goes under the stake at the top (A).

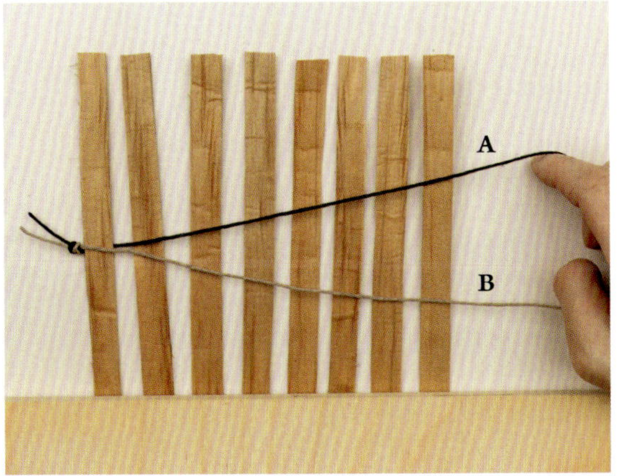

3. Cross strand B over strand A and under the next stake to the right.

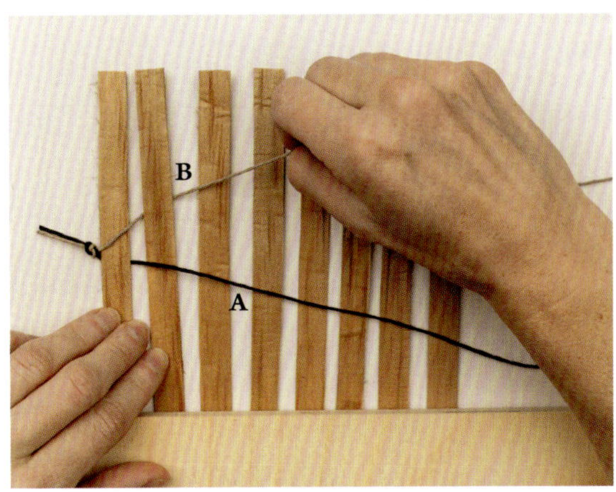

4. The two twining strands have now switched places. Bring strand B down in line with the knot and comb both twining strands to the right so they are positioned in a <-shape without tangles. This is a very important step to do with each twine.

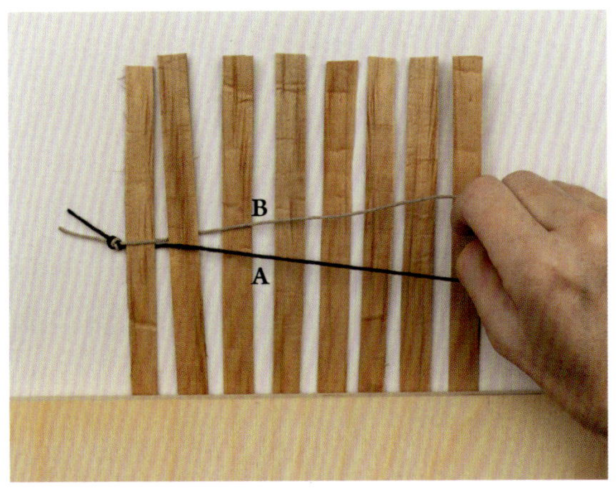

Continued on next page

5. Bring strand A over strand B and under the next stake to the right. Comb out the strands.

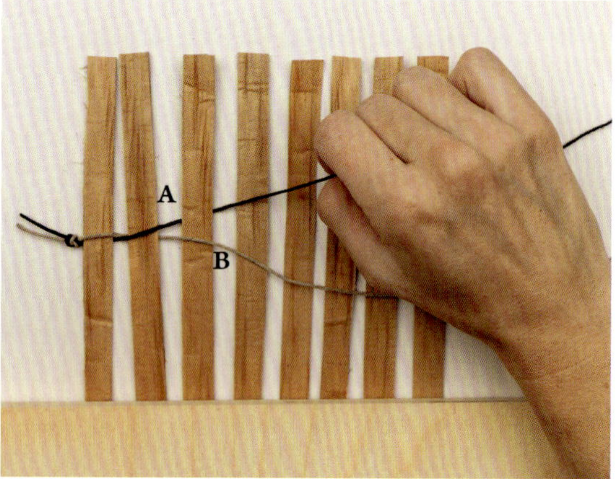

6. Repeat steps 3 to 5 to continue twining.

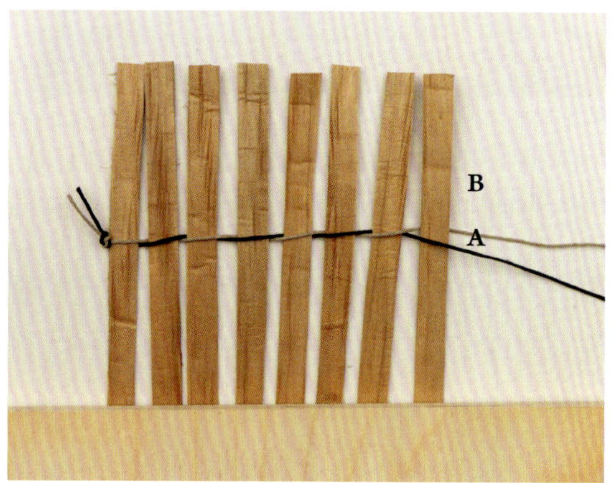

twining around a corner

Several projects call for one row of twining around a square base to secure the stakes together before continuing. Going around the corners of the base can be confusing. Take it slow and follow each step carefully.

1. Begin a square base. (See Square Bases on page 167.)

2. Twine one side using the Basic Twining Technique beginning on page 169.

TIPS FOR TWINING

- Go slowly and do each step methodically to gain muscle memory before moving faster.
- Always comb the two strands to the right and be sure they are positioned in a <-shape over the next stakes before doing the next twine.
- Note that the strands should not twist completely around each other between each stake. They are simply switching places. It is common for novice basket makers to twist them too many times.
- If you suspect that you have done an incorrect twine, undo a couple until it looks correct. You can spot an incorrect twine if the line of the twine is parallel across a stake instead of diagonal, which usually means the two strands have twisted around each other.

3. At the first corner, pause the twining and turn the base counterclockwise so that the next side of untwined stakes is at the top. Maintain the position of the strands: The thread that was in the top position should still be in the top position after turning. This is important to do at every corner.

4. Comb the two twining strands out to the right so they are both over the stakes.

5. The twining pattern does not change. Bring the bottom strand under the first stake of the new side.

6. Comb the two strands out to the right and continue twining as usual until you reach the end of the new side. Repeat steps 3 to 6 until you reach the knot.

securing a twined base

Once you've twined one row around the whole base, use any knot to tie the two strands together around the very first stake. Use needle-nose pliers to tuck the ends between two layers of base weaving.

TWINED TREASURE BASKET

THIS STYLE OF BASKET IS A PERFECT USE for easily foraged garden foliage like daylily, red hot poker, dandelion and daffodil flower stalks, crocosmia, Siberian iris, corn husks—you name it! This project is all about the details. The difference between a messy twined basket and a well-woven one is seriously slowing down and doing each twine methodically and tightly, always packing each row down. The basket shown features green Siberian iris leaves, cattails, and whitish corn husks as well as brown iris leaves harvested late in the season, with a regular twine pattern and a braided rim. Many variations in plant materials, twining patterns, and rim styles look great.

BASKET SIZE

3½-inch diameter at base; 2¼-inch diameter at rim; 3¼ inches high

TOOLS

- Spray bottle of water
- Measuring tape
- 4 × 4-inch piece of thick cardboard
- Pin or tack
- Basketry scissors
- Straight-tip packing tool
- Needle-nose pliers
- Tapestry needle

PLANT MATERIALS

- **Stakes.** Seven cattail leaves cut to a length of 14 inches and a width just shy of ½ inch
- **Twining strands.** A handful of Siberian iris leaves, red hot poker, crocosmia, corn husks, daylily leaves, dandelion and daffodil flower stalks, or any other leafy, long material

See Material Variations on the next page for other plant material options.

PREPARING MATERIALS

See Chapter 3, Leaves, Grasses, and Soft Stems, for details on harvesting and processing cattails and other leaves. Keeping the materials from drying out while working is essential. Dampen them occasionally with water from a spray bottle.

TIME REQUIRED

Because of the detailed twining, this project might take a long day or a couple of sessions over 2 days despite its small size. Hint: The slower the better; don't rush this one.

Leaves degrade in quality when repeatedly dried and rehydrated, so it's ideal to keep them damp and work on the basket over a couple of days. If you do want to dry it out in between work sessions, try to finish turning up the sides of the basket and tie the stakes loosely together at the top before pausing so the vulnerable dried stakes don't break.

MATERIAL VARIATIONS

For the stakes, yellow flag iris, yucca, or other wide and somewhat sturdy leaves are best. Thin inner bark stakes are great, too. If using thinner leaves like Siberian iris, either scale the project down in size or use a bundle of three or more leaves for each stake.

For twining strands, very thin vines, retted inner bark, fibers, and anything else flexible enough to not overpower the soft stakes will work.

prepare the base

1. Soften soaked cattail stakes by twisting them a couple of times.

2. Measure and mark the exact center of each stake with a small pencil line. Lay two of the stakes across each other in a cross shape with the middle marks lined up on top of the piece of thick cardboard.

3. Add the remaining stakes in an arrangement like the spokes of a wheel so they are all evenly spaced with the middle marks lined up. Place a pin through the center of all the stakes and into the cardboard. Don't worry if the stakes shift. Just take your time and try to keep them evenly spaced as you work.

4. Use any knot to tie two iris leaves together by the wispy tips to make your first two twining strands.

5. Turn the base so the bottommost stake in the pile is oriented vertically. Hook the knot of the tied iris around this stake and slide it toward the center.

twine the base

This is a basket where a lot happens in the beginning and, as a novice, you are learning a good deal at once. Take your time. If you aren't happy with the way your base looks because you are just getting the hang of it, you can always start over with what you've learned. Patience will pay off.

1. Twine around each stake in a circle. (See Basic Twining Technique on page 169.) The goal is to make an even circle of twining approximately 1¾ inches in diameter with the pin at the exact center, but the exact dimensions will vary depending on your basket.

Tip: *Pull each twine snugly and push them toward the center pin a bit, but not so far that the circle becomes uneven, or the twines slide beneath the stakes. Turn the base counterclockwise as you work, so the stake you are currently twining around is in the vertical position.*

2. Go around three times. Splice in new twining strands toward the end of the third round, even if it means cutting the twining strands short. (See Splicing Twining Strands for a Basket on page 176.) Use a measuring tape to ensure that each of the stakes is still even. Pull to adjust them.

Continued on page 177

SPLICING TWINING STRANDS FOR A BASKET

As each twining strand ends, splice in another to replace it. Always wait to splice until the strand that is running out is in position *behind* a stake. Don't splice both twining strands at the same place. If they are ending at the same time, cut one a few inches shorter. If you want to switch to a new material, you don't have to wait until the twining strands come to their natural end. Simply cut them off where you want the new material to begin.

1. Wait until the twining strand that is about to end is behind a stake. Use scissors to cut it so that it ends directly in the middle of the front of the next stake to the right.

2. If the piece being spliced in has a tapered end, cut the thin material off so the twining width stays even. Insert the end so that it is sandwiched between the stake and the ending twining strand. Let it stick out a little to the left of the stake to keep it from pulling out while you twine. It will likely tug a bit to the right and end up behind the stake.

3. Since the strands only overlap behind one stake, the new twining strand easily pulls out. Use your fingers to pinch the overlap between the old and new twining strands for several twines. If done precisely, the ends of both the old and new twining strands will be hidden. If not, don't worry. You can trim them later.

3. Remove the base from the cardboard and flip it over toward your body, laying it flat on the table. The tails should extend to the right, toward your body and underneath the stakes. This is a very important step and positions you to turn up the sides of the basket while still twining from left to right.

turn up the sides

To successfully turn up the basket, you need to hold three or four stakes in a row upright while you twine around them tightly. For a rounded base, hold the stakes at an angle as you twine. For a more straight-sided base, hold them straight up.

1. Bend several stakes upward and hold them in that position while twining. The twining technique doesn't change, but it might feel unfamiliar since you are holding the basket in a different position.

2. Turn the basket clockwise, bend another three or four stakes up, and twine around each individual stake snugly. Continue around the basket, splicing in new twining strands as needed. It takes several rows before the stakes will stay upright.

3. After five rounds of twining, use scissors to carefully cut the width of each stake exactly in half. Be careful not to cut through the twining: Split the last bit by hand. This doubles the amount of twining in each row, allowing the basket to swell in shape as it turns up.

Continued on next page

4. Continue twining around each split piece individually. Push the two sides apart so they separate and try to twine right against the previous row.

5. Pack the first few rows by grabbing two stakes and holding them steady while pushing down on the weaving between them with a packing tool. For best results do this between all the stakes, particularly between the ones that are newly split. Give the basket a spritz of water. Remember to keep the basket from drying out.

Tip: *After twining a few rows around the split stakes, you have the option of adding two or three additional leaves to each twining strand, which makes the basket more solid and densely woven.*

6. Continue until there are about 2 inches of twining. Splice in new materials if desired to create stripes of different color and texture.

UNDERSTANDING PACKING

Packing is one of the most important principles in basketry, and it simply means pushing down each row of weaving so that the gaps between rows are eliminated. This method makes a basket that is tightly woven, neat, and sturdy. Even though it might not seem like there is much space between rows at first, when the material dries and shrinks the space will increase. Typically, you use a packing tool to press each new row down right after it's woven, which compresses all the rows below it as well. Don't worry if the new row pops back up after packing. Just remember that each row you pack really serves to pack all the rows below it. Each project in this book will detail some techniques for effectively packing the rows of weaving in that type of basket.

shape the basket and seal the twining

1. Once the basket is 2 or 2½ inches high, begin to narrow the opening. Cross two stakes. (It doesn't matter which is in front.) Twine around the two stakes as if they were one. Do this four times on different sides of the basket for an even result.

2. After two rows cut out the back stake of the two that are crossing. Cut close to the twining.

3. Twine until the basket is 3 inches high or there is a minimum of 3 inches of each stake left over for folding over the rim. It's frustrating to weave the rim without enough length.

4. Cut one of the twining strands to 10 inches and thread it onto a tapestry needle. Insert the needle between a stake and four rows of twining and pull to the outside of the basket. Repeat with the second twining strand, passing through the same space or an adjacent one.

5. Tug both strands downward and then cut the ends carefully right next to the twining, so they slide beneath a weave when you let go.

braid the rim

1. Make sure the stakes are adequately soaked and flexible before starting so they don't crack and break. (If one does break, cut it off close to the twine and continue the braiding pattern without it.)

2. Fold any stake (A) to the right at a 45-degree angle *in front* of the stake directly to its right (B).

Continued on next page

3. Bring the folded stake (A) *behind* the next stake to the right (C) and *out* again.

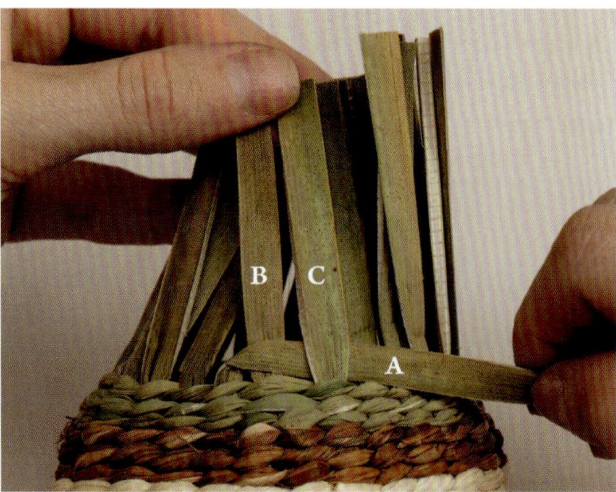

4. Now fold stake B *in front* of stake C, *behind* stake D, and *out* again.

5. Continue this pattern until only two standing stakes remain. If the stakes are too close together to work with easily, cut one out occasionally by trimming it close to the last row of twining and braiding over the top of it.

Tip: *The rim tends to angle upward as you braid, and the vertical stakes can bend to the inside of the basket and get lost. Mitigate this by tugging all but the first three folded stakes downward as you braid, while holding the vertical stakes upright.*

6. When there are only two stakes left standing, the pieces that they need to weave around are already folded over. Use a packing tool to pull the first two folded stakes up ⅜ inch so there is a visible gap.

7. Fold the next stake in line in front of the last standing stake to its right. To complete the "behind and out" part of the pattern, thread it behind the first folded stake and back out to the front. Use needle-nose pliers to pull through.

8. Thread the final standing stake "in front, behind, and out" around the first two folded stakes. If it is difficult to see where to thread it, pull the first two folded stakes up further. It should come out in the space directly above the top row of twining in the only space between stakes that is not already occupied by the end of a previously folded stake.

Tip: *Use needle-nose pliers to pull through.*

9. To create a flatter top, tighten each stake by pulling down on it using needle-nose pliers. Take care not to rip the stakes.

10. After the basket has dried, cut off each end. I prefer angled cuts. Leave at least 1/4 inch so the rim doesn't come apart. You can always cut more, but you can't put it back!

WILD FIBERS TWINED BAG

TAKE THE OPPORTUNITY TO SLOW DOWN while creating this twined bag. Embrace the meditative practices of harvesting and processing fiber, twisting cordage, and finally twining the bag—truly a balm for a fast-paced world. This project calls for regular twining, but the construction method is unique. It uses a mold to maintain its shape and is created from the top down instead of from the bottom up. You can adapt the project directions to other sizes by changing the size of the mold and adjusting the number and length of the warp strands. Just be sure to factor in extra cordage for the lark's head knot and finishing the bag at the bottom.

BAG SIZE

3½ inches wide × 4 inches high

TOOLS

- Piece of ¼-inch-thick foam core or cardboard cut to 3¼ × 5 inches for the mold; tape two pieces of cardboard together if needed to get ¼-inch thickness
- Masking tape or small piece of beeswax or candle
- Basketry scissors
- Tapestry needle
- Packing tool
- A few 2-inch spring clamps

PLANT MATERIALS

- **Warp pairs.** 28½ feet of cordage, ⅛ inch in diameter. Make or split the cordage into one 20-inch piece and twenty-three 14-inch pieces. Try to keep the diameter even throughout the cordage. Use a soft fiber, such as basswood, banana plant, yucca, agave, dogbane, nettle, milkweed, snake plant, or something similar. Note that it will be almost completely covered by the twining.
- **Twining strands.** Use any kind of cleaned and processed soft plant fiber that has not been made into cordage. Handling long, ribbonlike fiber, such as basswood or banana plant fiber, is easier than shorter, stringy fiber, such as nettle or milkweed, but both work.

The first twining strand must be a minimum of 50 inches. If using shorter fiber, tie two bundles together. The diameter of the fiber strip or bundle should be approximately ¹⁄₁₆ inch when twisted tightly. After this first long strand, you will splice individual strands onto each end.

Tip: *Depending on the fiber you are using, the thickness of your cordage, and your personal preferences, you may want to use thinner or thicker pieces of fiber for the twining strands. Experiment and see what feels better in your hand and what creates a fabric in the bag that is neither too bulky nor too loose.*

PREPARING MATERIALS

See Chapter 6, Wild Fibers, for details on harvesting and processing materials. See pages 128–132 for details on making cordage.

TIME REQUIRED

This is a great project to work on bit by bit over time, although I'd recommend doing the setup and getting 10 rows of twining in during the first sitting. If you've premade cordage and wanted to push through to completion, it might take 2 or 3 full days.

Anatomy of a Twined Bag

With construction methods that are quite different from the twined basket, there is some special terminology to understand.

Top strand. An extra-long piece of cordage tied around the top of the mold that forms the rim of the pouch. Each warp pair is knotted onto it.

Warp pairs. In weaving, warp threads stretch vertically on a loom and other threads are passed over and under them horizontally to make cloth. In this context, a warp pair is a piece of cordage folded in half and knotted to the top strand to form the vertical elements of the bag. The two legs of the warp pair are twined together as one.

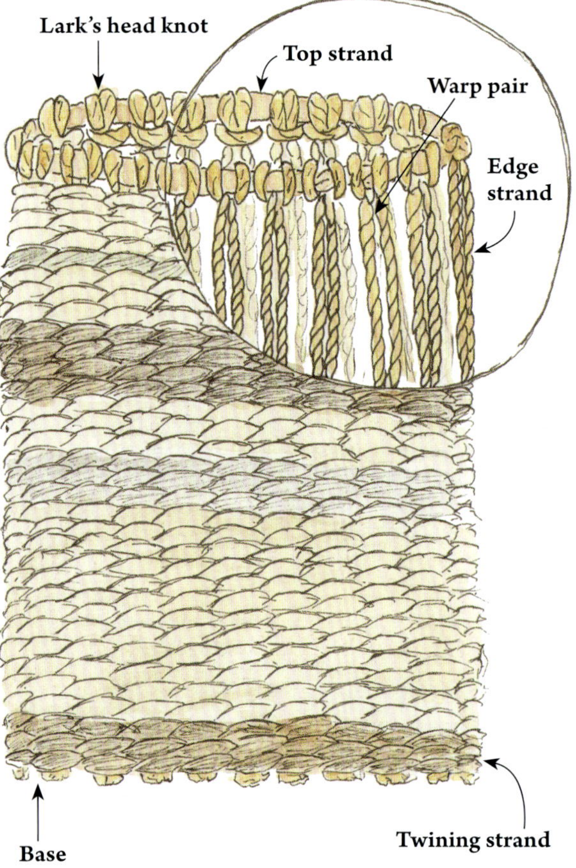

Edge strands. The two pieces of cordage on the short ends of the mold. One is a regular warp pair, and one is the tied ends of the top strand.

Lark's head knot. Used to attach each folded warp strand to the top strand.

Twining strands. Two horizontal elements made of loose fiber that twist around each of the warp pairs to create the fabric of the pouch.

Base. The bottom of the pouch, which is finished by knotting or sewing the cordage on each side of the bag together.

prepare the top strand and warp pairs

1. Tie the 20-inch strand of cordage around the top of the mold with a square knot (see Tying a Square Knot on page 160) so that the knot is on the edge and the ends are equal in length. If it seems very bulky, tie only the first half of the square knot and tighten it occasionally until you've twined a row or two.

2. Fold a piece of cordage exactly in half. Slide the fold between the mold and the top strand. This is your first warp pair.

3. Pass the two ends of the warp pair through the loop from the front to the back in what is known as a lark's head knot.

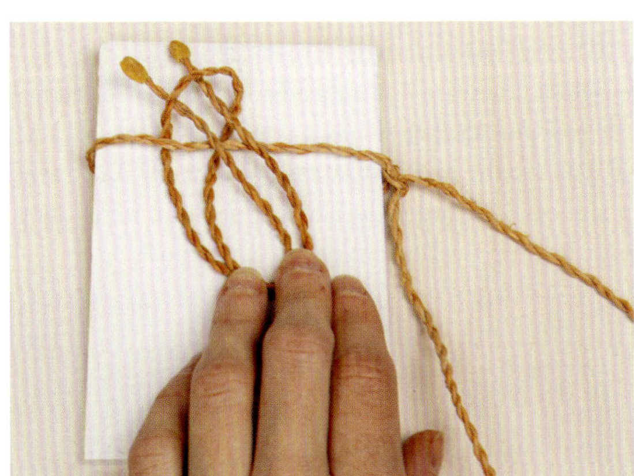

4. Pull snugly upward, and then downward so that the ends are flat against the mold. Make sure the two ends are exactly even and adjust if they are not.

5. Working left to right, repeat steps 2 to 4. Each warp pair should touch its neighbor without being crowded.

Tip: *Be sure to put one warp pair on the edge of the mold not occupied by the top strand knot.*

Continued on next page

6. Continue adding warp pairs until there are approximately 12 on each side and 1 on the edge opposite the top strand knot. Note that everyone's cordage will be a bit different, and you may need fewer or more warp pairs. What is most important is to space the warp pairs closely without squeezing them in.

7. Seal the tips of the cordage to prevent unraveling. Use either warmed wax or tiny pieces of tape pinched over each end. Note that the cordage will tangle if the tape is too large.

twine the bag

1. Starting at the left of the mold, fold the long piece of fiber for the first twining strands around a warp pair so the ends are uneven by 3 inches. (If using two shorter pieces tied together, position the knot on the left side and be sure one strand is 3 inches longer than the other.)

2. Slide the fold to the top. Brush the strands out to the right so they are not tangled and are positioned like <. Be sure the half that is resting in front of the warp pair is above the half that wraps underneath. This is the top half of the < and is the starting position for every twine. Pick up the bottom of the two strands.

3. Carry the bottom strand to the top of the mold, crossing over the top strand.

4. Pull the other twining strand down.

5. Pick up the next warp pair to the right and carry it to the left so it rests on top of the bottom half of the twining strands. This is a subtle movement.

6. Pull the top and bottom twining strands to the right, giving each a gentle tug to settle them in place. (Don't tug so hard that all the warp pairs start to angle to the right.) Comb the strands out so they form a <- shape, without tangles, and the strands rest on top of all the other warp pairs.

7. Repeat steps 3 to 6 to continue twining around each warp pair. Treat the two tails of the top strand knot on the edge of the mold as a warp pair and twine around them together.

Tip: *The tension with which you are pulling, the diameter of the cordage, and the thickness of the twining strands all combine to affect how many warp pairs you need. If a gap has developed between the last twine and the first one, add more warp pairs to fill the space.*

8. Go around the first warp pair a second time, closing the first round.

Continued on page 190

SPLICING TWINING STRANDS FOR A BAG

There are several different methods for adding new materials, depending on whether the twining strands are thinning out or ending abruptly and what kind of fiber you are using. Personal preference matters, too! No matter what method you use, always splice onto a twining strand when it is on the bottom position, underneath a warp pair. For clarity, contrasting colors are used for the new twining strands in these photos.

Method 1: Folding In

This method is good if both twining strands are thinning out. Take a new piece of fiber and fold it in half. Slide the fold onto the warp pair so that each half is integrated into one of the twining strands.

Method 2: Overlay

Use this method if only one twining strand is thinning out. You need 2 to 6 inches of material left on the strand. As it begins to thin, lay a new piece of fiber in, tucking it beneath a warp pair and twisting the ending strand and the new strand together.

Method 3: Tying On

Tying on uses a knot, which creates bulk, so this method works best when joining two thin single strands. Tie the two ends together with a square knot (see Tying a Square Knot on page 160). Try to position the knot so it will be on the inside of the bag.

Method 4: Tucking In

Use this method when the twining strands end abruptly or are very stringy. It is the most seamless transition. It also works well for creating abrupt changes between stripes of different-colored twining materials.

1. Thread the twining strand that is ending onto a tapestry needle and push the needle upward, underneath the top layer of four rows of twining (not all the way to the inside of the bag) and then pull tight to the outside.

2. Thread the new twining strand on the needle and go back one warp pair to the left. Push the needle downward, under the top layer of four rows of twining.

3. Pull through until there is an inch of tail hanging out of the top. Continue twining and trim the tail ends flush after a row.

OPEN-TWINE VARIATION

In open twining, you leave up to ¾ inch of space between each row, which makes the project go much faster! The cordage shows in the gap. I recommend at least starting and ending the bag with a 1-inch band of regular, packed twining to make it sturdier.

9. Continue twining. After completing several rows, hold two adjacent warp pairs steady and use a packing tool to push the twining strands upward between them so that all the twining is flush against the top strand. Do this between every warp pair.

10. Tighten the warp pairs to create a flat top. Grab each pair and pull down strongly while holding the rest of the bag in place with your other hand. If more than four rows of twining are in place, it will be hard, so don't wait on this step.

11. Continue twining. Pack the twining strands upward every two rows. When the shorter twining strand has 1 inch remaining or is thinning out noticeably, splice in a new strand. (See Splicing Twining Strands for a Bag on page 188.)

finish the twining

1. Continue twining until 2 to 2½ inches of cordage remain on the shortest warp pairs. At least 2 inches are needed to easily finish the bag.

2. Seal off the twining strands by threading each half on a needle and pushing the needle up along a warp strand, underneath the twining. The twining will completely hide the strands. Pull the strands through a bit and trim, so the ends sink back beneath the twining.

3. Remove the bag from the mold. If it sticks, use scissors or another bladed tool to cut the mold and collapse it. Be careful not to cut the plant material!

4. There are a couple of methods for finishing the bottom of the bag, depending on the look you like and the thickness of your cordage. Whether you choose knotting (this page) or threading down (page 192), be prepared to spend some time on this step as it is a slow and precise process.

knotting the bottom of the bag

This is the simplest method of finishing the bag. The knots create bulk, so I often flip the bag inside out to hide them afterward, which can take some effort, but it's definitely possible! If you don't flip the bag and choose to leave the leftover cordage fringe, note that the tape or wax will need to be removed and the cordage will unravel eventually.

1. The warp pairs that are on each edge are handled differently than all the rest. Using a piece of tape or clips to hold most of the cordage out of the way, start with a warp pair on the edge. (Otherwise, dealing with so many pieces of cordage can be visually overwhelming.)

2. Slowly tie the two pieces of cordage together in a square knot, positioning the knot closely against the bottom of the twining. (See Tying a Square Knot on page 160.) When the knot is in position, pull tightly.

Continued on next page

3. Unclip the next adjacent pieces of cordage. Note that you are *not* unclipping a warp pair, defined as two lengths next to each other, left to right. You are freeing two single strands opposite each other, front to back. Knot them together as in step 2.

4. Repeat the knotting process on all cordage lengths, tying the front of the bag to the back.

Tips: *If your cordage is too thick to knot easily, it's too crowded for knotting, or you think the knots are too bulky, then untwist each piece of cordage and cut one half flush with the bottom of the bag. Knot using only half the cordage thickness.*

threading down the bottom of the bag

I like this method for its elegance. Rather than knotting the ends of the cordage, you sew them into the twining. Don't worry if you miss a piece occasionally or get mixed up and thread it into the wrong space. If there is at least one element threaded into the opposite side, the bottom of the bag will be secure.

1. The warp pairs on the edges don't fit in with the pattern. We will integrate them later. Starting with two lengths of cordage adjacent to an edge pair, clip or tape the rest of the cordage out of the way. Note that you are *not* working with a warp pair, defined as two lengths next to each other, left to right. You are working with two lengths that are opposite each other, front to back.

2. Untwist one of the pieces of cordage and cut one half flush with the bottom of the bag.

3. Thread the uncut half on a tapestry needle and push the needle under five to eight rows of twining on the opposite side of the bag, alongside the opposite piece of cordage.

4. Pull tight, sealing the bottom of the bag in that spot. Remove the needle and trim the fiber flush with the twining.

5. Repeat steps 2 to 4 with the other unclipped piece of cordage on the opposite side.

6. Unclip the next two pieces of cordage opposite each other, repeating the process until only the edge warp pairs remain. Note that there will be multiple untwisted strands threaded under the same rows of twining, because each warp pair has two lengths of cordage to seal off. If it is just too bulky and more material will not fit underneath the rows of twining, it can be cut off. As long as one element from each side gets threaded onto the opposite side, the bag will be sealed.

7. Untwist the lengths of cordage in the edge pairs and sew half of each into the adjacent warp pair, choosing the side that still has space.

8. Trim any ends that are sticking out, being careful not to cut any of the twining strands.

CHAPTER 12

WOVEN BASKETRY

Basic weaving—known more specifically as plaiting—has many variations, and the results are often quite sturdy, making the baskets both versatile and beautiful. The techniques in this chapter cover plain and twill weaves using flat materials. I particularly enjoy weaving with bark from various species of trees, each of which has its own colors and textures that create distinctive results. I also love to combine weaving and twining patterns to create colorful and textured sampler baskets, demonstrating many materials and techniques in one basket.

Anatomy of a Woven Basket

Many of the structural elements and terminology in a twined basket are shared by woven baskets.

Stakes. Provide structure for both the base and the sides of the basket; should be sturdier than the weavers.

Weavers. Horizontal elements woven in rows around the stakes. Weavers should be a bit more pliable than the stakes so as not to overpower them.

Twining strands. Material that secures the base of the basket before you turn the stakes up the sides. Twining strands are either left in place or cut out when the basket is finished.

Attached rim. The top part of the basket, composed of inner and outer rim pieces that secure the stakes and the last row of weaving.

Lashing. A thin, flexible weaver that wraps around the inner and outer rims, securing them to the top layers of weaving.

Rim filler. A decorative piece of cordage or braid that sits in a trough between the inner and outer rim, covering the folded and cut stakes.

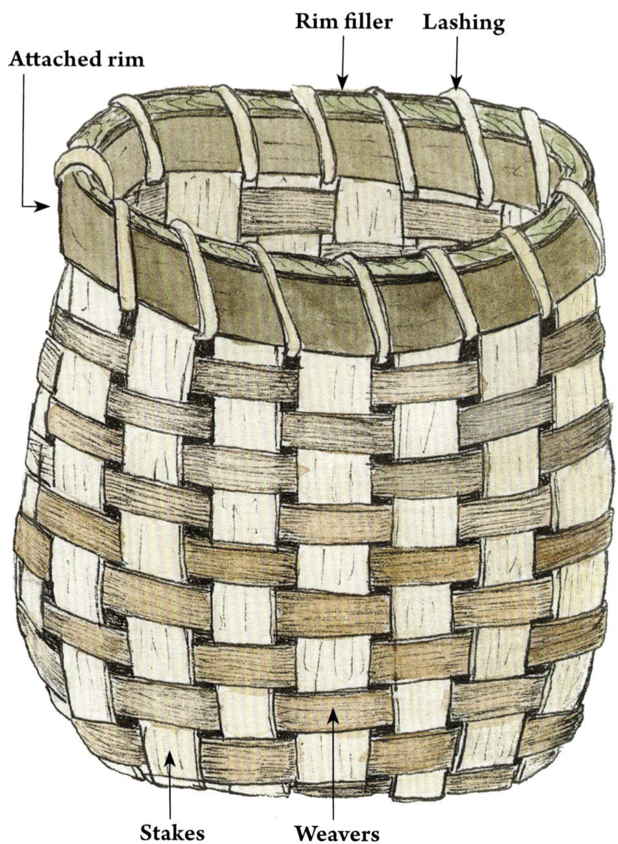

Base. The bottom part of the basket, which is woven first as a grid using the stakes.

VARIATIONS FOR WOVEN BASKETS

The project in this section focuses on the use of flat inner bark strips for weaving, but other sturdy flat materials could be substituted, including cattail, palm, or yucca leaves, especially if they are doubled up. You can also use store-bought flat reeds as stakes, which is an easy way to get started.

See pages 166–168 for other possible base shapes and rim styles. You can also add stripes of any twining pattern to a woven basket. I love putting several rows of twining into my designs, which adds a beautiful contrast of texture, color, and material.

weaving patterns

The weaving patterns that follow can be incorporated into twined baskets as well.

Plain Weave

Also known as basic weave, checkerboard weave, or regular weave, the plain weave is a repeating pattern in which a horizontal weaving element goes over one vertical, under one vertical, over one vertical, under one vertical. An odd number of vertical elements, called stakes, are required in the basket for this pattern to work. If you have an even number, cut a stake on one side of the basket in half lengthwise to split it into two. Note that after a basket base is complete, each piece on all four sides of the base counts as a stake. For example, if you started a base with 5 vertical stakes and wove in 5 horizontal stakes, once the base is complete you will have 20 uprights to weave around individually, and 21 after cutting one stake in half.

Twill Weaves

Twill weaves are any pattern other than a plain weave. Twills can be very complex, with the weaver going over and under different numbers of stakes in each row to create an image, or the pattern might be the same for each row.

Two × one twill. In this basic twill the weaver goes over two stakes and under one. For the pattern to work, the total number of stakes in the basket must be either one more or one less than a number that is divisible by three. For example, 16 stakes works because it is one more than 15, which is divisible by three.

Two × two twill. In this lovely twill, the weaver goes over two stakes, then under two stakes. Because the weave is looser, the tensioning is a bit trickier. Take your time to make sure the basket walls stay even. An odd number of stakes is required for this weave.

Plain weave, over one under one

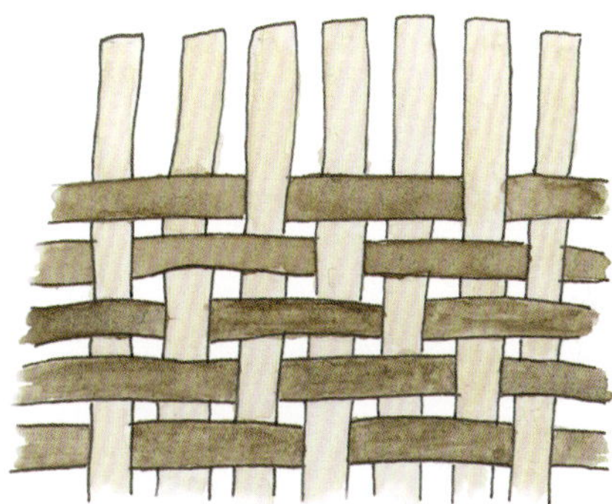

Two × one twill

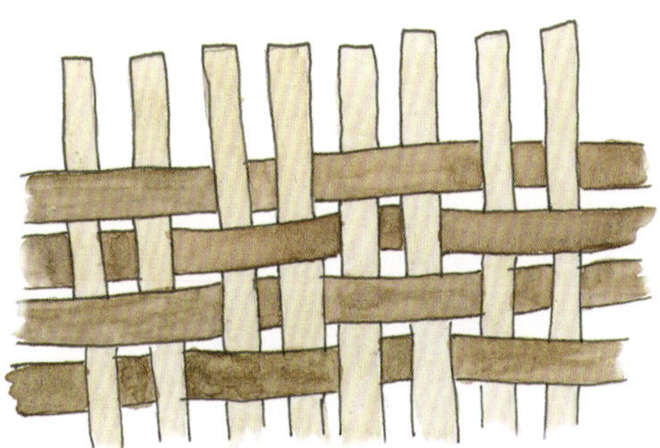

Plain weave, over two under two

Two × two twill

WOVEN BERRY BASKET

TO MAKE A BASKET FROM A TREE IS PROFOUND. Every time I use my woven bark baskets, I appreciate the life of the tree and the many hours I spent peeling and processing the bark into weaving material. This project is the perfect introduction to weaving square-bottomed baskets and can be scaled up easily by adding additional stakes and making them longer. Experiment with different colors, patterns, and sizes using whatever materials you have access to. For the basket shown, I used tulip poplar for the stakes and willow with the bark on for the weavers.

BASKET SIZE

4½ inches in diameter at top; 3½ inches square at bottom; 4¼ inches high

TOOLS

- Ruler or measuring tape
- Four micro alligator clips
- Basketry scissors
- Straight-tip packing tool
- Needle-nose pliers
- Utility or fixed-blade knife
- Four 2-inch spring clamps
- Chenille needle with an eye large enough to fit sewing strand

PLANT MATERIALS

- **Stakes.** Ten strips of inner bark ½ inch wide x 15 inches long, either a little thicker or the same thickness and flexibility as the weavers
- **Weavers.** Approximately 16 feet of bark strips (outer bark on or off), with each strip being ⅝ inch wide and as long as possible, ideally less thick and more flexible than the stakes
- **Twining strands.** 4 feet of thin twine or basswood fiber
- **Rim.** Two pieces of bark ¾–1 inch wide, depending on your project. Wait to cut these until the basket is woven.
- **Rim filler.** 16 inches of cordage ¼–⅜ inch in diameter
- **Lashing.** 7 feet of any kind of twinelike strand. One piece is ideal, but two can be overlapped, if necessary. Thin cordage, basswood fiber, long narrow strips of strong inner bark, raffia, or a human-made material are all good options.

PREPARING MATERIALS

See Chapter 7, Bark, for harvesting and processing inner bark strips and peeling bark from saplings. Rehydrate stakes, weavers, and rim materials just before working with them, soaking in hot water until flexible. Split bark can rehydrate in as little as 2 to 10 minutes.

TIME REQUIRED

For beginners, expect this to take a full day. I often recommend splitting the project into 2 days to allow the sides to dry and further pack down before completing the basket rim.

Pause your work at any point since you can dry and rehydrate bark two or three times without harming the quality of the material. Tie the stakes up and store your progress in a safe place as the stakes break easily. If pausing for under 24 hours, you can keep the project damp in a plastic bag stored in a cool place.

weave and secure the base

1. Measure and mark the exact center of the wrong side of each stake with a pencil. (The wrong side is the side you don't want to show on the exterior of the basket, which is an aesthetic choice.)

2. Lay five of the stakes vertically on a flat table with the middle marks lined up and ⅛ to ¼ inch between them. The wrong side should be facing up. If any of the stakes have a natural curve, position them so they are curving outward toward the corners. Weight the bottom with any available item, such as a scrap of wood or a book.

3. Weave a new stake horizontally from right to left across the vertical stakes so that it covers up the middle marks. Go over the first stake, under the second, over the third, under the fourth, and over the fifth in a plain-weave pattern. Pull the horizontal stake through until its middle mark matches up with the center vertical stake.

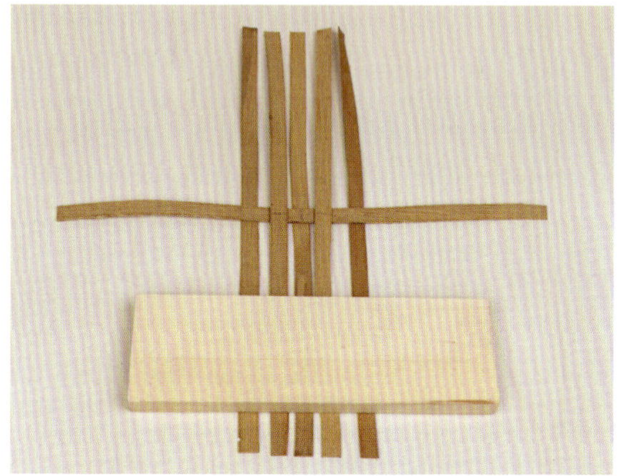

4. Weave in the remaining stakes—two above and two below the middle one—alternating whether you start over or under. Since the first stake started over, for example, the next stakes above and below start under. There should never be two overs or unders next to each other in any direction. Pull each stake through so the middle marks are lined up with the center stake and they have ⅛ to ¼ inch of space between. The base should be about 3½ inches square. Adjust so the spaces are all equal and clip each of the corners to secure.

Tip: *Less space, such as ⅛ inch, creates a basket with a smaller base and higher sides. More space, such as ¼ inch, makes a wider basket with lower sides.*

5. Add one row of twining around all four sides to secure the grid of the base so it doesn't come apart when turning the sides up. (See Understanding Twining and Twine the Base on pages 169 and 175.) When the basket is finished you can either leave the twining in or cut it out.

6. If any stakes shift out of alignment, hold the base in place and reposition the off-kilter stake. Measure each side to make sure the stakes are very close to equal.

Tip: *One of my favorite adages is that a basket can only be as high as its shortest stake. If a single stake or an entire side is shorter than the rest, you've limited the height of the basket.*

turn up and weave the sides

Turning up the sides of the basket takes some time and patience. At first you may wonder if it will ever happen! Just keep going and use clips to secure your progress. It takes three rows before it starts to feel like the basket is held together and turning up.

1. A plain-weave pattern needs an odd number of stakes. Since there are currently 20 stakes, cut 1 middle stake in half lengthwise—but only to the twine. Do not continue the cut on the other half of the stake.

2. Bend each stake upward against the base and press very firmly. They will not stay upright but will remember the crease. It helps if the stakes are not extremely wet during this process. Since the right side of the stakes is facing the table, when you bend them up the right side should now be facing outward, where it will show on the outside of the basket.

Continued on next page

3. Choose the first weaver—preferably a long one that can go around the basket three times or more. Use scissors to taper the last 10 inches on one side so the weaver ends in a point. This taper allows the weaver on the second round to slope over the beginning of the first round, rather than stepping up and leaving a hole.

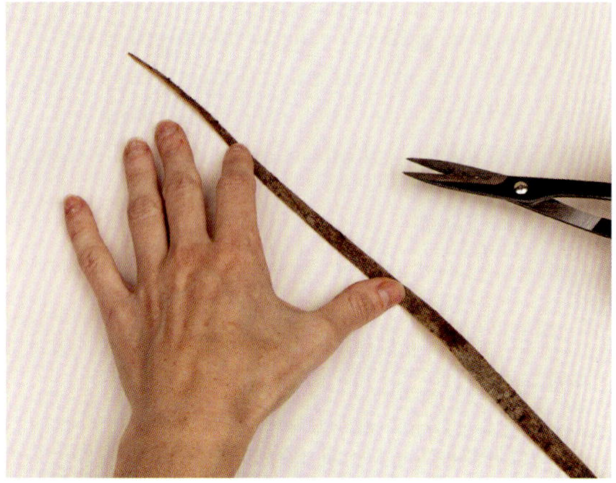

4. Choosing a side that does not have the split stake, use a clip to secure the end of the weaver behind the stake that is farthest to the left. The weaver should stick out a bit to the left of the stake.

5. Weave the first side in the plain-weave—over, under—pattern. After each weave, push the weaver toward the base using your fingers or a packing tool. It will always pop back up a bit, but packing is essential.

Tip: *To make the movement of each weave easiest, tilt the stake forward and slip the weaver over and behind it while holding the weaver in place over the last stake with your left hand. Try to keep the weaving as close to the previous row or the bottom of the basket as possible.*

6. Before continuing to the next side, place a clip to secure the weaver to the last stake. Check closely to make sure the pattern is correct. If there are any places where the weaver goes under or over two stakes in a row, unweave and correct it. Going forward, double-check your weaving after finishing each side and each round.

7. Rotate the basket clockwise so the new side is facing you. Weave the second side. Be extra careful not to disrupt the plain-weave pattern at the corner.

Continued on page 204

SPLICING WEAVERS

When a weaver ends, splice in another to continue, overlapping the new piece and old piece across four stakes, copying the same weaving pattern.

1. Cut the ending weaver so that it stops directly in the middle in front of a stake.

2. Slide the new weaver back four stakes so that it is in front of the ending weaver. The tip should rest behind the fourth stake back or stick out to the left a bit. (You can pull it forward later.)

3. Pack the new weaver down until it overlaps the ending weaver. Essentially it is sandwiched between the ending weaver and two stakes in a way that hides the ends of both weavers behind stakes.

8. Weave around each half of the split stake as individual pieces, pushing them far enough apart so that the weaver can pack down flat. The split stake is often a spot of difficulty on the basket. Making sure there is space between the halves will help keep the rows flat and even.

9. When the first round is complete, double-check that your weaving pattern is correct, then remove the clip holding the tapered end down and continue weaving. You can use the clip on top of the new row to help secure it.

10. After every row, pack the weavers toward the base by holding two stakes at a time, placing the packing tool between those two stakes, and pushing down all rows of weaving beneath it. Then move to the next two stakes to the right. Be careful not to crush the weavers with the packing tool. Again, packing is essential with each weave and each row. Secure the top row with one clip per side if desired.

finish weaving and pack the walls

1. Weave the sides, or walls, of the basket until there are 2 to 2½ inches left on the shortest stakes. The rim will cover the top two or three rows so don't save your best weavers for last.

2. If possible, let the basket dry, packing all the rows tightly a couple of times throughout the drying process. Start at the bottom and work your way to the top so that there is no space between them. As the materials dry, they shrink, and small spaces get bigger.

3. After the final packing, dip the stakes and top several rows of the basket in hot water to get them flexible again. Weave in more rows if packing has made room, but be sure to leave 2 to 2½ inches of stake for folding over.

4. Taper the last 10 inches of the last weaver, cutting along one edge so that it narrows to a point. The slope allows the top of the basket to be flat and even. Finish the weave.

finish the stakes

1. Cut the ends of the stakes that are on the *outside* of the final row of weaving into arrowpoints.

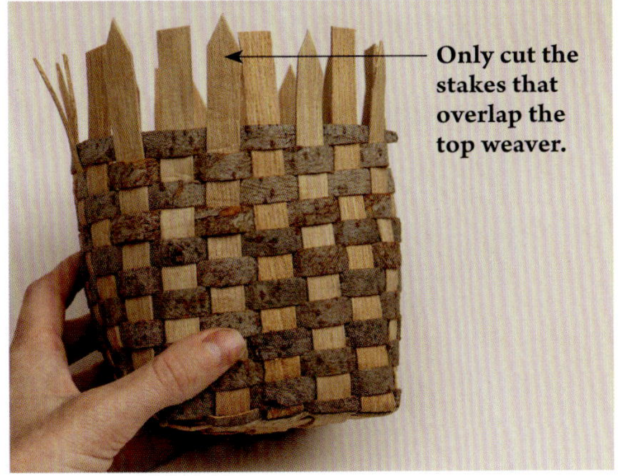

2. Position the basket so you are looking across the open top to the opposite side of the basket. Starting anywhere, use the packing tool to open a space between an arrow-tipped stake and the second weaver down. Make sure you are in a place with good light so you can see into the basket easily.

3. Using needle-nose pliers, if needed, tuck the stake into this open space and pull it down until it's tight against the top row of weaving.

4. Tuck in all the remaining arrow-tipped stakes. If the final tapered weaver does not seem secure enough at this point, cut an extra stake into an arrow tip and fold it in. If one or two stakes are too short to tuck in, cut them off instead.

Continued on next page

5. Cut all the flat-tipped stakes flush to the top of the weaving or slightly below.

add the rim

1. To cut the rims to width, measure from the top of the folded stakes to the bottom of the second row down and add ¼ inch. (For a wider rim, measure it to cover three rows of weaving.) The tapered ending of the last row can be a bit tricky to account for, but measure and cut a rim that will generally cover two or three rows.

2. To cut the rims to length, measure the circumference of the basket top and add 1½ inches for an overlap. The inner rim can be a little shorter than the outer one since the inner circumference of the basket is a bit smaller. Wrap them around the basket top to make sure each fits.

3. Shaving down the ends of the rim pieces to reduce bulk where they overlap is called creating a scarfed joint. Starting 1½ inches from each end on both rim pieces, use a knife to whittle away half the thickness.

4. Secure the inner rim to the inside of the basket top with clamps so it sticks out ¼ inch above the top edge of the basket.

5. Place the outer rim on the outside of the basket so it also sticks out ¼ inch above the top. Don't line up the overlaps of the inner and outer rims. Reposition the clamps so they secure both rim pieces. Squeeze all the slack out of both rims so there are no bumpy areas.

Tip: *Since clamps can leave permanent indents, cut a few pieces of bark into small pads to place between the metal and the rims, if desired.*

6. Add the rim filler to the trough between the two rim pieces. You can overlap the ends or thread them down between the outer rim and the wall of the basket.

lash the rim on

The lashing strand can wrap every space between the stakes or every other space. Aesthetically, I prefer every other space. Depending on how you angle and position it on the inside of the basket, you create either diagonal or straight lines of sewing.

1. Thread a lashing strand onto a needle. On the outside of the basket, push it up along a stake underneath one row of weaving and in between the two rims so that the needle and lashing strand come out the top of the basket. Pull the needle until there are about 4 inches of lashing left on the outside of the basket, which you will trim later.

LASHING STRAND VARIATION

The project instructions are for lashing strands on the rim that can be threaded on a needle. If using very narrow strips of inner bark, cut arrowpoints in the ends of the strips so each becomes its own sewing needle. Use an awl to open space between the weavers and stakes to thread the bark strands through.

2. Position the needle on the outside of the basket, just below the rim, in the space between the next adjacent stakes. Push straight back, drawing the needle through to the inside of the basket. (Note that you always insert the lashing strand from the outside of the basket to the inside.)

Continued on next page

3. Bring the lashing strand over the top of the rim and push the needle through the same hole. It should layer on top of the first wrap as closely as possible. You only double the lashing this first time, so it doesn't slip loose.

4. Bring the lashing strand over the top of the rim and position the needle just under the rim, two stakes to the right on the outside of the basket. Push the needle through the space between the stakes. Pull tight and continue to sew through every other space. As you sew, keep the tension of the lashing strand tight without tearing it. Squeeze all the slack out of the rims as you work along.

Tip: *Because the last weaving strand tapers, sometimes the bottom of the rim crosses over a row of weaving. In this case angle the needle up or down to go above or below the row. If necessary, punch through the weaving itself.*

5. After one complete round, tighten the lashing strand again. Slide a packing tool beneath the beginning of the lashing. Pull it toward you. Use the packing tool and your fingers to work all slack out of the lashing strand until reaching the end. You will likely gain a couple of inches of material.

6. Lash another round to finish securing the rim. For the second round, work in the opposite direction, from right to left, pushing the needle through the same holes as the first round.

Tips: *I angled the lashing strand to make V-shaped stitches on the front. For a plainer and simpler top, work the second round of lashing in the same direction as the first and overlap the stitches. Alternatively, you could create X-shaped stitches by shifting your needle positions one stake over.*

7. To finish, insert the needle between the inner rim and the outer rim and behind at least one row of weavers on the inside of the basket. If it's difficult to push through, you have succeeded in securing the lashing strand! Use needle-nose pliers, if necessary, to pull it tight. Trim the remainder of the lashing strand with scissors.

SPLICING LASHING STRANDS ON A RIM

If you don't have a lashing strand that is 7 feet long, splice a second strand on midway.

1. Secure the ending lashing strand by threading it with a needle between the rim pieces and behind at least one row of weavers on the inside of the basket. Use needle-nose pliers, if necessary.

2. Go back two stitches and thread the new lashing between the inner rim and the wall of the basket. Leave a few inches of tail hanging to trim later.

3. Overlap the last two stitches of the ending lashing strand with the new one and continue lashing until the end.

CHAPTER 13

DIAGONAL-PLAITED BASKETRY

Cultures all over the world practice diagonal plaiting to make baskets, hats, and even shoes. The technique uses flat materials and, unlike regular plaited baskets, the pieces are woven on the diagonal. I find the technique endlessly fascinating, because precision is important but so is instinct. Sometimes new students of mine find that they are weaving correctly but have no idea how! The rhythm of going over and under as you weave makes intuitive sense but also can be hard to wrap your mind around, inviting both a keen eye and trust in the flow of the process.

Anatomy of a Diagonal-Plaited Basket

These baskets use only a single material, but the way the elements cross to build the form always amazes me.

Rim. The top edge of the basket. Both projects use a flat rim where the weaving pieces fold at a 45-degree angle and tuck back down to the base.

Plaiting strips. The long, flat strips of material that are woven on a diagonal to create the basket.

Base. The bottom of the basket, which is worked as a tightly woven grid.

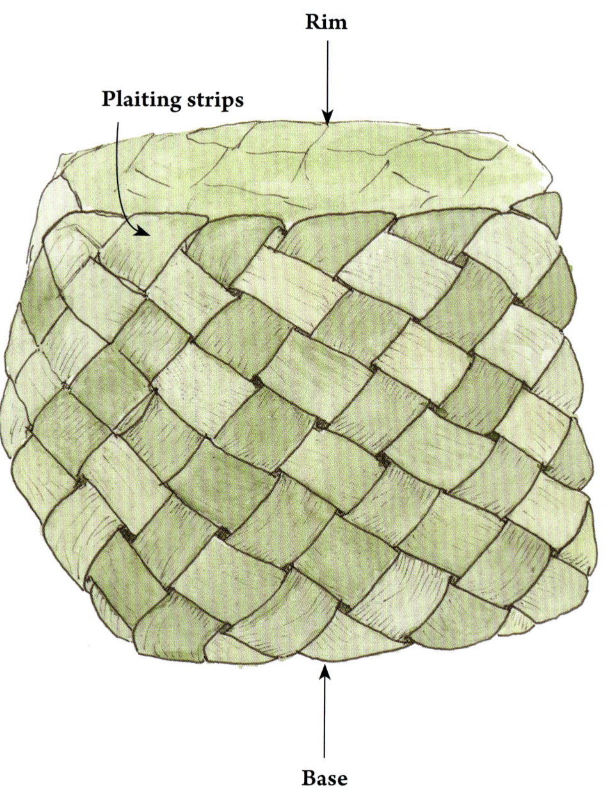

choosing material for diagonal plaiting

Any flat material is suitable, such as strips of inner bark, birch bark, cattails, western red cedar, and yucca, to name only a few. All elements should be cut to an even width. You could even complete these projects using decorative paper.

VARIATIONS FOR DIAGONAL-PLAITED BASKETS

Playing with the color patterns, number, and length of the stakes, as well as where the corners are placed to make different shapes, are all fun ways to create variations in diagonal plaiting. Even by using only a couple of randomly placed stakes of different colors, you can create interesting patterns as the colors cross each other and wrap around the basket.

To make a larger basket, increase both the number and length of stakes used. Square shapes are the easiest and must always have an even number of both horizontal and vertical stakes in the base.

To create a rectangle, use an odd number of stakes in each side so there are an uneven number of stakes on either side of the corners.

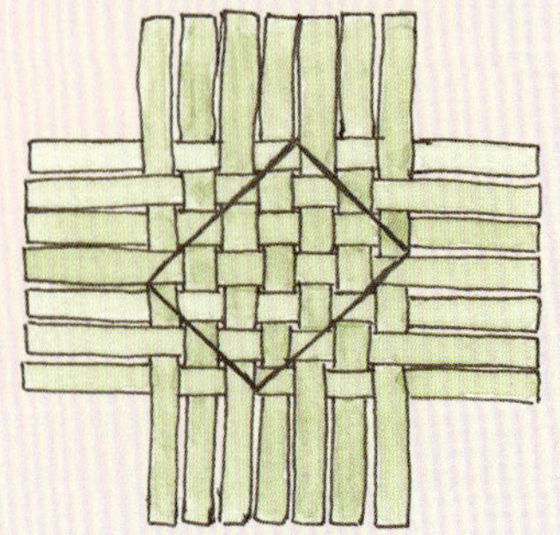

DIAGONAL-PLAITED CATTAIL BASKET

DIAGONAL PLAITING IS PERFECT FOR CATTAILS since four layers are woven on top of each other, fortifying the leaves' relative weakness. The walls of this basket are quite sturdy and rigid. This project takes a surprisingly long time for its size, mostly because of the very last part—weaving each and every piece back down the wall of the basket to the base. At that point, set yourself up with a movie and a spray bottle to keep the basket damp, and enjoy the process!

BASKET SIZE

3¾ inches wide × 3¾ inches deep × 3½ inches high

TOOLS

- Ruler
- Small piece of cardboard
- Pin or tack
- Six micro alligator clips
- 16-inch piece of thin twine or string (to be cut out of basket at the end)
- Spray bottle of water
- Basketry scissors
- Straight-tip packing tool

PLANT MATERIALS

16 cattail leaves, each 30 inches long, cut to an even width. This project shows leaves that are approximately ½ inch when dry (or substitute any flat, flexible material, such as birch bark, inner bark strips, or paper or other human-made materials).

PREPARE MATERIALS

Mellow cattails (pages 48–49). Take care not to oversoak them or the basket will loosen as it shrinks. Choose leaves without holes or blemishes. Cut material from the middle portion of the whole leaf, discarding the thicker, whitish end and the thin, wispy tip.

TIME REQUIRED

This project is best completed in a single day, since cattails degrade if they are dried and rehydrated. If necessary, store an incomplete basket overnight in a plastic bag in a cool place and finish the next day.

weave and twine the base

1. Use a ruler to mark the exact middle of each plaiting strip with a pencil line. It doesn't matter which side.

2. Lay two pieces vertically on a small piece of cardboard so that the middle marks line up. Hold the two vertical pieces in place while weaving a horizontal piece from right to left under the first vertical piece and over the second, just below the middle marks. Pull it through until the middle mark is right between the two vertical pieces.

3. Weave a second horizontal piece from right to left *over* the first vertical piece and *under* the second, directly above the first horizontal piece. Pull through until the middle marks match up. Put a pin in the center space between the four pieces, securing it in the cardboard and marking the center.

4. The rest of the base pieces are added in groups of two. First, add one vertical piece on the left side and one on the right, weaving over and under the horizontal pieces. After adding each piece, check that no two overs or unders are next to each other. Make sure the center lines all line up. Pack tightly inward toward the center.

5. Next, add two horizontal pieces: one above the existing pieces and one below. Weave each new piece tightly against the previous one. The goal is zero space between plaiting strips. Weaving tightly now will make packing them easier later.

6. Continue adding the rest of the pieces in pairs of verticals and horizontals.

Continued on next page

Tip: *When weaving a new strip, it's easier to lift the pieces that your new piece goes under. After the strip is in place, lay the lifted pieces down flat again.*

7. When all 16 pieces are in place, check that there are 8 verticals and 8 horizontals. Pack them very tightly toward the center, starting with the center pieces and working outward. Use clips in the corners to secure your progress. Make sure the final base is square and the ends of the pieces are even on all sides.

8. With a temporary piece of string, add one row of twining on all four sides to secure the grid of the base. (See Understanding Twining on page 169.)

REPAIRING A BROKEN PLAITING STRIP

Use a packing tool to open the weaves on top of the broken cattail and trace a replacement leaf along the same path until it overlaps the broken strip for at least two weaves.

create the corners

This is where the magic happens! The strips fold up diagonally and weave into each other to make the walls of the basket. No additional weavers are added. Also notable is that the corners of the base become the basket's walls and the sides of the base become the corners.

1. Pick up two center cattails. Bring the cattail that's in the over position on the last row of the base *behind* the other so the two lock in place. (Whether it's the right or left strip that goes behind depends on your base weave.) Pull them tightly and at a very wide, open angle.

Tip: *If you completed the base as instructed, the weave order in these steps should match your basket. If you varied anything—particularly the number of plaiting strips—the order of overs and unders may be different. However, the principle stays the same: Use a plain-weave (over, under) pattern and make sure the two corner pieces lock in place against each other.*

2. You will continue to work in pairs on either side of the new corner. Weave the right piece first, simply overlapping the adjacent strip.

3. Weave in the left piece, going under, then over. The four woven pieces should create an even grid of diamonds, with no two overs or unders next to each other. Pull all four tightly together at a wide angle. Secure with a clip.

4. Repeat steps 1 to 3 for the other three sides of the basket. Turn the basket each time so that the side you are working is farthest from you.

Continued on next page

5. For the next round, position the basket so you are now working from the exterior on the side closest to you. Otherwise, your arms will get in the way while weaving. You will continue to work in pairs.

6. Weave in the next pair of pieces on either side of the already woven grid, using the plain-weave—over, under—pattern. Pull the sides tightly in a wide angle. Place a clip over the weave so both hands are free and don't obstruct your view as you check for mistakes: No two "overs" or "unders" should be next to each other. Turn the basket and repeat on each side, working from the exterior.

7. To weave the last round of base strips, rotate the basket 45 degrees and fold one corner of the base up so the twine creates a triangle shape. The original corner of the base weave becomes the flat wall of the basket.

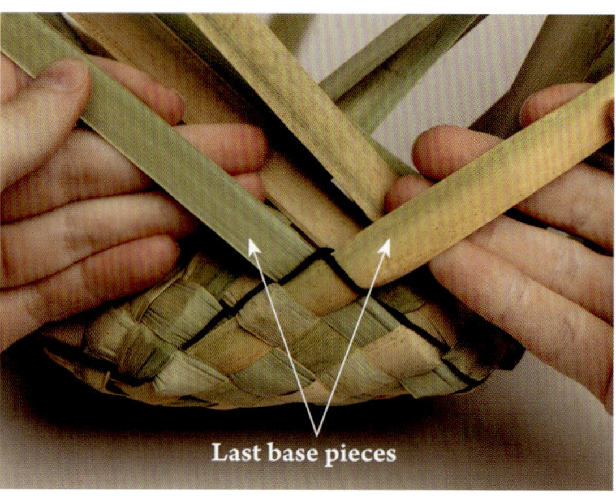

8. Weave each of the last base pieces in, going over and under (or under and over) two strips. Add a small clip over the weaving to secure your progress. Repeat to create the other three sides.

9. Once the final base strips are woven into all four sides, look at the bottom of the basket. Don't be surprised if the corners are lopsided or the edges are puckered. Tensioning evenly is a skill that takes time to develop. Go around the perimeter of the basket, pulling tightly on all the strips to eliminate puckering and square up the corners.

Tip: *There is a balance between moving too quickly past imperfections and obsessing over details. Especially as you are learning, seek to find a balance. I find this particularly important for diagonal plaiting!*

Continued on page 220

TIPS FOR WEAVING THE SIDES

After creating the base and corners, there isn't a formulaic step-by-step process for weaving the rest of a diagonal-plaited basket. What's most important is understanding how your movements affect the basket. Following are principles for diagonal plaiting I've learned from practice.

Keep moving!

Do one or two weaves in a spot, then move on. Don't get lost weaving a single piece upward until it runs out. This will result in uneven tension and mistakes.

Weave in the lowest unwoven areas first.

The goal is to weave at an even height around the perimeter. It's easy to accidentally get carried away and weave too high in one section. Weave a low area and then move over to weave another low area, steadily building height around the whole basket.

Maintain even tension.

Tug firmly on every strip every time you work it. Pull weavers apart and downward at a wide angle. The goal is to eliminate any space between the rows.

Stop and look.

Pause frequently, moving your hands out of the way to look at how the basket is going. Is one side woven too high? Are you pulling enough for good tension? Is your weave correct, with no skipped overs or unders? Once you've made a mistake (going over two, for example), it continues to compound. The only option is to unweave and fix it.

Check often for mistakes. This strip goes over two adjacent pieces instead of over one, under one.

Use clips.

Clips are indispensable in this basket for keeping the weaving you've already done from unraveling and maintaining good tension. I use about six while weaving the sides of a basket this size.

Keep the basket damp.

Cattails dry out quickly and start breaking, especially if the weather is hot. Have a spray bottle or a pot of warm water on hand to dampen the basket often.

weave the sides

Read Tips for Weaving the Sides (page 219) before continuing.

1. Remove one clip and pick two pieces that are crossing each other. Pull tension on both and then weave each for only a move or two. Replace the clip.

2. Move to the right and pick two more pieces that cross each other to weave in for just a move or two. After going around the entire perimeter once, cut the twine out of the base, which will allow you to pack the plaiting strips tighter and help the basket base round out.

3. Keep weaving until the basket is seven diamonds high in all places (as measured by counting upward from a corner). The final project height is five diamonds, but it's important to weave a little higher so that the tension and weave don't come undone as you turn the rim over.

mark the rim

1. Choose a corner where the diamond on the bottom is part of a plaiting strip that angles up and to the right. While you can fold either the left- or right-angling pieces first on the rim, following along with the photos will be easier if you are working in the same direction. Mark each of the five diamonds going up from that corner with black dots. The marks will get covered later. (To reference a project where the left-angling pieces are folded first, see the diagonal-plaited Birch Bark Tool Sheath on page 225.)

2. Draw a horizontal line through the middle of the fifth diamond up, marked with a dot, connecting the diamond's corner points. Continue the line through the side corners of the next diamond. Then continue around the basket until reaching your starting point. The starting point and end point of the line should connect.

Tip: *If the line doesn't connect, check carefully that you picked the correct diamonds to draw through: They may angle up or down significantly. If the line is right, there was likely a weaving mistake lower in the basket or uneven tensioning. You can tinker with the uneven spot on the rim (for example, tucking two pieces into one spot) or partially unweave and weave the sides again.*

fold the rim and weave down to the base

What makes this basket so sturdy is that each piece is threaded underneath the top layer of weaving on the walls back down to the base, which eventually creates four layers of weaving in each diamond. The pieces are folded in two rounds. In the first round are all the pieces angling up and to the right—the ones with the lines drawn through them. In the second round are the left-angled pieces. When the rim is finished, it will be flat.

1. Use scissors to trim the end of each of the pieces into a rounded arrowpoint to allow them to thread down more easily.

2. Choose a strip with a line drawn through it and unweave it down to the line.

3. Fold and crease the unwoven piece forward along the line so it is angling down and to the right. It should line up with the angle of the piece it is crossing over.

4. Tuck the folded piece under the first available weaver along its path: Insert a packing tool from the other side and turn it on its side to open the space under the weave. While drawing the packing tool out, push the rounded tip of the rim cattail in.

Continued on next page

5. Pull the cattail through all the way and crease the top so that it creates a flat edge. Don't tug it tightly yet.

6. Moving to the right one piece at a time, repeat with all the pieces that have lines drawn through them. Be careful to thread each piece under the correct space. When finished, the folded pieces should create a flat edge.

7. Next, fold and tuck in all the remaining pieces (which angle in the opposite direction, to the left), so the crease lies against the already established rim of the basket. These left-angled pieces fold down to the left, just as the first round of right-angled pieces folded down to the right.

8. Start with any piece and thread it down to the left under the first weave available, which will be just underneath the right-angling folded piece from the previous round. (It goes under this piece only, not the one beneath it as well.) Pull through and tighten.

9. After tucking in the remaining pieces, go back and tug every strip again to even up and neaten the top edge.

10. Thread each strip through to the middle of the base, matching the existing weave. There is no specific order to go in: Work in one area or move around the basket.

Tip: *Each strip only needs to thread through two spaces to be secure, so it's okay if a few break. Also, if you are short on time, you could consider the project complete if all the strips weave through two spaces, but there will be a noticeable raised area at the top of the basket.*

11. When two pieces from opposite sides meet on the bottom of the basket, cut one so it stops in the middle of an over and weave the other piece on top of it.

12. Trim any excess by pulling the end of the piece snug and cutting it right next to the weaver it is threaded under so it slides back under when let go.

BIRCH BARK TOOL SHEATH

BIRCH BARK IS SMOOTH, WEAVES EASILY, AND THE COLORS ARE GORGEOUS—a lovely material for diagonal plaiting. Tool sheaths are fun and relatively quick projects that don't require much material. After practicing with this project, adapt the directions for the tool you want to sheathe by changing the width, length, and number of strips woven. For example, use four instead of six pieces of birch bark to make a sheath for scissors. Shaping around edges and working out the measurements for different tools is great practice. You can also substitute for birch bark any inner bark strips, western red cedar bark, white cedar bark, cattails, or other slightly sturdy, flexible, flat materials. Note that these sheaths aren't suitable for knives, which will cut the bark.

SHEATH SIZE

1¾ inches wide × 3½ inches high

TOOLS

- Micro alligator clips
- Rigid paper, such as chipboard, matte board, or watercolor paper for a mold (cardboard is too thick)
- Basketry scissors
- Straight-tip packing tool

PLANT MATERIALS

6 birch bark strips, ⅜ inch wide and 19–21 inches long (longer is better)

PREPARING MATERIALS

See pages 118–120 for preparing birch bark so it's thin, pliable, and lightly oiled.

TIME REQUIRED

Several hours or less once you get the hang of it. I suggest making a mock-up with strips of paper before completing the final with your natural materials. You can pause your work on this project at any point.

weave the bottom

This project uses a plain-weave method: Each strip weaves "over one, under one," making a checkerboard-like pattern. Keep an eye out for places where you've accidentally woven two overs or two unders next to each other and correct them.

1. Fold all six strips in half at their center point and crease. Lay one folded piece (strip A) on the table, angling to the right. Thread the *bottom* half of the second folded piece (strip B) underneath the *top* half of A so that they hook together and B angles to the left.

Tip: *The side of the strip that is inside the fold is the one that will eventually show on the outside of the project. The choice is aesthetic.*

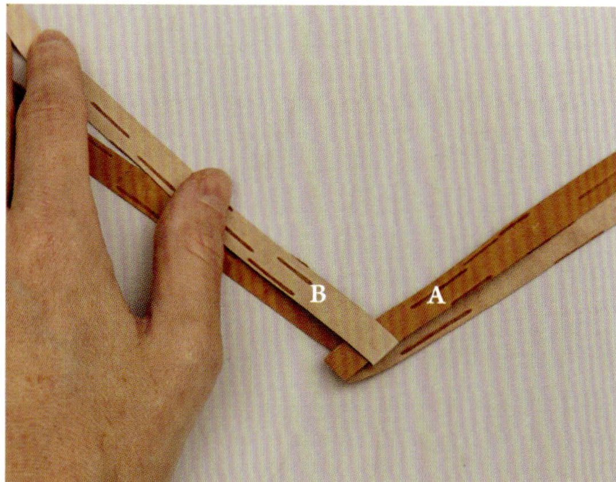

2. Hook the third folded piece (strip C) onto the *bottom* half of A, angling to the left.

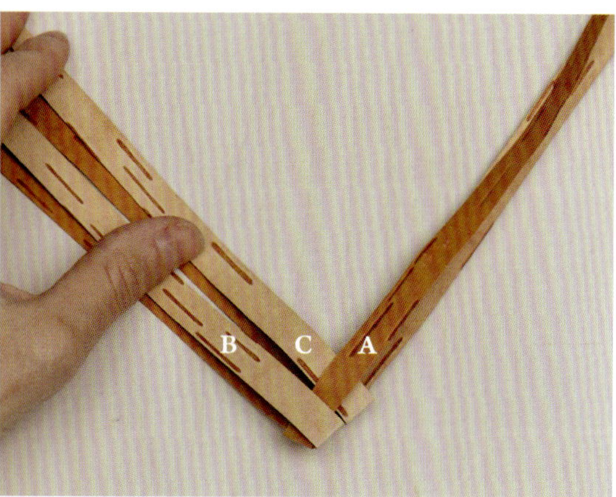

3. Add the fourth piece (strip D) to the right side. Take one end and weave it over the top half of B and under the top half of C. Pull the strip up so it aligns with A and place a clip on the front to secure the weave.

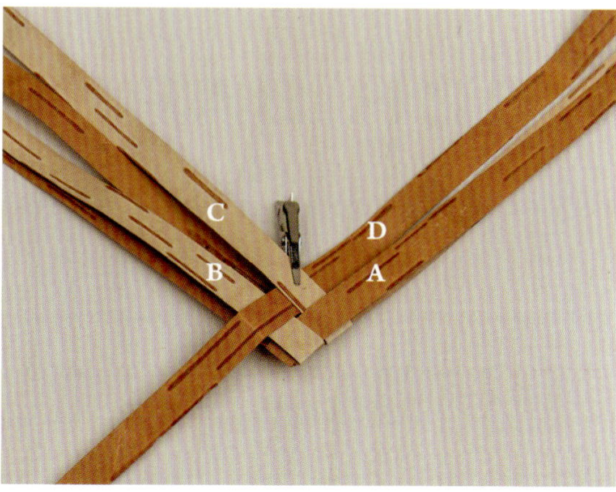

4. Carefully flip the project over and weave in the second half of strip D (now angling to the left) under and then over.

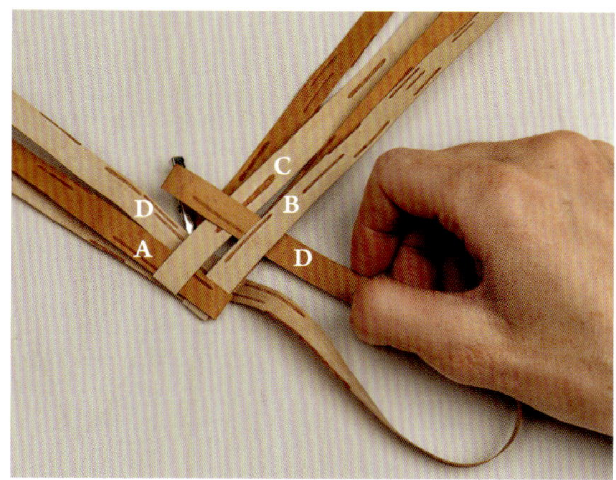

5. Use the template on the next page to draw the dimensions of the mold onto a piece of rigid paper material and cut it out. The mold is a flat piece that you weave around, keeping the front and back of the weaving separate. You will trim it down later to match your project exactly.

SHEATH MOLD TEMPLATE

1¾"

5"

⅞"

⅞" ⅞"

6. Place the mold, point down, in between the front and back halves of weaving.

7. Weave in the top half of the fifth piece of birch (strip E), angling to the right.

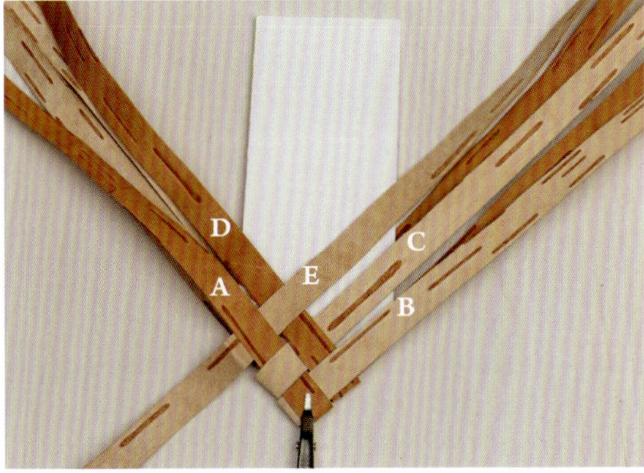

8. Flip the sheath over carefully and weave in the second half of strip E. Pull so that the fold is snug against the mold.

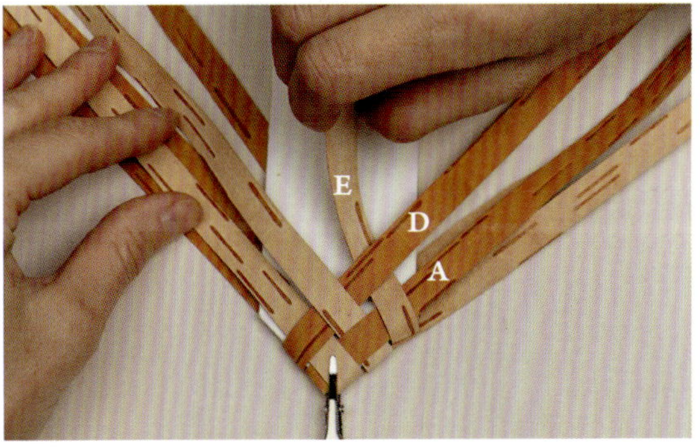

Continued on next page

9. Weave in the sixth piece (strip F) using the over, under pattern on both front and back. Tighten all the strips so they are snugly up against the mold and there is no space between them. The angled corners of the mold should match up with the top corners of the weaving. If they don't, adjust the mold, either cutting a thin strip off each side of the mold or adjusting the mold's angles. Remove the mold from the weaving to trim it to size.

weave the sides

1. View the project from the side edge for the next steps. You will weave two strips around the edge at a time—one from the front and one from the back—starting with the two strips closest to the bottom of the project (strips G and H). Weave the one that goes under first (strip G), which is the lowest loose strip.

Tip: *While weaving the sides you need to keep turning the project, viewing it from both edges as well as the front and the back.*

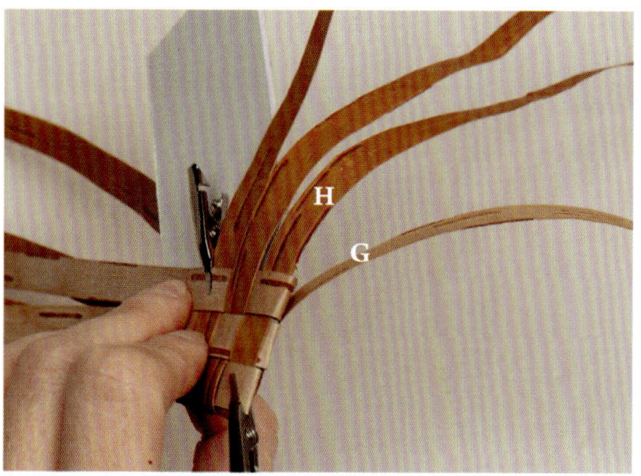

2. Wrap strip G around the right edge from the back to the front, crease snugly against the mold, and weave it under strip H, then over and under the remaining two strips.

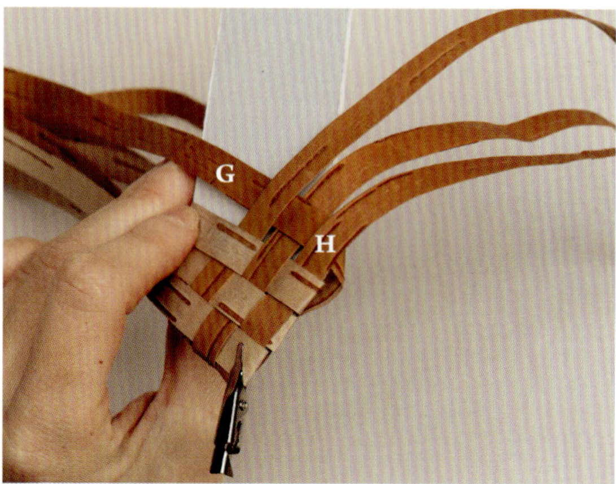

3. Wrap strip H around the edge of the mold from the front to the back, going over G, then under and over the two strips on the flip side of the mold.

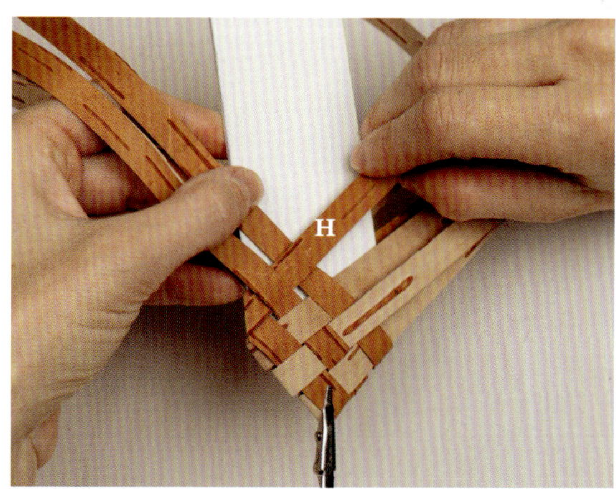

Tip: *After weaving a pair from each edge, tighten each of the strips so it is flush against the mold and pressed down closely against the previous row, leaving no space between them.*

4. In the same way, now weave the two strips on the other edge of the mold that are closest to the bottom of the sheath. Weave the lowest loose strip first. When finished, the two sides of the sheath completed so far should be woven to an even height.

5. Continue alternating sides, weaving the two bottom strips on each edge until the weave at the middle of the front and back measures 4½ inches high from the bottom point. Mark seven of the diamonds in the center from the bottom to the top. (The marks will get covered later.) There should be one or two rows woven past the seventh diamond as shown in the photo below. If not, then weave another round.

Tip: *Use micro clips as needed to keep one side from unweaving while you are working on the other.*

fold the rim

1. Clip the weaving to secure it. Count seven diamonds up from the point at the bottom (this diamond should be one that is angling up and to the left). Draw a horizontal line through this diamond and then through the ones just to the left and right of it so the line goes across the top. Turn the project over and continue the line in the same position.

Tip: *If you want to make the project shorter or higher, you can measure and draw a line through a different row of diamonds. If you adjust the height, it could affect which group of strips you fold first. In the following directions, we fold the left-leaning strips first. If you are folding right-leaning strips first, the visuals for the Diagonal-Plaited Cattail Basket on page 213 are a better match for your process.*

2. Cut the tips of all strips into an arrowpoint.

Continued on next page

3. Starting on the side with the dots, unweave the rightmost left-leaning strip with the line drawn through it (strip I).

4. Crease strip I toward you along the line.

5. Thread the strip under the first opening in the weaving along its path, labeled J. Pull it through until it lies flat and the top edge is crisply folded. Use a small straight-tip packing tool to open up the space, if needed.

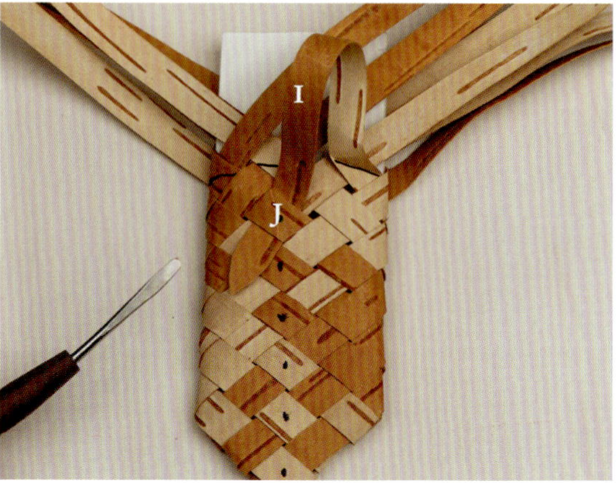

6. Crease the next strip to the left (the middle strip on this side) toward you along the line. Thread it under the first opening in the weaving along its path and pull until flat.

7. Continue with the leftmost strip that has the line drawn through it on this side. Because it needs to fold around the edge, it appears a little different. Remove the project from the mold, look at the sheath from the edge, and squeeze it a little to open the side. This will make it easier to see where to thread the last strip through.

8. Turn the project to the back side. Fold and thread each of the three strips with lines drawn through them.

9. Now fold and tuck the right-angling strips. Start with the middle strip on either side. Fold it toward the right, creasing it over the top edge that has already been established. Thread it under the first opening available along its path, under the left-angling piece that was just tucked in. Note that there are now two layers of weaving; only tuck under the top layer.

10. Repeat this with all the right-angling pieces. When finished, tighten each piece so the rim is even and crisply folded.

11. Weave all the pieces down in any order by threading them under every opening available along their path until they reach the bottom. Use a packing tool to help open the spaces, if necessary. They only need to go under the top layer of weaving.

12. Weave as many strips as possible over the edge of the bottom and back up the other side as far as they will go, which creates strength in the bottom of the sheath.

13. Trim any pieces that stick out by pulling them taut and then trimming, so they sink under the weave when let go.

CHAPTER 14

FOLDED BARK BASKETRY

If you want to make a fast, useful container with minimal effort, then folded bark is the answer. By making a few cuts in a sheet of bark, folding it, and then stitching, you will have an impressively beautiful basket. However, even though this formula is simple, there is tons of room for creativity. Every time I teach a folded pine bark class, a student comes up with something that I have never seen before!

Anatomy of Folded Bark Basket

No matter the size or shape of a folded bark basket, there are structural elements that unite them all.

Basket body. The cut and folded shape of the basket made from a sheet of bark.

Side stitching. The stitches holding together the sides of the basket.

Attached rim. Holds the shape of the basket. Usually composed of inner and outer rim pieces that sandwich the top edge of the basket body.

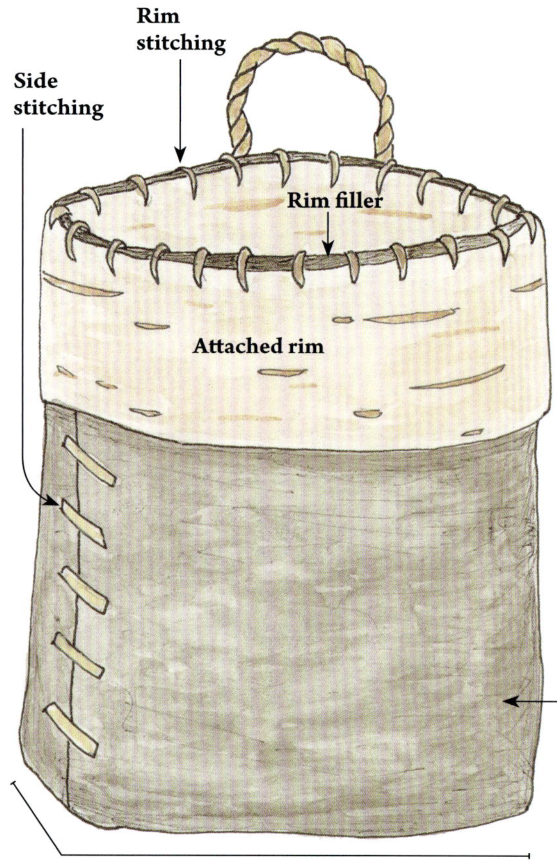

Rim filler. A decorative piece of cordage or braid that sits in a trough between the inner and outer rim, hiding the top edge of the basket body.

Rim stitching. A sewing strand that attaches the rim to the basket.

Footprint. The size and shape of the bottom of the basket. Some designs have a big enough footprint to sit on a table, while others are meant to hang.

choosing and preparing bark for folding

The method of working with bark sheets that I have developed is best for white pine, which has particularly thin, flexible outer bark, but birch, tulip poplar, and other similar barks can be used as well. I recommend using bark sheets with furrowed, thick outer bark only for larger projects, and expect some cracking when folding unless you use the cat's-eye cut on pages 250–251.

You can use bark fresh or dried and rehydrated. If rehydrating bark, submerge in a pot of steaming hot or lightly simmering water for 5 to 15 minutes (for very thin outer bark) or 20 to 45 minutes (for thicker outer bark). See pages 118–120 for birch bark, which has unique requirements.

Designing a Folded Bark Basket

This basket style is ripe for improvisation—every piece of material is unique, and the techniques are simple. To understand the basics, I suggest that you make either the Bark Necklace Pouch on page 239 or the White Pine Bark Catch-All on page 245. Then get creative! Here are some guidelines for designing your own.

choose a shape and make a paper template

Look at your bark and evaluate the form to which it is best suited. In general, square (or squarish) pieces of bark work well for flat-bottomed baskets. Narrow rectangular pieces are good for simple fold and hanging pouch baskets. To create your desired shape, you will either simply fold the bark or cut it to create flaps before folding. You then sew the basket body in place and add a rim to hold everything together. But before you start cutting your bark, make a paper template by tracing the exact shape and size of your bark on a piece of newsprint or other paper and practicing different cuts on it to test your plan and experiment.

Simple Fold

This is the most basic shape (see Bark Necklace Pouch on page 239). Fold a sheet of paper in half horizontally or vertically and tape it in place on each side. Adjust the size of the paper and the orientation of the fold to change the pouch shape and the size of the opening.

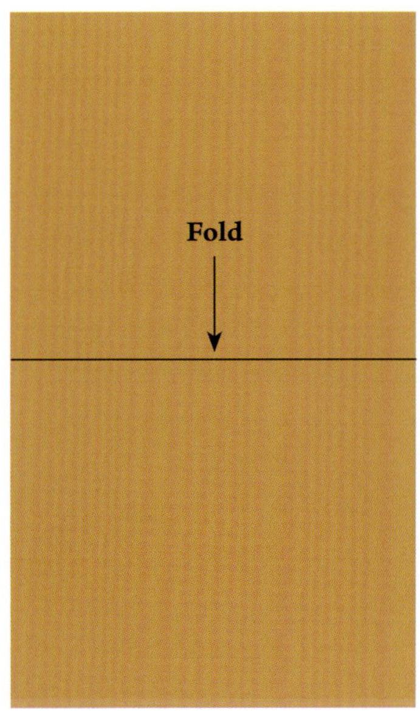

Flat-Bottomed Square or Rectangle

This shape can have a large footprint and low sides or a small footprint and high sides. In either case, the footprint should be big enough so the basket can sit flat on a surface. (See White Pine Bark Catch-All on page 245.)

The cut lines should be as long as your desired basket height. The distance between each cut line and the edge of the paper should equal the length of the cut lines. Otherwise, the sides of the basket will not line up evenly. Cut and fold all the flaps in toward the center to test the dimensions, securing with tape or clips.

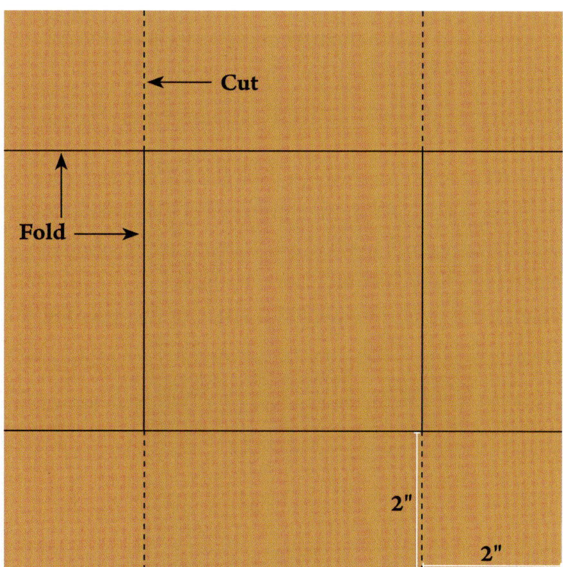

This example results in a basket that is 2 inches high. Experiment with different sizes and heights.

Hanging Pouch

This basket has a very narrow base and will not sit flat on a surface. It is best suited for belt pouches, purses, or wall hangings. The distance of the lines from the center and the length of the lines will change the width and depth. Cut and fold all the flaps in toward the center to test the dimensions, securing with tape or clips. If the side flaps don't overlap, cut the lines longer.

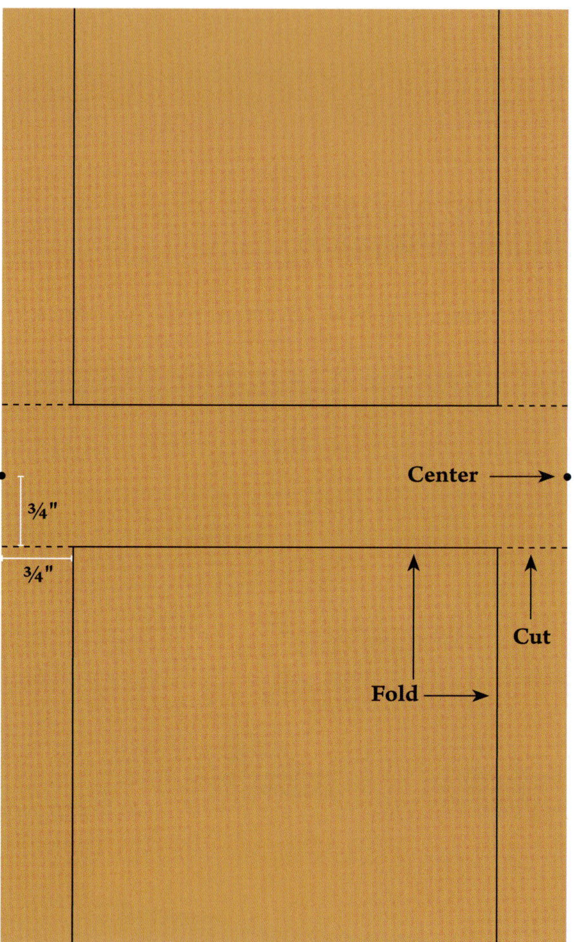

This example results in a basket that is ¾ inch deep. Experiment with different heights, widths, and depths.

cut the bark

Once you are happy with your paper template, measure and mark the cutting lines on the bark. Marking on wet bark can be tricky. Try a water-soluble colored pencil or a charcoal pencil. Using basketry scissors or a utility knife, slice through the cutting lines. Fold the basket to see how it looks.

Folded bark baskets almost always require some adjustment at this point. Even with precise measurements, the top might look uneven. While you can adjust the cuts and trim the top of the basket to make it straight, don't obsess. The irregularity of bark is part of the beauty of this material, and the rim will conceal small imperfections.

sew the basket

In a folded bark basket, you stitch the sides together and attach a rim to hold its shape. Many different stitches are possible, including straight stitch, whipstitch, and any variations on these you want to experiment with, including decorative ones. To avoid tearing the bark, keep your stitches at least ¼ inch from the edge of the bark on small baskets and ½ inch on larger ones. Space the stitches at least ¼ inch apart. If your bark tears, increase the stitch distance.

The material and design choices of the sewing strands and rim are opportunities for aesthetic touches. I recommend sewing your first projects with store-bought materials that are long, strong, and predictable, such as hemp, twine, artificial sinew, strong yarn, or waxed linen. Natural materials that are good for sewing folded bark baskets include basswood fiber, cordage, very narrow strips of inner bark, and spruce or pine roots. Whatever you choose, strength is essential. If your sewing strand is too thick to thread on a needle, use an awl to poke a hole big enough to pass the end of the sewing material through.

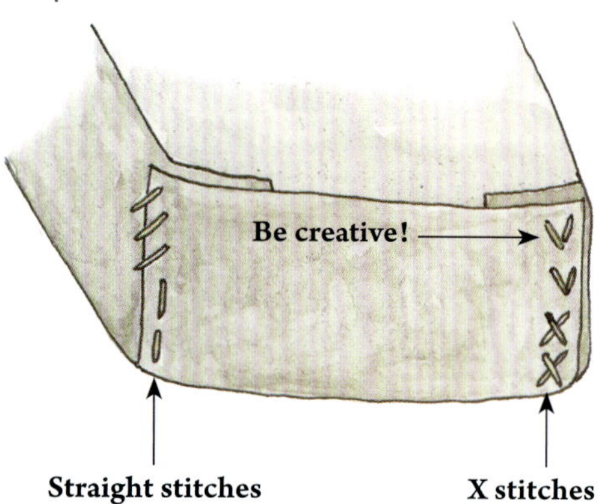

attach the rim

The rim can be narrow or wide, depending on the material you have and the look you prefer. It should be sturdy enough to support the basket, but not so thick that it won't bend around the diameter of the opening. Any inner bark is suitable as well as willow rods that are ½ inch thick or more and split in half. Most folded bark baskets have both an inner and an outer rim, unless the opening to the basket is very narrow and an inner rim won't fit. You can loop stitches around the rim or sew through the rim itself if the material is thin enough to pierce without splitting.

decorate

I love embroidering patterns or sewing cutout shapes of birch bark onto pine bark. Add any decoration before folding and sewing the basket into shape since it's often hard to get your hand into a finished basket to stitch on decoration. Take care not to make stitches too close together or pull them too tightly or the bark can tear.

BARK NECKLACE POUCH

SIMPLE AND QUICK, THIS IS A PERFECT INTRODUCTION to folded bark basketry. The small size is well suited to miniature pieces of thin, smooth bark, peeled from willow rods or from white pine branches that are as little as 3⁄4 inch in diameter. Harvest a small branch from a tree or a sapling and you will have enough material for several small pouches. Vary the stitch patterns and add decoration to the rim to create one-of-a-kind pieces that make great gifts.

BASKET SIZE

1¾ inches wide × 1 inch deep × 2½ inches high

TOOLS

- Basketry scissors
- Micro alligator clip
- Waxed linen, artificial sinew, or waxed embroidery floss for sewing
- Chenille needle with an eye large enough to fit sewing strand

PLANT MATERIALS

- Piece of smooth, flexible willow bark, approximately 1¾ × 6 inches; the best material will come from willow rods that are 1–3 inches in diameter
- 28-inch length of cordage (or longer)—see pages 128–132 for directions on making cordage
- Piece of paper birch bark, approximately ¾ × 6 inches

PREPARING MATERIALS

See Chapter 7, Bark, for details on harvesting and processing materials.

TIME REQUIRED

A couple of hours at most. You can pause this project at any time by placing it in a plastic bag to keep it moist. You can also let it dry and rehydrate.

trim bark and secure cordage

1. Use basketry scissors to trim the sides of the bark so they are straight.

2. Fold the bark in half and place the necklace cordage in the fold. Either the inner or the outer bark can face outward. Arrange so the two ends of the cordage are even and use any knot to tie the two ends together. Secure the fold of the bark with a clip.

3. Press the folded bark closed, sandwiching the necklace cordage between the two sides at the edge. Insert the needle through both layers of bark right near the knot. You don't want it to get caught in the knot, but it can go through the same hole. With each stitch, always push the needle straight through the bark, not at an angle.

Tip: *Hold the necklace cordage in place against the side of the bark so that each stitch wraps around it. Use a clip if you need a third hand.*

whipstitch the sides

1. Triple-knot the end of an 18-inch length of sewing strand. Insert the needle from the inside to the outside of one layer of bark, ¼ inch above the fold and ¼ inch from the edge, to secure the knot on the inside of the pouch.

2. Pull through until the knot is pressed against the bark. Don't pull too hard or the knot will tear through the bark.

4. Pull gently but firmly to tighten. Again, you can rip through the bark if you apply too much force. Stitching that wraps around the edge of two pieces of material to join them is called a whipstitch, which is the best choice for this project since it will secure the cordage.

Continued on next page

5. Take another stitch through both layers of bark 1/4 inch above the last, being sure to go around the cordage strand, which is sandwiched between the two. This is what secures the cordage to the pouch. Continue to whipstitch up the side, keeping the distance between each stitch even.

6. To tie off the stitching, put the needle back into the same hole as the last stitch at the top.

7. Pull through until there is a small loop remaining. Pass the needle through this loop and pull tight. Cut the thread, leaving a 3/4-inch tail. (This will get covered up by the rim later.)

8. Using a 4-foot-long piece of sewing strand, repeat the whipstitch along the full length of the opposite side of the pouch. Don't forget to capture the cordage strand in your stitches on this side, too. At the end do not cut off the tail. You will use the remaining thread to sew on the rim.

attach the rim

1. Wrap the birch bark scrap around the top of the pouch to estimate what height you want the rim pieces to be. Trim the long sides to the desired height.

Tip: *The bark you use for the rim needs to be flexible enough for folding and sewing without cracking. If your bark is too stiff, split it into thinner pieces (see Splitting Bark Strips on page 113).*

2. Wrap the rim around the top of the pouch again and cut it so that it overlaps itself by 3/4 inch. Secure it with a clip.

3. Tuck the necklace cordage into the pouch so it isn't in your way while stitching. Using the sewing strand already attached from sewing the second side, insert the needle from the outside to the inside about 1/4 inch from the top and loop it over and around the top edge. Be sure to go through the birch bark and the pine bark beneath it.

4. Whipstitch the rim to the pouch, working stitches ¼ inch apart and pulling firmly between each one.

Tip. *If the birch bark is cracking, then it is either too thick or too dry. Try splitting it thinner, oiling it, or making the stitches farther apart. The stitches can also loop entirely around the birch bark if you prefer that look.*

5. After stitching all the way around the rim once, stitch on top of the first five stitches (or more if you like the look of doubled stitches), going in and out of the same holes to help secure the end of the thread.

6. To hide the end of the thread, insert the needle between the rim and the pine bark, entering from the top and pulling out at the bottom. Then trim the thread so it can't be seen.

WHITE PINE BARK CATCH-ALL

WITH A WIDE FOOTPRINT AND LOW SIDES, this basket is a perfect catch-all. I have several of them dedicated to tools and supplies in my studio. You can modify this into many different shapes and sizes. My favorite material to use is white pine bark because it's so thin and flexible, but birch bark and other materials could be substituted.

BASKET SIZE

11 inches square × 3 inches high (or see Design Variations on page 246 for other options)

TOOLS

- Ruler
- Basketry scissors
- Four 2-inch spring clamps
- Waxed linen, twine, raffia, strips of ¼-inch-wide basswood fiber, or any similar material for sewing
- Chenille needle with eye large enough to fit sewing strand
- Awl
- Straight-tip packing tool

PLANT MATERIALS

- **Basket body.** Sheet of white pine bark, 14 × 14 inches
- **Rim filler.** 32-inch braid of iris leaves, ¼ inch wide
- **Outer rim.** Strips of thin, flexible white pine bark, totaling 39 inches long and 1¼ inches high; overlap two shorter pieces to achieve this length if needed. (Bark strips from any other species of tree can be substituted for the rim pieces.)
- **Inner rim.** Strips of thin, flexible white pine bark, totaling 35 inches long and 1¼ inches high; overlap two shorter pieces to achieve this length.

Tip: *Because each person's basket can turn out a slightly different size, I recommend leaving the rim pieces a little long and then cutting them to the exact size after the body of the basket is complete.*

PREPARING MATERIALS

For the basket body and rim pieces, see Chapter 7, Bark, for details on harvesting and processing materials. Soak the bark sheet and rim pieces by submerging them in a pot of steaming water for 10–20 minutes or until very flexible. Trim the sheet to 14 × 14 inches so the edges are straight and even. A metal straightedge ruler, utility knife, and a cutting mat are optimal tools if you have them available. Otherwise, measure and mark the shape on the bark before using your basketry scissors.

For the rim filler, see pages 132–137 for directions on making multistrand braids. Spray the iris braid with water to keep it flexible.

TIME REQUIRED

A day or less. I usually make these baskets in one sitting to avoid resoaking; pine bark can lose its shape if it dries without the rim on.

DESIGN VARIATIONS

This project invites many variations in size, material, and decorative effects. See Designing a Folded Bark Basket on page 235 for more ideas.

Size. Smaller baskets require less material while being just as beautiful and useful.

- For a basket with a finished size of 9 × 9 × 3 inches, use a 12 × 12-inch sheet of bark.
- For a finished size of 5 × 5 × 3 inches, use a 10 × 10-inch sheet of bark.

Stitching. You will secure each corner of the basket with stitching. The project shown has three short stitches in a line, but you could substitute one large straight stitch, one or more Xs, or other decorative variations. The stitches will be visible on both the inside and the outside of the basket, except for the top ones, which the rim will cover.

cut and fold the basket body

1. Cover your work surface if necessary to protect it from pine sap. Place the trimmed bark square light side up. Measure and mark 2½-inch-long vertical lines at top and bottom that are also 2½ inches from the side edges. Cut along the four lines with basketry scissors, taking care to cut each to the exact same length.

2. Fold the right corner flap upward and inward.

3. Fold the left corner flap in and the side wall up, securing both corner flaps with clamps.

Tip: *The corner flaps can be tucked on either the inside or the outside. It's an aesthetic choice.*

4. Repeat on the other side of the basket. The sides of the basket body should be even. Trim or cut the lines further as necessary.

sew the sides

1. Thread a 10-inch piece of sewing strand onto a needle and push the needle from the inside to the outside of a basket wall, ¼ inch from both the bottom and the side. (Stitches need to be at least ¼ inch from the edge to avoid tearing the bark.) Pull through until about 3 inches of tail remain. At first the needle goes through only the single outer layer to hide the knot, but subsequent stitches will go through both the wall and the flap.

Tip: *If it's too hard to push the needle through, use a sharp, thin awl to pre-poke the hole.*

2. Push the needle back through the flap from the outside of the basket wall to the inside, ¼ inch up from the first hole. Tie the tail and the working strand together in a double knot. This secures the sewing strand to the basket.

3. Push the needle through the inner flap just about where the knot would touch the inner flap when they are folded together.

4. Pull tight to the inside, anchoring the wall to the flap and hiding the knot.

Continued on next page

5. The next stitch goes from the inside of the basket to the outside. Insert the needle through both the inner flap and the outside wall, ¼ inch up from where the sewing strand comes out, and pull snug.

6. Continue stitching up the corner until reaching the top. Tie off the sewing strand by repeating the top stitch, which loops around the top of the bark. Pull the stitch almost all the way, and when there is a small loop remaining, pass the needle through this loop and pull tight.

7. Pass the needle between the two layers and pull out at the edge, securing and hiding the tail.

8. Repeat on the other three corners. For the final corner, use a sewing strand 6 feet or longer, which you will later use to sew the basket rim. Coil it inside the basket until that point.

attach the rim

1. Starting with the inner rim, use 2-inch spring clamps to secure both the inner and outer rim pieces ¼ inch above the top edge of the basket. If you are overlapping multiple pieces for either rim, use enough clips to secure the overlaps. The sewing strand should hang beneath the inner rim on the inside of the basket. Either side of the rim pieces can show—it is an aesthetic choice. In this example the outer rim shows the inside part of the bark and the inner rim shows the gray, textured outside of the bark.

Tip: *Since clips can leave permanent indents, cut a few pieces of bark into small pads to place between the metal and the rims, if desired.*

2. Feed the rim filler into the trough between the inner and outer rim pieces. Tuck the ends of the rim filler down between the basket wall and either rim piece. Be sure to squeeze all the slack out of both rims so they both lie as flat as possible.

3. Carry the sewing strand over the top of the rim, holding the rim filler in place. Insert the needle straight through the pine bark, below the rim, from the outside to the inside of the basket.

4. Pull the sewing strand to the right at a diagonal and bring it over the rim again. Take another stitch, spaced about ¾ inch from the first.

5. Continue stitching around the perimeter of the rim. At the end, tighten the sewing strand by sliding a straight-tip packing tool under the first stitch. Pull firmly toward you. Use the packing tool and your fingers to work all slack out of the sewing strand, stitch by stitch without ripping the strand.

Continued on next page

6. Sew over the first several stitches. This overstitching will hold the end of the sewing strand in place.

Tip: *You can create Xs or Vs with the rim stitching by going around the rim a second time in reverse, using the same stitch holes and angling the sewing strand. See Woven Berry Basket on page 199 for an image of an attached rim done with Vs.*

7. Push the needle between the outer rim and the wall of the basket. Pull tight and trim the sewing strand to hide the end.

8. As the pine bark dries over the next 2 or 3 days, it might begin to warp. Having a sturdy rim helps prevent this. Monitor, adding clips to the rim overlaps to keep them flat or massaging and bending the basket shape throughout the drying time to alter it.

CAT'S-EYE BASKET

Cat's-eye baskets are named for the shape of the cut that creates the base. I love using them for foraging or storing basketry materials. Tall versions are fun as quivers. The cat's-eye cut is best for thick or textured outer bark, such as tulip poplar, ash, elm, thicker white pine, and fruit trees. It does not work well with the thin bark found on younger trees or on smooth white pine bark because they tend to tear. However, the thicker the outer bark is, the tougher these baskets will be to make, especially when wrestling a rim on. Freshly peeled bark is best. If using dried and rehydrated bark, be sure to soak it very well. An awl is essential for making sewing holes.

1. With charcoal or chalk, draw a cat's-eye shape in the middle of the outside of the bark.

2. Using a sharp utility knife, score partway through the outer layer of bark only. If the cut is too deep, your basket will break into pieces. Cut lightly at first and then if the basket won't fold up, cut a little deeper where necessary.

3. Overlap the sides ½ to 1 inch and sew them together. Sewing the sides on this style can be tough! Here are some tips:

- Use a sharp awl to pre-poke holes for the sewing strand. Poke the holes large enough so you don't struggle to thread the strand through.
- Sew from the bottom up. It's a tight space to fit your hand in, so take your time. The first side is easier than the second because you can leave one side unclipped for more room. Alternatively, sew both sides at the same time—using two different needles—working from the bottom to the top.
- Use a headlamp to see into the basket, if needed.

4. Use sharp basketry scissors to straighten the top of the basket before attaching the rim. Adapt the directions for the White Pine Bark Catch-All to make and attach a rim for your unique basket size. Since this bark is thick, use an awl to pre-poke holes for stitching.

5. To add a wall hanger or strap, sew it to the wall of the basket either before or after attaching the rim.

CHAPTER 15

RIBBED BASKETRY

Ribbed baskets, also called frame baskets, are a great way to use the random vines, long leaves, and other plant materials you inevitably gather as a basket maker. This style of basket originated in Europe and was brought to North America by settlers, particularly in the Southeast, and is now associated with the Appalachian Mountain region. There are many kinds of ribbed baskets whose names reference either their shape or intended use, including egg, hen, potato, gizzard, kidney, two-pie, and buttocks. (I'll bet you can guess the shape of the last one!) I almost always have a couple of frames ready to weave in my studio, so I can pick one up and work whenever a material inspires me.

Anatomy of a Ribbed Basket

Ribbed baskets are made up of four components: hoops, lashing, ribs, and weavers. Beyond that, there are many different variations in shape possible. The illustration below shows a two-hoop basket with a four-point lashing.

Hoops. One to three sturdy circles on which a ribbed basket is built.

Handle. Top part of the vertical central hoop.

Spine. The bottom part of the central hoop, which forms the bottom of the basket.

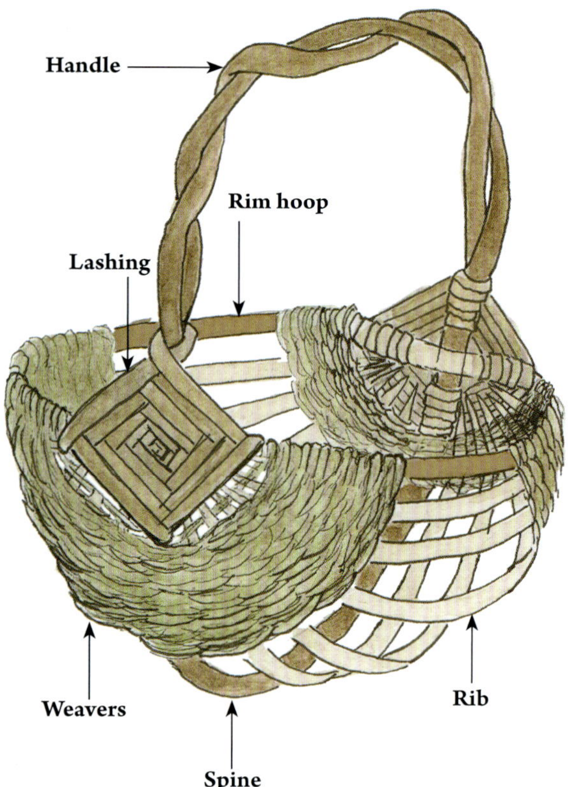

Rim hoop. The horizontal hoop that forms the rim of a two-hoop basket.

Lashing. Long, flexible pieces that secure the hoops where they intersect and form a place for the first ribs to rest.

Ribs. Structural elements that create the shape of the body of the basket.

Weavers. Elements woven around the ribs to create the fabric of the basket.

choosing materials for ribbed baskets

Each part of a ribbed basket has different requirements. Here are some of my favorites, though there are undoubtedly many more, depending on your geographic location.

Hoops require the most strength. Choose sturdy vines, such as grapevine, bittersweet, porcelain berry, wisteria, and thick honeysuckle, or rods, such as willow and red osier.

Ribs must be straight and strong, with a consistent thickness. While sturdiness is important, ribs shouldn't be stronger or thicker than the hoop material or they will push the hoops out of shape. Willow, red osier dogwood, or any other similar stems are ideal. Straight sections of grapevine and bittersweet are also usable.

Lashing strands require length and flexibility. Kudzu, wisteria, or similar vines are ideal. I like to split the vines so that they lie flat as they layer. Less pliable vines, like grapevine, bittersweet, and Virginia creeper, suffice but are finicky. Thick jute or another processed cord as well as very flexible willow are also options.

Weavers should be flexible. Choose long ones in the beginning, reserving shorter pieces for the end of a project when space is tight. Kudzu, akebia, honeysuckle, wisteria, Virginia creeper, willow, red osier, inner bark strips, twisted cattails, and other long leaves are all good options for weavers. You can heat bittersweet and thinner grapevine to make them more flexible.

making vine hoops

The goal is to make a tight, streamlined hoop without gaps that will hold its shape permanently. *Tight* is the key word here; keep it in mind throughout the process. After you've made your hoops, they should ideally sit for a while to dry and solidify the shape. However, I often skip the drying step and start making my basket right away without any problems.

1. Cut vines of the diameter specified in the project to the correct length. Cut away any knobs or other protrusions.

2. Stand upright, holding one end of the vine in your right hand. Grab the vine with your left hand about 3 feet away and brace the length in a U-shape against your stomach. The rest of the vine hangs down.

3. Cross the right end of the vine *over* the other side, making a circle about the size that you want for the final hoop.

4. Bring the right end (now on the left) through the circle as if you were beginning to tie a shoelace and pull it over a bit to tighten the loop. This circle will be the size of the hoop. If you want it to be bigger or smaller, start over and adjust the size.

5. Shift your left hand over to hold the place where the long part of the vine hangs from the circle.

Continued on next page

6. Bring the entire long part of the vine through the center of the hoop, starting with the tip.

7. Pull the vine through, wrapping the original hoop tightly. Shift your left hand over again to capture your progress.

8. Continue until you have gone around the circle once, making a two-layer hoop. If you're using a thin vine and the hoop feels very flexible, you could go around a third or even a fourth time.

9. Cut the two ends at an angle so they are streamlined and don't stick out. Be careful to cut them in a way that they are still braced under tension and the hoop doesn't unravel. If the hoop is loose and large gaps are showing, try again and practice keeping the tension tight with each wrap.

Tip: *Want a final test of your coil-making skills? Toss the hoop across the lawn like a Frisbee! If it comes undone, keep practicing.*

lashing styles

When it is time to connect your hoops, you can choose among a variety of lashing styles.

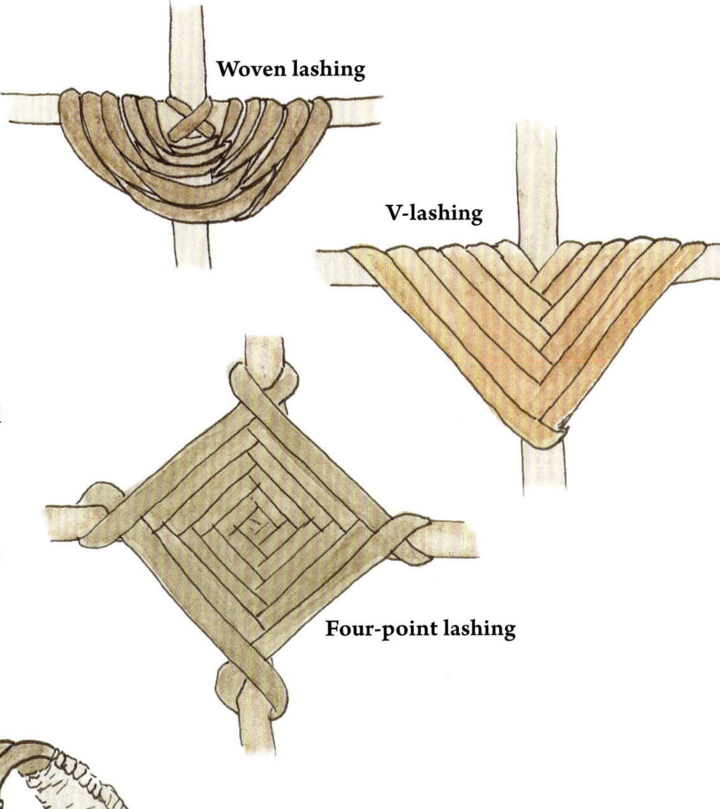

Woven lashing. Essentially you just start weaving around the two rims and the spine until pockets form where the first ribs can be inserted. This is the style described step-by-step in the Two-Hoop Harvest Basket on page 259.

Four-point lashing (a.k.a. God's eye). This lashing goes around four elements—the handle, two rims, and the spine—to create a diamond. The ribs are braced against the back of the diamond inside the basket.

V-lashing. This lashing goes around three elements—two rims and the spine. The first ribs are usually pierced directly through the lashing between the rims and spine.

basket shapes

A frame basket can take an amazing variety of shapes, from the traditional one-hoop potato basket to innovative sculptural masterpieces.

1 hoop

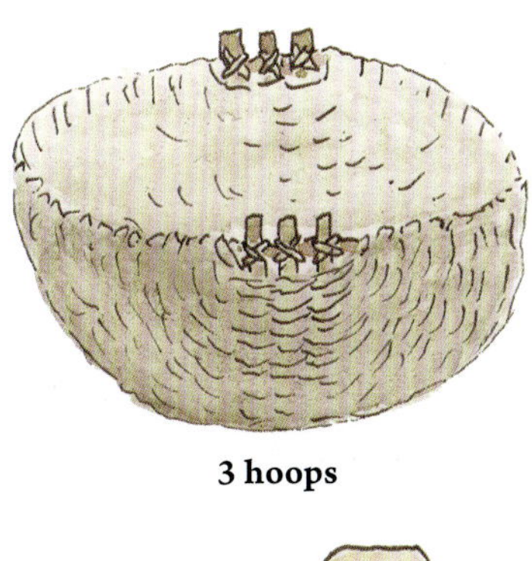

3 hoops

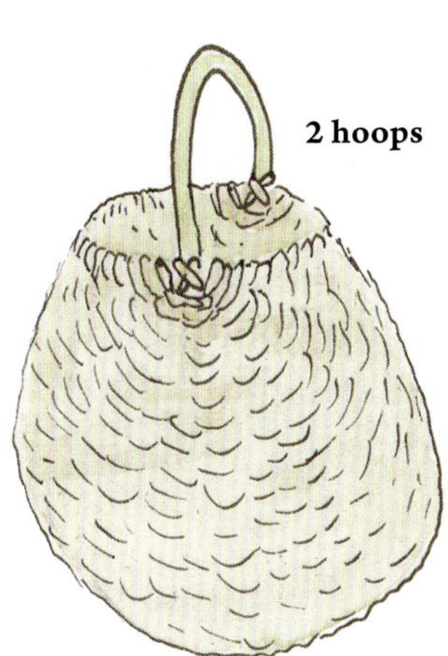

2 hoops

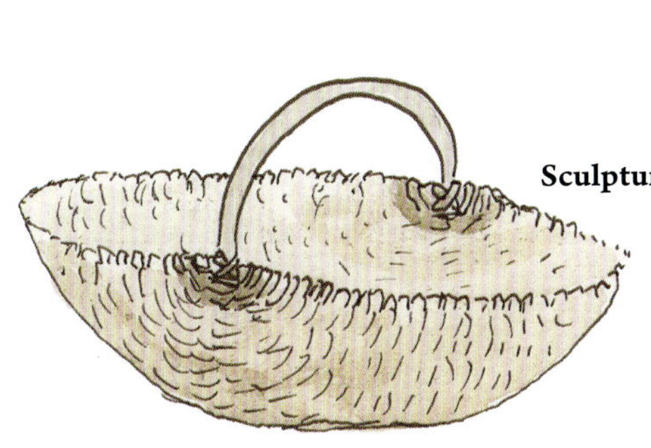

Sculptural forms

TWO-HOOP HARVEST BASKET

THIS IS HANDS-DOWN ONE OF THE MOST USEFUL BASKETS OUT THERE. I use mine for everything—harvesting from the garden, carrying supplies to and from my studio, and holding fruit on the kitchen table. This project focuses on invasive vines, but you can use any species, and I recommend taking advantage of whatever vines are local to your area. You can also use willow, red osier dogwood, twisted ropes of cattails, inner bark strips, and other similar materials for the weavers. I even had a student use only cordage for the weavers! After making a couple of two-hoop baskets, try experimenting with other shapes and sizes.

BASKET SIZE

13½ inches wide × 10½ inches deep × 6 inches high (12 inches high, including handle)

TOOLS

- Masking tape or thick twine
- Straight-tip packing tool
- Two 2-inch spring clamps
- Pruning shears

PLANT MATERIALS

- **Hoops.** Two 12-inch-diameter hoops, each made from bittersweet vine ⅜–½ inch in diameter and 5 feet long (see Making Vine Hoops on page 255)
- **Lashing.** Two 6- to 8-foot-long pieces of flexible lashing material, such as split wisteria, split kudzu, or akebia
- **Ribs.** Ten 15- to 18-inch-long pieces of bittersweet or grapevine without any kinks or bends
- **Weavers.** 18–25 coils of split kudzu, wisteria, honeysuckle vine, akebia, English ivy, or other material that is thinner and more flexible than the ribs

PREPARING MATERIALS

See Chapter 4, Vines, for details on harvesting and processing materials. The hoops and ribs can be made with either freshly harvested or dried and rehydrated material, since grapevine and bittersweet do not shrink too much. Use dried and rehydrated material for the lashing and weavers to mitigate shrinkage.

TIME REQUIRED

This basket takes a full day or two to make, depending on the number of ribs and the fineness of the weaving material. Creating the initial frame and weaving in the first round of six to eight ribs for 2 inches or until they are secure is best done in one sitting. After that you can pause the project at any point and pick it up again easily. The only added preparation would be rehydrating any new weaving materials.

position and lash the hoops

There are two hoops—the handle and the rim. Try different combinations to see which one looks and feels the best in your hand as a handle.

1. Position the two hoops so that the handle hoop is on the outside of the rim hoop and the rim hoop is at the middle point of the handle hoop. Make sure none of the pokey ends are on the handle part of the hoop or where the lashing will be.

2. Use a piece of masking tape or thick twine to secure the intersection of one side of the hoops by wrapping diagonally in both directions. Mark which is the handle using a small piece of masking tape.

3. Begin on the side that does not have the masking tape. The lashing begins with an X across the intersection. Place the end of a long lashing strand diagonally behind the intersection of the two hoops so that a few inches of the tail are visible in the lower right corner and the rest is at the top left corner.

4. Holding the tail in place behind the intersection of the hoops, bring the lashing strand over the front to meet the tail.

TIPS FOR LASHING

What looks like a lot of steps will eventually feel intuitive—a rhythm of going over the rim, across the front of the spine, over the rim, across the back of the spine. If you get a wrap right, it will lock in place. If you get it wrong, the strand will be loose and diagonally cross the X. You can also look to see whether the weave on the previous round was in front or behind the spine and then do the opposite.

5. Wrap the strand behind the spine to the lower left corner. Make sure to catch the tail.

6. Wrap the strand diagonally over the front of the hoops to the upper right corner, completing the X.

7. Wrap the strand behind the right rim to the lower right corner.

8. Wrap the strand across the front of the spine to the lower left corner.

Continued on next page

9. Wrap the strand behind the left rim to the upper left corner.

10. Wrap the strand over the top of the left rim to the front and down to the lower left corner.

11. Bring the strand behind the spine straight over to the lower right corner.

12. Wrap the strand over the front of the right rim to the inside so it ends in the lower right corner again.

13. Repeat steps 7 to 11 to build the lashing until there are pockets below each side of the rim and along the spine that are big enough to fit two ribs. If the lashing strand runs out, see Splicing Woven Lashing Strands on the facing page.

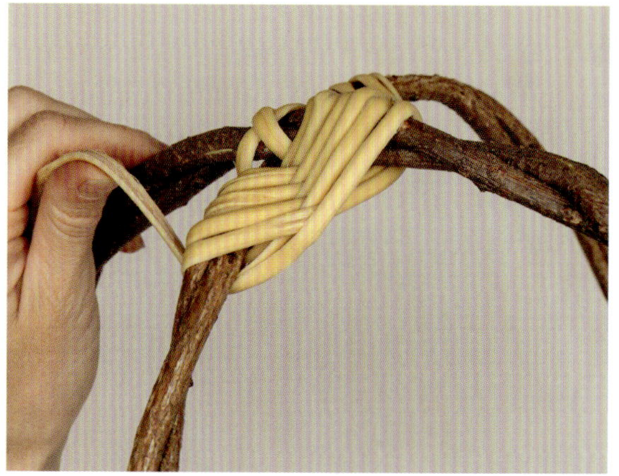

SPLICING WOVEN LASHING STRANDS

To add new material, tuck the ends of both the new and ending strands under the lashing that is already completed.

1. Tuck the end of the lashing strand underneath two or more layers of lashing that has already been created. Pull tight.

2. Use the packing tool to open space either alongside or near the place where the ending strand is tucked in and thread the end of the new lashing strand through.

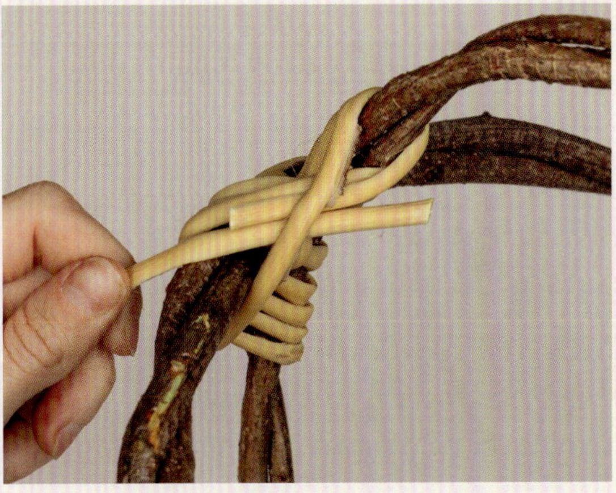

3. Continue lashing with the new strand, being careful not to pull it out for the first round.

14. Ideally you have at least 16 inches of lashing strand left when the lashing on one side is complete, which you will use to start the weaving once you insert the ribs. Use a clamp to secure it to one side of the rim.

15. Remove the tape from the opposite side of the basket and check that the hoops are still arranged evenly. Look from above. Is one side sticking out farther than the other? Adjust before lashing the second side.

16. Repeat steps 3 to 13 to complete the lashing on the second side, matching the size of the first lashing with pockets large enough to fit two ribs and at least 16 inches of lashing strand remaining. Secure the second side of lashing to the rim with a clamp.

add the ribs

Hold the basket upside down for this process. The goal is to add two ribs in each pocket, four ribs on each side. If the pockets in the lashing aren't quite big enough for two ribs in each space, then just add one or keep lashing a little bit until they are larger. It is okay if some pockets have two and others have one.

1. Freshly harvested ribs are less flexible than rehydrated material, so you must pre-bend them into an arc shape to prevent them from poking through the lashing. Along the entire length of a rib, gently and evenly bend one section at a time into an arc. If the rib kinks or breaks, discard it, but don't worry if this happens—it's all part of the learning experience. When complete, the rib should remain somewhat curved. If it presses outward after being inserted and warps the shape of the hoops, it has not been pre-bent enough.

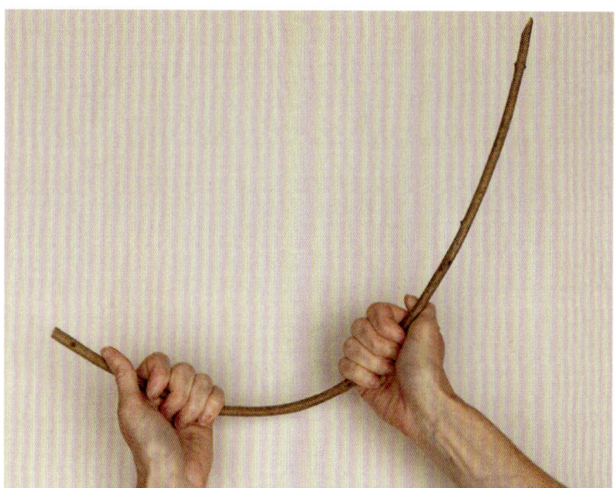

2. Cut the end of one of the rib pieces at an angle with pruning shears. Place it into one of the pockets in the lashing.

3. Shape the rib to match the arc at the bottom of the spine and meet the lashing on the opposite side.

MAKING AND ADDING RIBS

Ribbed baskets are all about the ribs! Whether the basket needs 8, 10, 20, or more, be prepared to take your time. You insert them gradually throughout the process of making the basket, beginning with 2 to 4 on each side and then adding as needed. Even if only a few inches of weaving are left, you still need to add a rib to keep the weave tight.

Taking a lot of time to shape ribs to the perfect length is just part of the process. In the beginning they need to be constantly adjusted, removed, made shorter, added in, and at some point, they will all fly out and whack you in the face before you've securely woven them in! Rib rage is a well-known phenomenon in my basket classes. I recommend taking a break before doing the first round of ribs and going easy on yourself as you learn.

4. Cut the second end at an angle and insert it into the pocket. (Better to start with it a little long since you can always cut more off.) It should still match the curve of the spine and remain loosely in place. If it starts to straighten and poke through the lashing, take it out and bend it more.

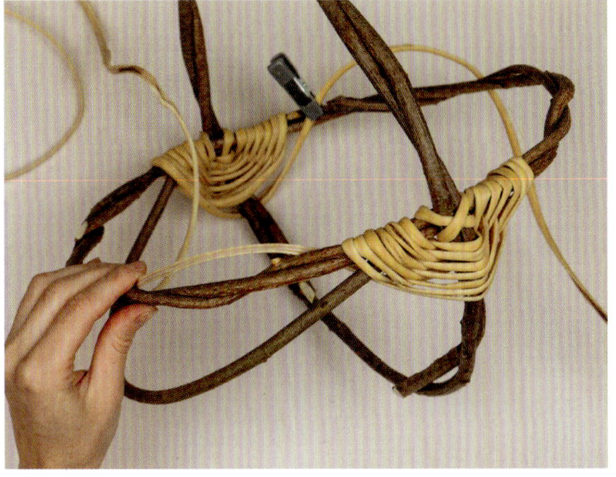

5. Keep adding ribs into all the pockets using the same process until there are two ribs in each pocket on the basket (or one if two won't fit). The goal is an even half-circle shape matching the arc of the basket's spine. Avoid having the spine stick out farther than the ribs next to it, which will make the basket less likely to sit flat. The ribs can either sit at the exact level of the spine or stick out a little farther.

Tip: *Loop a string around the ribs to help see the shape of the basket more clearly. Look at the basket from all angles. Is one rib sticking out farther than the others? Take it out and cut a little off. Is one too short? Replace it with a longer rib. The more you fine-tune now, the more evenly shaped the basket will be. Refer to Making and Adding Ribs (facing page) for more tips.*

weave the basket

The pattern is a plain weave—over, under, over, under—around the ribs and the rim. For the first two rows of weaving, the ribs can easily fall out, which is normal. If they do, just put them back and hold them there until secure.

1. Unclamp one length of lashing and weave it over the rim, under the first rib, and over the next rib, continuing the plain-weave pattern across all ribs. In the photo below, the weaver starts on the left side of the lashing and begins by going over and in front of the rim to begin the pattern. Your pattern may start by going over and behind the rim, depending on where your lashing ended its weave pattern.

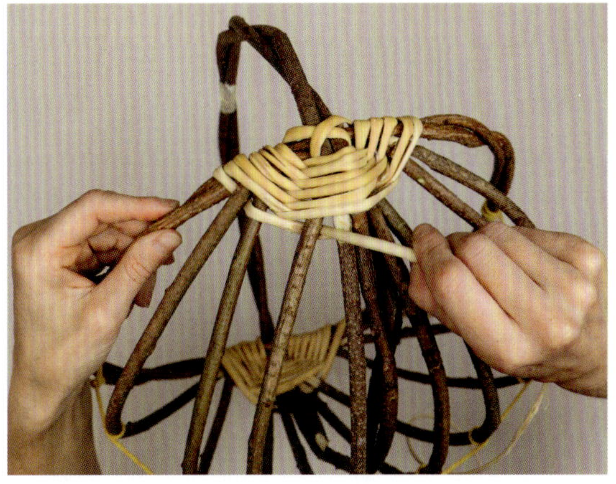

Tip: *Weave as close to the lashing as possible since you can't pack these first rows tightly later.*

Continued on next page

2. When you reach the rim on the other side, bring the weaver around it, keeping the pattern. (It may go in front of the rim, as shown, or behind, depending on your pattern.) When it wraps around the other side of the rim, it is in position to weave across the basket in the opposite direction, and the pattern should be opposite of the first row. (Every rib where this is an over on the first row should be an under on the second row.)

3. Carefully weave the next several rows, being sure to pull each weave close to the lashing. After three rows, the ribs should be secure enough that you can put the basket down without the ribs coming out.

4. When the first weaver runs out, switch to the other side of the basket and weave those rows in using the leftover lashing strand. For the rest of the basket, continue going back and forth between the two sides evenly.

Tip: *Packing each row in a ribbed basket is important to create a solid weave. After every row or two, pack down thoroughly, using your fingers or a packing tool.*

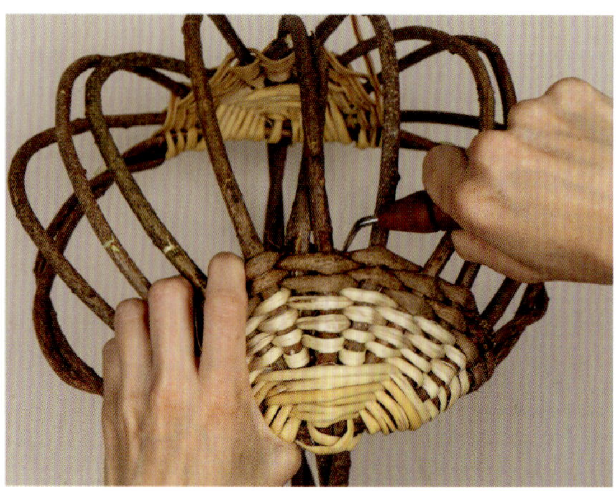

add more ribs

As the weaving progresses away from the lashing, the space between the ribs increases and the weaving becomes loose unless you add more ribs. A general rule of thumb is to add ribs as soon as possible when the weaving starts to feel a little loose. There shouldn't be more than 1½ inches between ribs, and I usually aim for 1 inch. For a fine weave, maintain a distance of ½ inch.

The only way to avoid disrupting the plain-weave pattern is to add two ribs at a time, placing them in adjacent spaces, one on either side of an existing rib or the spine. The exception is when adding a rib adjacent to the rim, which does not disrupt the pattern.

Tip: *When ribs are slightly different sizes and shapes, adding two at the same time isn't always practical. Sometimes one space needs a new rib and the adjacent space doesn't. In that case, add a new rib where it is needed and keep weaving over and under, even if it isn't opposite the previous row. Once you go around the rim and come back again, the pattern will self-correct. Pack tightly to help hide the incorrect weaves.*

SPLICING WEAVERS

You can create patterns of color and texture by weaving this basket with different materials. Add material according to your design or when the current weaver runs out.

1. A weaver can end on either side of any rib except for those adjacent to the rim or the rim itself. Cut a few inches off the weaver if it ends in the wrong place.

2. The end of the new weaver overlaps the old weaver by two ribs. It does not need to tuck in. Take the new piece and trace it back over the end of the old one until it is underneath the previous rib. Secure the overlap with a clamp until the next row is woven to hold it in place. Trim any ends once the basket is complete.

1. Cut the end of the new rib at an angle and insert it into the weaving alongside an existing rib, pushing as far as it will go. Use an awl or a packing tool to open space if it's tight. Bend the new rib to the other side of the basket and estimate the correct length, accounting for the part that will push into the weaving. Cut that end at an angle and insert. Adjust as needed by either cutting more off or pushing it deeper into the weaving.

2. Add the second rib in an adjacent space.

add filler rows

Due to the bulbous shape of many ribbed baskets, the two sides of weaving often meet at the rim before meeting at the bottom of the basket or vice versa. Prevent this by weaving filler rows to keep the edges straight. Pay attention to your unique project and add filler rows throughout instead of all at the end, which would be very visible in the finished basket. The following instructions are for a long filler row. Sometimes you may just need to fill across one or two ribs.

1. Instead of weaving all the way up to the rim, stop one rib before the rim. Turn around and weave to the other side. Again, stop one rib before the rim. This is a filler row.

2. If your basket does not need much correction to maintain a straight weaving edge, then do a regular row after the filler row and pack it in. If it needs more, do a second filler row but turn around two ribs before the rim. On the other side, also stop two ribs before the rim. Do as many in a row as necessary, even if it is just weaving over three ribs at the bottom, to straighten the edge. Pack the next regular row very tightly to help hide the edges of the filler rows.

Tip: *If using wider material, do the filler rows every other rib to create a smoother line.*

finish the basket

When there is only 1 inch left, the two sides tend to get tangled with each other, so stop weaving evenly, alternating side to side, and finish in one direction.

1. Cut a weaver on one side so that it rests behind a rib. Tape the end to secure it temporarily to the previous rows until the weaving is complete, which will secure this row.

2. Continue weaving the other side to fill the remaining space. Then pack the rows and weave one last round. Sometimes the last rows become a bit of a free-for-all. You can embrace this or take your time and try to keep it very organized. Remove all the tape from the basket.

Anatomy of a Tension Tray

This is a unique form that is somewhere between a wickerwork and ribbed basket. I love its elegant simplicity.

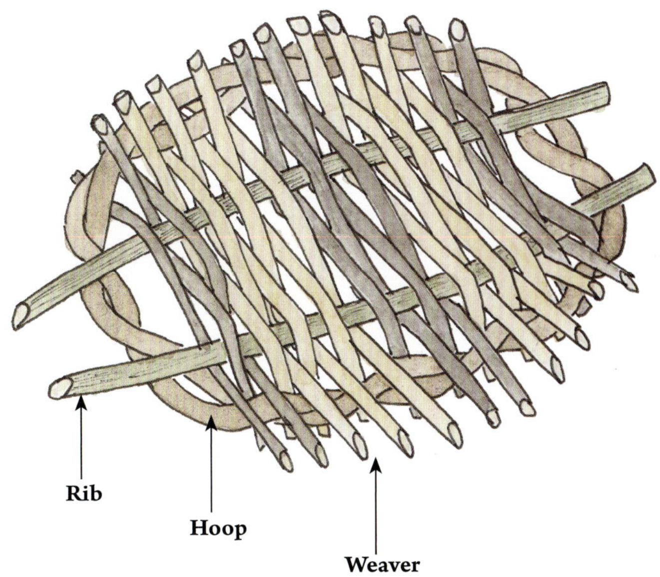

Hoop. Initial structure, which provides the shape of the tray.

Ribs. Two groupings of one to three somewhat stiff, vertical lengths of material that rest on top of the hoop.

Weavers. Short pieces of material that form the structure of the basket. They should be a little sturdy, but not so much that they bend the ribs out of place. They do not bend around the hoop as in regular ribbed baskets, relying instead on tension to hold them in place.

TENSION TRAY

THIS FLAT TRAY IS FASCINATING BECAUSE IT RELIES ON TENSION to hold its form. I categorize it as a ribbed basket because it has a hoop, ribs, and weavers. Traditionally made with willow and used to serve bread or add interest to a table setting, tension trays are quick and fun to make. They don't require very long or flexible materials, and you can use freshly harvested plants—just about any thin, straight stick from a shrub, tree, or vine. I used multiflora rose, bittersweet vine, grapevine, and Japanese barberry. Note that fresh materials will shrink, but you can easily remedy that by adding a few extra pieces after the tray dries.

BASKET SIZE

11 inches wide × 12 inches long

TOOLS

- Pruning shears

PLANT MATERIALS

- **Hoop.** 12-inch-diameter hoop made of a piece of grapevine or bittersweet about ⅜ inch in diameter and 6½ feet long (see Making Vine Hoops on page 255)
- **Central ribs.** Four straight, 25-inch-long rods ¼–⅜ inch in diameter; rods should be a consistent diameter. Use grapevine, multiflora rose, willow, or similar material.
- **Weavers.** About 45 weavers, approximately 16 inches long and ¼ inch in diameter. (The number of weavers needed depends on thickness.) They should be long enough that they stick out 2 inches on either side of the hoop. Use multiflora rose, brambles, forsythia, willow, red osier dogwood, grapevine, bittersweet, or similar material.

PREPARING MATERIALS

See Chapter 4, Vines, and Chapter 5, Woody Stems, for details on harvesting and processing materials. They can be used fresh or dried and rehydrated. If using freshly harvested materials, no rehydration is required, although letting them dry for a couple of days to a week allows them to shrink a bit, while remaining flexible enough to weave.

TIME REQUIRED

This is a half-day project even if you are harvesting materials as you go. You can pause at any point after approximately 2 inches of weavers are in place.

secure the ribs

1. Place a pair of ribs vertically on top of the hoop, left of center. While holding them in place, tuck the first weaver under the left side of the hoop, but over the ribs and the right side of hoop. It should be about in the center of the hoop.

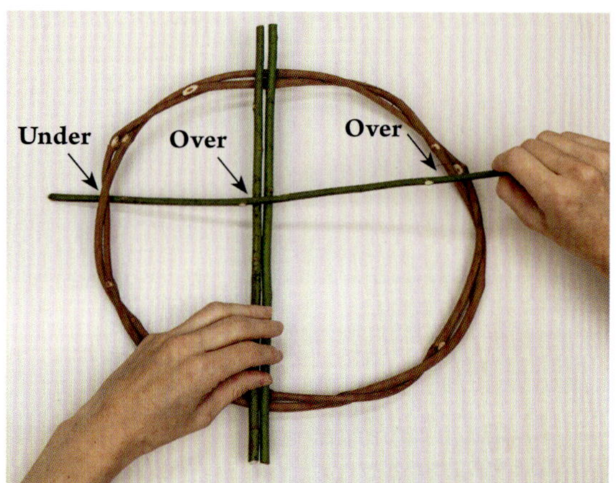

2. Place the second pair of ribs right of center, on top of the first weaver. The ribs and weavers will be loose for the first several steps. Do your best to hold them in place and then adjust after they are secure.

3. For the first seven weavers, each new weaver is placed below the ones already in place. While holding the ribs in place, tuck a second weaver under the right side of the hoop, over the right ribs, under the left ribs, and slide it up over the left side of the hoop.

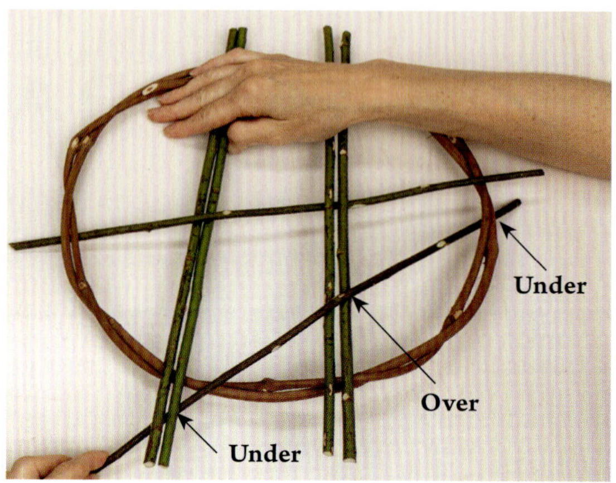

4. Slide the new weaver up until it is pressed against the first weaver. Both weavers are only braced against four elements: the two hoop edges and the two pairs of ribs. The weaving creates tension that holds everything together.

weave the tray

1. Tuck the next weaver under the left side of the hoop and over the left ribs. Bend it down to weave under the right ribs and over the right side of the hoop, sliding it up against the rest of the weavers.

2. The next weaver goes under the right side of the hoop, over the right ribs, under the left ribs, and slides up over the left side of the hoop. Always start the new weaver on the side where it needs to go under the hoop, which will alternate back and forth from right to left for the whole tray. This will allow for the easiest weaving. Continue going back and using the plain-weave pattern of over and under, alternating how you begin each row so no two overs or unders abut each other. After adding several more rows, shift all the weavers until they are centered in the hoop. Adjust their placement so they are equidistant and straight.

3. As you continue, add three or four weavers above the centered set, then three or four below so that you work each side equally. Alternate colors to create a pattern, if desired. As you work, continue to pack all the weavers tightly against each other toward the center.

4. Add weavers until no more will fit. Toward the ends, thinner pieces might be easier to weave into the smaller spaces. If using fresh materials, let the tray and some spare weavers dry for a week. As shrinkage allows, weave in a couple more pieces before moving on to the finishing steps. If using materials that were dried and rehydrated, you can finish right away.

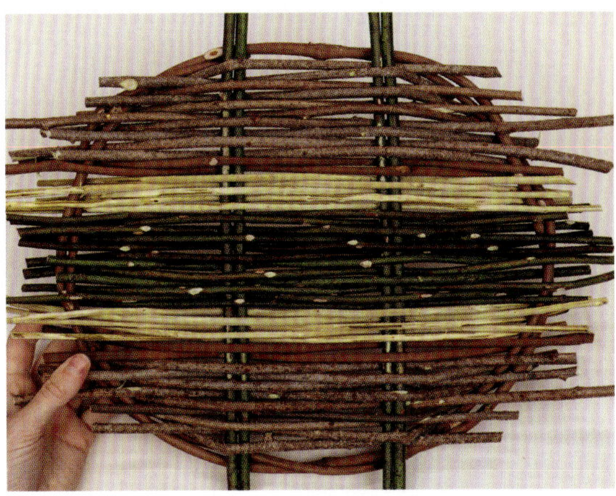

5. When the tray is dry, trim the weavers at a diagonal, leaving enough that they are braced against the hoop. Whether they are cut directly over the hoop, as in this example, or stick out past the hoop is an aesthetic choice. You can always cut off more material, but you can't put it back, so take your time to get an angle you like. As you trim, follow the hoop's curve.

CHAPTER 16

RANDOM-WEAVE BASKETRY

Wild, spontaneous, artful, exasperating, fun, dynamic—all these words describe both the process and the outcome of random-weave baskets. The word *random* may suggest that there are no rules, but there are in fact principles to follow that create a solid, well-balanced basket both in structure and appearance. Random weaving is one of my favorite methods to teach because it involves collaboration with wild materials at its best, asking us to work with what the materials offer, rather than to force them into a specific shape. It is also a wonderfully versatile technique that you can use with thicker vines to create large baskets and structures, or flexible materials, such as grasses, to make soft sculpture.

Anatomy of a Random-Weave Basket

The following components pertain to random-weave baskets in general. The illustration depicts a two-hoop version of the Grapevine Market Basket. One-hoop baskets such as the Random-Weave Bowl (page 285) are less structured; they share the same elements except for the handle hoop and lashing.

Hoops. Provide the initial framework to weave around.

Handle hoop. Top part of the vertical, central hoop.

Spine. The bottom part of the handle hoop, which forms the bottom of the basket.

Lashing. The first round of weaving, which secures the hoops together on either side.

Base weavers. The sturdy weavers that create the shape of the basket.

Surface work. The last weavers added that fill in spaces and create aesthetic interest. They often do not weave all the way in and out, traveling more on the outside surface of the basket.

Rim hoop. The top edge of the basket.

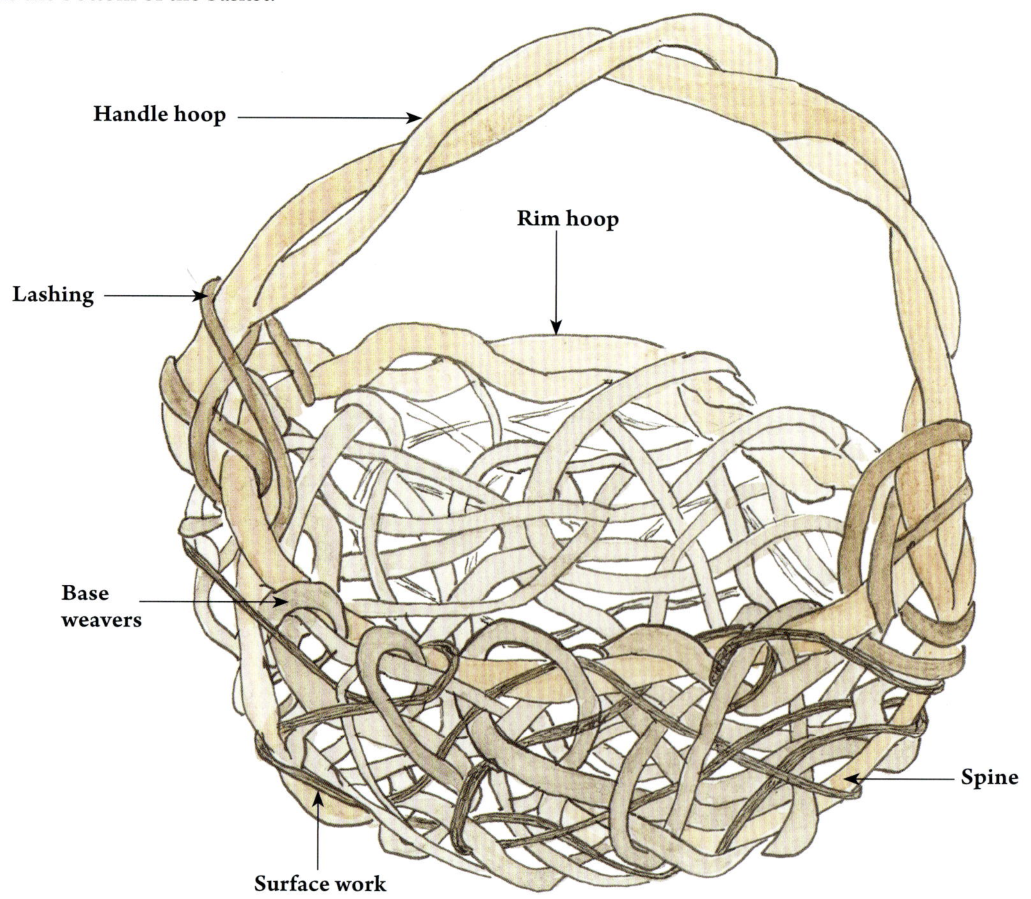

choosing plants for random-weave baskets

The projects here focus on vines, but many materials are ripe for experimentation. Vines are excellent for large containers and baskets with an open weave. Fibers, foliage, and grasses create soft, nestlike forms. Bark strips are wonderful for solid containers. Almost any natural material is possible to use with widely varying results. When designing your own project, remember this: Any sort of frame can be filled in with random weaving to create an artful and uniquely textured basket.

principles of random weave

Despite the name, achieving a sturdy, random-looking weave takes attention and intention, but not by following step-by-step instructions. Instead, use a combination of intuition and the following guidelines. Refer to these principles often during the process.

Weave for tension. In a plain-weave pattern, each new round is woven opposite the one before it. For example, if the first row weaves over, under, over, under, the next row weaves under, over, under, over. The goal is to create a consistent pattern and a solid structure. With random weave, the rhythmic sameness of the pattern is not a goal, but you still need a basket that holds its shape and can carry weight. Every time a weaver crosses an element you must decide whether going over or under that element will be opposite of the nearest weaves already present, creating tension and building strength in the basket. As more elements cross each other from different angles, creating the tightest weave becomes experimental. You might go over two, under one, then change the angle and go over several. Try different ways and see what creates tension. With practice, you'll develop an eye for building a tight weave.

WEAVING FOR TENSION TEST CASE

Each time the working vine crosses an element, this is an opportunity to weave, adding tension that solidifies the basket's form.

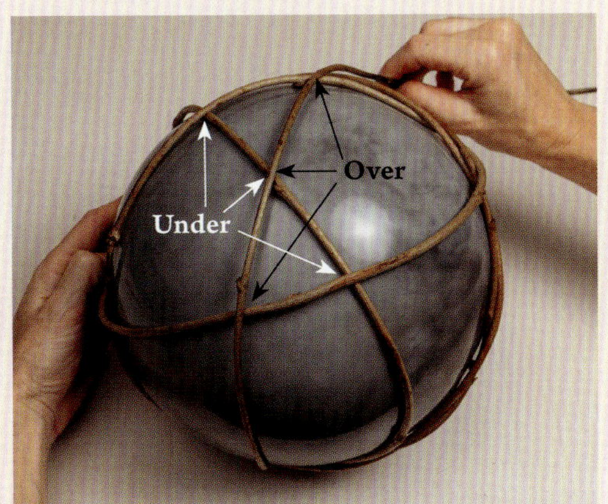

NOT CORRECT! Note how one vertical weaver goes over three consecutive elements and the other vertical goes under three, creating no tension.

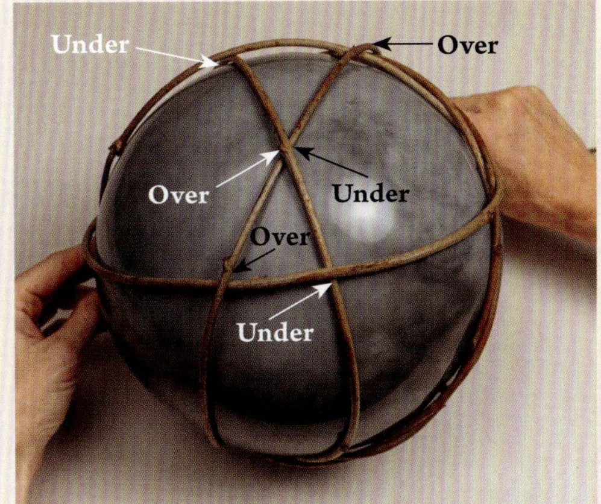

CORRECT! Here is a successful weave.

Fill in the biggest spaces first. Weave the vines across the biggest spaces first, eventually filling in smaller and smaller ones.

Use a lot of clamps. Clamps are necessary for holding the shape of the basket as you weave. Don't skimp on them!

Secure intersections with weaving. After several vines are in place with clamps, begin to weave the next ones with the goal of replacing clamps with vines. Go over and under intersections to secure them. Feel for loose sections and purposefully use new vines to secure them.

Vary your movements. Don't go up to the rim with every sweep of the vine across the basket. Also go around the circumference, loop backward, create S-shapes—anything to fill the basket in evenly in an aesthetically pleasing way to your eye.

Work from thickest to thinnest materials. Whether working with vines or grasses, use the thickest, longest, and most sturdy pieces first to build structure. Progressively thinner and shorter materials can be added as the basket takes shape.

Take a step back frequently. Hold the basket away from you and look at it from all angles. It's easy to get tunnel vision and then realize the shape is squashed in a strange way or there are huge gaps.

Evaluate aesthetics. Once a fair amount of weaving is filled in, begin looking at the surface of the basket with an aesthetic eye. Is one bulky vine sticking out? Do you like the way the vines look as they curve across the basket? How can you create a visual balance? Once you've developed a feel for weaving with good tension, start making conscious choices about the visual texture, colors, and design of the basket.

GRAPEVINE MARKET BASKET

I'M OFTEN ASKED WHAT TO DO WITH GRAPEVINE, an abundant, thicker vine that isn't very flexible. This open-weave market basket is my answer. Taking advantage of grapevine's sturdiness, this basket is also big, useful, and fast to construct. Plus grapevines don't shrink much, so you can use the material fresh. Some of my favorite workshop days have been taking folks into the woods, harvesting grapevines, weaving for an afternoon, and then seeing them go home with a finished basket on their arm (sometimes more than one!).

BASKET SIZE

18 inches in diameter × 16 inches high, including handle

TOOLS

- Masking tape
- Ten 4-inch spring clamps

PLANT MATERIALS

- **Hoops.** Three 15- to 17-inch-diameter hoops, each made from grapevine ½–⅝ inch in diameter and 9½ feet long (see Making Vine Hoops on page 255). Use two layers of vine (no more) in each hoop.
- **Lashing.** Two 4-foot lengths of thin, flexible vine
- **Weavers.** Nine 6- to 10-foot lengths of grapevine, ¼–⅝ inch in diameter

Due to the nature of random weave, everyone's basket will be very different in shape, size, and density of weaving, so it's difficult to say exactly how many vines to gather for this project. The amount listed here is an estimate. Gather a variety of vines of different diameters so you have some thicker pieces for the structural frame and thinner ones for filling in, plus extras in case any break. Substitute any sturdy, thicker vine, such as bittersweet, wisteria, Virginia creeper, or English ivy, if desired.

PREPARING MATERIALS

See Chapter 4, Vines, for details on harvesting and processing materials. You can use vines that are either freshly harvested or dried and rehydrated. If using fresh vines, weave some extra material in after the basket has dried for a couple of weeks.

TIME REQUIRED

A surprisingly quick basket to make, especially considering its size, you can construct it in a couple of hours. Pause the project at any point.

build the frame

1. Three hoops begin the structure of the basket. One is the handle and spine and the other two are the rim pieces. Choose a hoop for the handle and arrange the other two inside as shown. Loose pressure should keep them together. If the inside hoops don't stay in place, they are too small or need to be rearranged.

2. Temporarily secure the hoops with an 18-inch piece of masking tape wrapped around the connection points. Also mark the handle with a small piece of tape so you don't lose track of where the opening is.

lash the hoops

1. On the side that doesn't have tape, tuck one end of a 4-foot-long thinner vine in between the two layers of any hoop except the handle near where they intersect.

2. Weave around in a circle one time. Alternate going over and under the vines, either singly or doubly. Unders always follow overs, but the number of elements you go across should vary. As one example: Go over one layer of vine, under two, over two, under one. It can appear random, but the goal is always to create tension.

3. Weave in an outward spiral for three rounds, leaving space between each round so there is room to weave in more vines later. If the vine has run out, tuck the end in anywhere. If not, clamp it and leave the rest hanging to weave in later.

Continued on next page

4. Remove the tape from the other side and repeat the lashing. The aesthetics at this point aren't important. The three hoops should feel relatively anchored on both sides.

5. Take a step back and look at the overall shape of the basket. Imagine a skin going over the bottom. Is one hoop sticking out much farther than the rest? If so, adjust it. The shape of this basket changes a lot during the process, inviting a flexible mindset about outcomes, but it is still important to keep checking and adjusting.

Even shape

weave the basket

Before continuing, read the Principles of Random Weave on page 277. They are essential to weaving this basket with ease and success. Random-weave projects do not have exact steps to get to the end. Instead you must rely on experimentation and instinct, informed by the principles. The process is a lesson in letting go and finding a balance between spontaneity and an adherence to rules.

1. Fold a long and slightly thicker vine over the top of one side of the rim. Secure it with a 4-inch spring clamp. You can now work with the two halves of the vine independently to avoid pulling the entire length through with each weave.

2. Bring one half of the folded vine across the bottom of the basket so that it goes over most or all of the ribs until it reaches the rim on the other side. (This exception to the rule of always weaving over and under will help create a voluminous basket body.) Secure each intersection with a clip. Go over the rim from the outside to the inside, adding a clip.

3. Bring the vine back down across the bottom of the basket at a different angle, so that it crosses different elements. Each time it reaches a vine, go over or under it in whatever way creates the most tension. Add a clamp when needed to keep the weaver from moving around too much.

4. Keep weaving back and forth between the rims until the first half of the vine runs out. Leave the end braced somewhere and don't worry if it comes loose.

5. Weave in the second half of the vine, taking a different path each time so the vines crisscross each other at different angles. Fill in the biggest spaces first.

6. Add a second vine, this time by sliding it under an element anywhere on the side or bottom of the basket until you've reached the new vine's halfway point. Secure with a clip and proceed to weave each half of the vine.

7. Continue weaving. Don't go up to the rim with every sweep of the vine across the basket. Instead, vary it, going around the circumference, looping backward, creating S-shapes—anything to fill in the basket evenly. Pause often to look at the basket from a distance and all angles. Push and pull elements to adjust the shape as needed.

8. Continue adding one vine at a time and weaving it in. Remember to fill in the biggest spaces first with the thicker vines, moving to fill smaller and smaller openings with thinner vines. After several vines are in place, weave around intersections with the goals of securing them and replacing clamps as well as filling in areas with aesthetically pleasing surface work.

9. When the basket is filled in as much as you like, stop weaving. There are no rules for how densely woven this basket needs to be. How you want the basket to look, what you want it to hold, and how heavy it becomes are the only factors. Tuck in all the ends and trim anything that sticks out. Make a final evaluation, and if you don't like a certain vine, cut it and weave the ends in.

RANDOM-WEAVE BOWL

THIN, FLEXIBLE VINES ARE A DREAM TO WEAVE WITH. They flow beautifully and, as you're completing the basket, the process becomes like embroidery as you develop patterns, swirls, and lines for the eye to follow. For this basket I used honeysuckle, akebia, kudzu, and inner bark strips from various species. There is a lot of flexibility in the design of this bowl—you can weave it to a solid finish or leave it open and airy. Practicing random weave around a mold is a great way to become familiar with the principles of creating a strong weave without the challenge of working free-form. Once you remove the mold, the final product is beautiful as well as useful. I have three in my kitchen now, holding fruit, garlic, lemons, and whatever else needs a lovely place to sit.

BASKET SIZE

9 inches in diameter × 4 inches high

TOOLS

- 9-inch inflatable exercise ball for a mold*
- Five to seven 2-inch spring clamps

* Substitute a soccer ball, beach ball, or even wadded paper wrapped in tape. Adjust the directions for making the hoop to fit your substituted size. Deflating the mold after use is easiest, but if that's not an option, don't weave so tightly or high on the mold that the basket won't come off.

PLANT MATERIALS

- **Hoop.** Thin vine, such as akebia, honeysuckle, kudzu, or wisteria that is approximately ¼ inch in diameter and at least 7 feet long—ideally as long as you can find.
- **Weavers.** 10–15 coils of thin vines 4–10 feet long, 1⁄16–¼ inch in diameter. Optionally, add 5–10 coils of other materials at least 18 inches long and flexible, such as inner bark strips, grasses, leaves, cordage, and even yarn.

PREPARING MATERIALS

See Chapter 4, Vines, for details on harvesting and processing materials. Clean up the vines before weaving by cutting off all nobs, nodes, and anything that could snag on the mold.

TIME REQUIRED

A half to a full day, depending on how densely you weave the basket. You can pause the work at any time. To pause, store soaked vines in a plastic bag in a cool place for up to a couple of days or soak new material.

weave on the mold

1. Make a double-wrapped hoop that will fit around the middle of the mold using one end of the longest, thinnest vine you have (7 to 10 feet). (See Making Vine Hoops on page 255 for details.) The hoop should be snug enough that it won't slip off the mold, but not so tight that you can't weave around it. This will likely require some adjusting before you get it just right. This hoop is the basket's rim. The extra length of material will be used to begin the weave.

2. Start the basket upside down with the rim facing the table. Secure the hoop with masking tape onto the center or a little below the center of the mold. Then bring the vine across the top of the mold to the other side.

3. Turn the mold so the working end is facing you and wrap the vine around the rim from the outside to the inside.

4. Cross the vine over the mold at a different angle to a different part of the rim.

Tip: *Secure the vines on the mold temporarily with masking tape to keep them from shifting too much, if needed.*

5. Read the Principles of Random Weave on page 277. They are essential to weaving this basket with ease and success. Random-weave projects do not have exact steps to get to the end. Instead, you must rely on experimentation and instinct, informed by the principles.

6. Continue crossing the vine over the form, dividing the largest open spaces and wrapping over or around the rim. Remember to weave over and under as many elements as possible to create the tension that will hold the basket together. See Weaving for Tension Test Case on page 277 for tips.

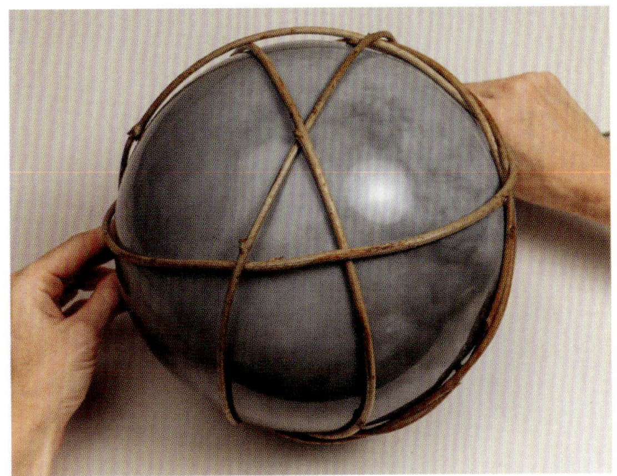

7. Weave the first vine until it runs out. The end does not need to be secured well at this stage of the basket. Don't worry if it pops out. Wrap it around another vine or let it hang loose.

8. To add a new weaver, insert under the rim or any other solid element and pull through until you reach the middle. Weave one half into the basket. When it runs out, weave the other half. Weaving in halves saves time and abrades the weaver less since you aren't pulling the entire length through.

9. Continue weaving. From now on there is no need to return to the rim as often. Begin swirling the weaving around the form and creating loops. Loops are a great way to build a strong basket with lots of overs and unders in the weave.

weave off the mold

There are many aesthetic approaches possible. Do you want to fill in the whole basket with an even texture or leave an open weave of organically shaped swirls? Do you want to create contrast with different-colored materials?

1. Once there are no big open spaces and the form feels solid, remove the basket from the mold to continue weaving with more ease. Some shifting is expected, but if it feels very loose put it back on the mold and add more vines.

Tip: *The photo shows a good stage to remove the basket from the mold. If you remove it too early, the basket can become deformed, shrink in on itself, and end up flat.*

2. Once removed from the mold, there will be new loose areas to solidify. Continue weaving. You can also adjust the shape by pushing and pulling on sections.

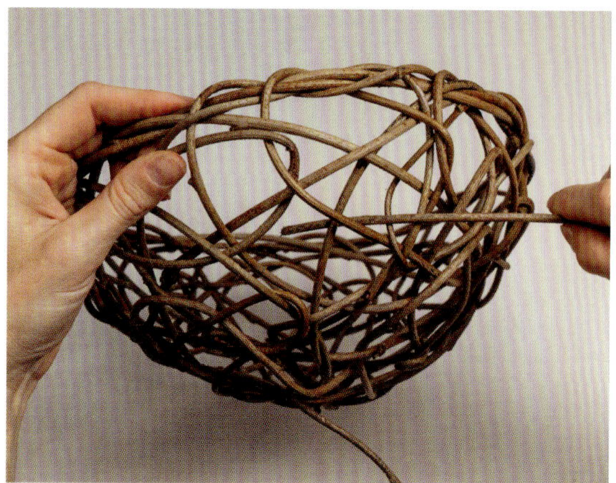

3. Optional: Once the basket form is established, weave in other flexible materials. Shorter pieces at this point have an advantage since they don't take long to pull through and there are plenty of places to tuck ends in.

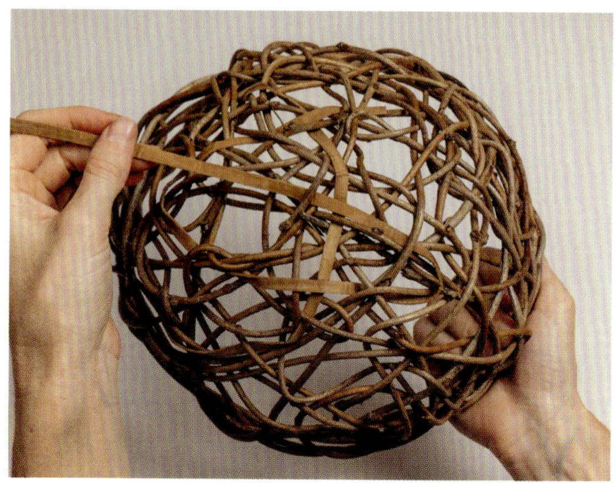

4. Eventually the basket becomes too dense to pull weavers under and over multiple elements at the same time. At this stage pull the working weaver all the way to the inside of the basket and pull it all the way back out at another spot. The weaving itself is the same, though the process is now slower. Alternatively, work on the exterior surface of the basket only, threading the weaver under or over one outside element at a time instead of pulling it all the way through.

5. Continue to shift elements and shape the bowl as you progress. To create a basket that will sit flat, turn it upside down and flatten the bottom occasionally. The further along it gets, the less you can affect the overall shape.

finish the basket

Random-weave baskets are finished when you want them to be. There is no rule for when to stop weaving, but I will say that folks tend to stop weaving early rather than going too far. This basket also tends to have an awkward middle stage where it seems uncertain that it will ever turn into a basket! If you find yourself feeling that way, just keep going. When you're finished weaving, tuck in any loose ends and trim any loose bits or nubs.

CHAPTER 17

WICKERWORK BASKETRY

Wickerwork is one of the most utilitarian types of baskets—think gathering baskets, hampers, storage baskets, and furniture. The style is known as stake-and-strand, meaning the basket is composed of a base, uprights, and weavers with woody material that is round, as opposed to flat—like a branch or a dowel. Most commonly it is done with willow, but red osier dogwood, vines, bramble canes with the thorns stripped off, and water sprouts from trees work just as well. Using these strong materials can feel a bit like wrestling alligators, but it also requires finesse and attention to detail. Wickerwork is also commonly done with rattan, a vine native to Southeast Asia that you can purchase from basketry suppliers.

Anatomy of a Wickerwork Basket

There are many different shapes and styles of wickerwork basket. The construction below illustrates a classic stake-and-strand–style round-bottomed basket.

Base. Bottom of the basket, composed of base stakes and twining strands. It is woven separately first, and then upright stakes are inserted into it.

Base stakes. Structural elements onto which you twine to create the bottom of the basket. The material must be sturdier and thicker than all other elements.

Upright stakes. Structural elements that are inserted into the base, bend upward to form the walls of the basket, then fold and weave to create the rim. Material should be less sturdy and thick than the base stakes but still strong enough to provide structure. Materials should also be sturdier than the weavers but still flexible enough to weave.

Weavers. Thin, flexible elements that weave around the upright stakes to create the walls of the basket. Materials should be thinner and more flexible than the upright stakes.

Twining strands. Thin, flexible elements that twine around the base stakes to complete the base. Materials should be thinner and more flexible than the base stakes.

Rim. Top of the basket, formed by weaving the upright stakes.

SIZE AND SHAPE VARIATIONS

To create different sizes and shapes of wickerwork basket, vary the number of base stakes and upright stakes, the types of weaving material, and the height and angle of the basket walls.

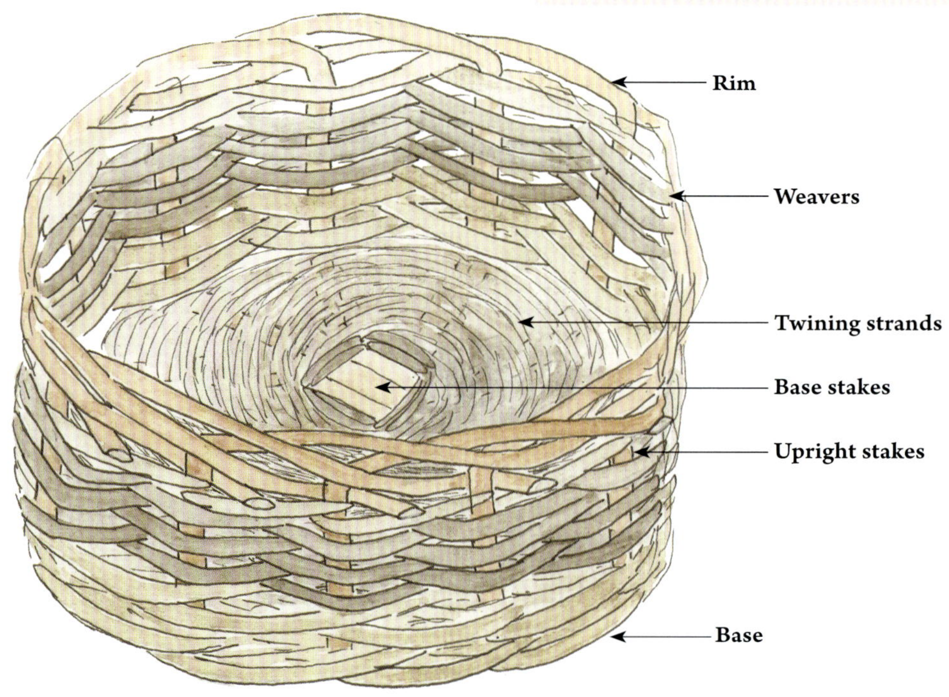

anatomy of a rod

Many terms used in wickerwork are historically rooted in the traditions of willow basketry.

Rod. A single length of first year's growth of willow or another similar material.

Tip end. The thinner end.

Butt end. The thicker end.

Slype. A cut that is long and angled.

choosing plants for wickerwork baskets

Use a variety of sturdy, woody or semi-woody materials, including willow, red osier dogwood, multiflora rose and other brambles, water sprouts, suckers from trees and shrubs, and even vines, such as grapevine, bittersweet, English ivy, Virginia creeper, wisteria, or kudzu. Look for any plant part that is a little sturdy and at least a couple of feet long.

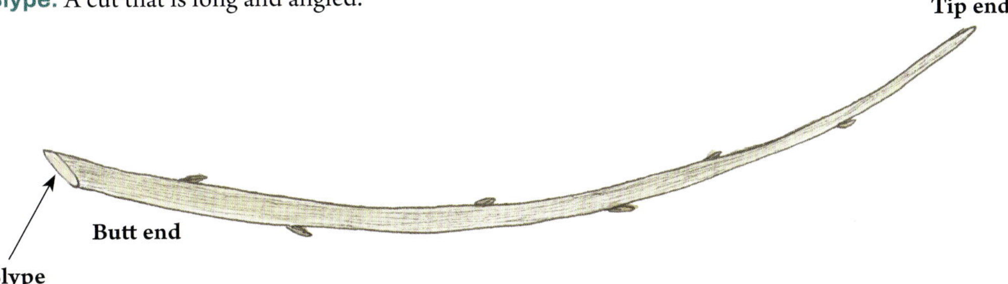

Willow is a classic material for wickerwork.

WILD WICKERWORK BASKET

A CLASSIC INTRODUCTION TO WICKERWORK, this useful basket has a separate base to which vertical stakes are added and then woven around with flexible material until they are bent over to weave the rim. Typically done with willow, any wild material that is round in cross section and relatively flexible will work. One of the first wickerwork baskets I ever made used red osier dogwood and goldenrod stems. I still have this basket and, while it is a little worse for wear after all these years, my memory of the gorgeous fall day I spent weaving it by the river is as fresh as if it happened yesterday.

BASKET SIZE

8 inches in diameter × 7½ inches high

TOOLS

- Pruning shears
- 5-inch awl
- Coconut oil
- 2-inch spring clamp
- Hammer or rapping iron

PLANT MATERIALS

I recommend that you gather extra material for each component of a wickerwork basket as some may break.

- **Base stakes.** Six 12-inch rods that are the same diameter along their full length—about ⅜ inch.
- **Upright stakes.** Twelve rods about 4 feet long that are thicker than the weavers, but thinner than the base stakes. Choose a flexible yet strong material that doesn't crack when bent over to weave the rim.
- **Weavers and twining strands.** A variety of slender, long rods, vines, or canes. You don't have to worry as much about the weavers cracking since they only go around in a circle, but they still need to be pliable and should not be thicker or more powerful than the stakes.

  For the base of this basket I used twenty-five 3-foot-long rods of willow ⅛–¼ inch in diameter. (I recommend 33 feet of material if using vines and brambles.) Your thinnest and most flexible pieces are best for this part.

  For the sides I used six 5-foot lengths of grapevine, 15 feet of bittersweet vine, thirty-two 30-inch rods of willow, red osier, and water shoots, and six 4-foot lengths of bramble (149 feet total)—all ⅛–¼ inch in diameter.

PREPARING MATERIALS

Prepare each kind of plant material according to its type. Refer to details for harvesting and processing in Part One. Ideally use dried and rehydrated materials (with the exception of bramble canes, which I prefer to use fresh). If using fresh materials, they may shrink, and the basket will loosen. Ideally, let materials dry for a week or so until they are still flexible enough to weave but have lost some moisture. Otherwise, remedy any looseness by weaving in additional rows after the basket has dried. If using material that is completely dry, soak woody stem rods for one day per foot of length and mellow for 12 to14 hours; soak brambles for several days; rehydrate dried vines in a pot of hot water for 20 to 45 minutes or more, depending on their thickness.

TIME REQUIRED

One full day or two half-days in a row. It is not ideal to dry and rehydrate woody materials more than once since they degrade in quality after that. The only exception would be to weave the separate base, allow it to dry, and then complete the basket another day.

prepare the base

1. Gently bend each base stake until straight. Test straightness by rolling it on a table.

2. Cut one end of three base stakes at a long angle; this is known as a slype.

3. Use an awl to pierce a hole directly through the center of a base stake without a slype. The piece may split significantly, which is normal. Take a piece with a slyped end, grease the end in coconut oil to ease sliding, and insert through the split. Push through until centered. Keeping the awl in place after piercing the hole makes this action easier.

4. Use the awl to pierce through the second and third base stakes without slypes and slide them on either side of the first base stake.

5. Slide the second and third slyped stakes on either side of the first one, greasing the ends to help them slide. Adjust the entire base so that all sides are equal.

twine the base

The start can feel challenging to a beginner. Take your time and expect a tight weave to take a couple of tries. (Note that even though woody stems feel and behave very differently than other materials, the twining in this project is the same technique previously covered in the book.)

1. Choose the two longest, thinnest weavers as the first twining strands. Insert the tips from right to left through all three split base stakes.

2. Holding the tips in place, bring the two twining strands down so one is in front and one is behind the base stakes on the right side.

3. Rotate the base 90 degrees counterclockwise so that the two twining strands are horizontal on top. (The base turns counterclockwise with every twine.) Bring the twining strand in the back under the twining strand in the front and over the base stakes on the right so it is tight against the corner.

4. Bring the other strand behind the base stakes. This completes one twine.

5. Rotate the base and twine around the next three base stakes. With each twine, the strand in the back comes to the front and the strand in the front goes to the back, crossing over the first strand. The place where they cross should be very tight against the corner. Use your fingers while twining to help push them down.

Continued on next page

6. Twine around the entire base twice, which also fastens the tips of the twining strands that threaded through the split stakes. After two rounds, secure the twining strands with a 2-inch clamp so they won't come undone. As a preparatory step, bend the base stakes in the corners at an angle, so it's possible to evenly space them like the spokes of a bicycle when you twine around them individually.

7. Twine around each base stake individually. As usual, bring the twining strand in the back to the front, so that it sits deep between the two stakes. Bring the twining strand in the front to the back, crossing it over the top of the first twining strand so that it sits very tightly against it. Take your time to pull each twine as tight as you can toward the center of the base; if it's loose after a couple of twines you can always go back and practice again. It's not unusual for it to take making several baskets before you can achieve a tight twining in the first few rounds.

8. Continue twining around each individual base stake, taking care to bring the two corner stakes very close to each other before twining around them. Holding the bend in place while twining will spread the stakes out. When you run out of material, see Splicing Wickerwork Twining Strands (facing page).

9. When the base reaches approximately 7½ inches in diameter and the twining strands are ending with the tips (which are much easier to tuck in), you are done twining. Bend each twining strand alongside a base stake and cut to 2 inches. Use an awl to open space along the stake and push both strands into the space until they are flush with the base edge. The photo below shows the bend of the twining strand before it is inserted into the space along the base stake.

10. Trim the ends of all twining strands, making the cuts close to the base at an angle.

add the upright stakes

This project has a single upright for each base stake. For a more finely woven basket, or a basket with a larger diameter, two uprights would be inserted for each base stake—one on either side. If your base is not flat, place it on the table like an upside-down bowl so the edges are touching the table. For the following steps, you'll need up to 6 feet of space to spread out.

SPLICING WICKERWORK TWINING STRANDS

Tip ends are always spliced to tip ends and butt ends are always spliced to butt ends. Twining strands should never end at the exact same place: Cut one to end early, if necessary.

1. When an ending strand is in the underneath position, cut it so that it sticks out no more than an inch from the basket. Make sure that the strand on top snugly holds it down.

2. Pull the ending strand backward and slide a new strand in so that it sits alongside the old end, not on top of it. The pressure of the other strand on top will hold the two flat and next to each other. They will not stay in place until the next round is woven. When you get to that spot on the next round, press the two ends into position before weaving over them.

1. Cut off the thickest part of each upright stake at an angle. Insert each one at least 1½ inches into the twining, greasing the ends, if necessary. It's not important to place them consistently on the same side of the base stakes. Space them evenly to your eye. If the upright has a curve, the concave part of the curve should face down.

Continued on next page

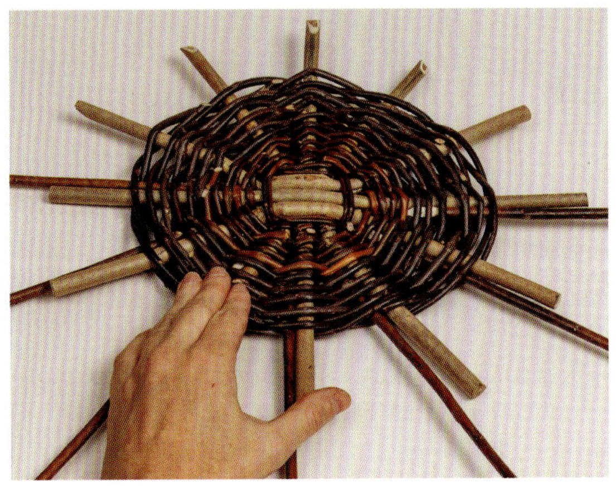

2. To prepare for bending the uprights, use an awl to make a tiny prick in each one a little less than ⅛ inch from the edge of the twining.

3. Bend each of the uprights and tie them at the top.

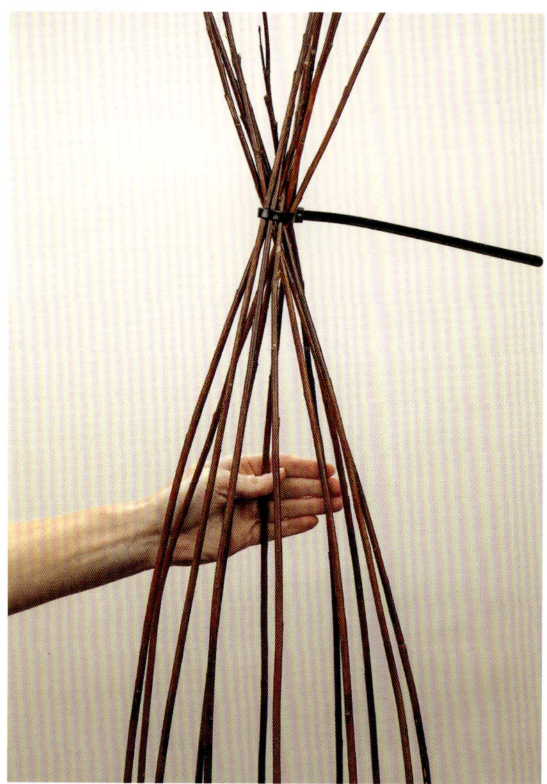

4. Use pruning shears to cut all the base stakes so they are flush with the edge of the base. Push the stakes away from the uprights, if necessary, to make the cuts.

secure the upright stakes

The weaving pattern we'll use for turning up the uprights is known as a three-rod wale, which uses three weavers at the same time and is very sturdy.

1. Choose three long, thin weavers that are all the same diameter and length. In this case I used grapevine. Lay the thinner ends in consecutive spaces between and next to the upright stakes. (For some vines, there may not be a thinner end, in which case it doesn't matter which side you start with.) Hold them in place with your fingers for the first couple of moves.

2. The weaver farthest to the left is the one that always moves. Bring it in front of two stakes, behind one, and out. It is now holding down the other two weavers.

3. Repeat with the new weaver farthest to the left. Bring it in front of two stakes, behind one, and out.

4. Continue the three-rod wale until the weavers run out. Since you started weaving with the thinner tip ends, you are ending with the butt ends. Splice in three new weavers one at a time, butt end first. (You will always match tips to tips and butts to butts.) Starting with the weaver farthest to the left, slide the butt of a new weaving strand in so that it is sandwiched between the ending one and the upright stake. The pressure of the rows above it will hold it in place.

5. Do one weave with the newly spliced weaver: in front of two, behind one, and out. Repeat the splice and a single weave for the other two ending pieces.

6. Continue the three-rod wale for four total rounds, which should be enough to keep the upright stakes vertical. If not, weave another two rounds. If there is a thin end, try to end with that and lay the ends inside the basket before packing the rows down.

7. Use a sturdy, heavy tool such as a hammer to forcefully pack—or rap—down the rows of weaving between the upright stakes. A specialized tool called a rapping iron was developed for this use in traditional willow basketry.

weave the walls

1. Weave the basket until it is 5½ inches high, using your choice of materials and any combination of twining, three-rod wale, and chase weave (see page 302).

2. Finish the walls with two to four rounds of three-rod wale, ending with the thin ends of the last set of weavers, which you can either tuck alongside a stake or rest inside the basket.

CHASE WEAVE

Chase weave is much like a plain weave, except you work two weavers at the same time. Unlike the plain weave, the chase weave works with an even number of stakes because the second weaver staggers behind and never overtakes the first one.

1. Insert one weaver behind an upright stake and go under and over five stakes in a plain-weave pattern.

2. Insert a second weaver in the space to the left of where the first weaver started. Go under and over three stakes.

3. Continue a plain-weave pattern with both weavers, but make sure that the second weaver never overtakes the first one. This requires some attention. Splice in new weavers as the old ones run out (see Splicing Wickerwork Twining Strands on page 299).

weave the rim

This rim style is known as a basic trac border.

1. Bend kinks in the first two upright stakes to the right, 1/4 inch above the top of the basket to account for the uprights that will be woven beneath them at the end. Then kink all the rest of the uprights a little lower at 1/8 inch above the top of the basket.

2. Fold the first ¼-inch-kinked upright and weave to the right, going in front of the first two stakes, behind the next, and out of the basket.

3. Take the next standing upright that is kinked at ¼ inch (it will be one to the left of the upright you just folded down) and repeat step 2, bending it over to the right in front of two upright stakes, behind the next, and out of the basket. Repeat step 2 with each standing upright in line from left to right until there are only three upright stakes standing.

4. Run the three remaining stakes along the edge of your hand to soften them for bending. They will have to thread through tight spaces, and this will help prepare them.

5. Fold upright A in front of the two others. Bring it to the inside of the basket and thread it back out underneath the first upright you folded over at the beginning of making the rim.

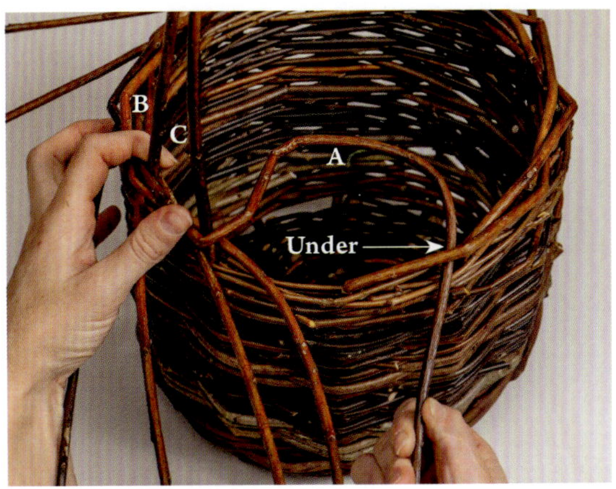

Continued on next page

6. Fold upright B in front of C and thread it to the inside of the basket in the space to the right of the second upright you folded over when starting the rim.

7. Bring the same upright stake out of the basket to the right of the third upright you folded over when starting the basket.

Tip: *It can be tricky to figure out where to bring upright stakes out. An end should thread out of every space between two stakes.*

8. Repeat with upright C. It needs to fold over the two stakes to the right that have already been folded down (A and B), threaded to the inside of the basket in the same space the end of stake B is coming out of, and then threaded back out the last space that doesn't have the end of an upright sticking out of it already.

9. Trim all the ends at an angle but be very careful to make sure they rest with tension against a stake. If you trim them too short, they will pop out to the inside of the basket.

RESOURCES

Basketmaking Supplies

Basket Maker's Supply
https://basketmakerssupply.com

Suzanne Moore's North Carolina Basket Works, Inc.
https://ncbasketworks.com

HH Perkins Co.
https://hhperkins.com

Basketry Groups

United States

National Basketry Organization
https://nationalbasketry.org

Local Basketry Guilds
Most states or regions have basketry guilds with gatherings and workshops. Search for a guild in your state or consult the national group for a recommendation.

United Kingdom

The Basketmakers' Association
https://basketmakersassociation.org.uk

BIBLIOGRAPHY

General Basketry

Here are a few books that focus on wild harvested basketry or will further your knowledge of specific basketry techniques.

Baskets from Nature's Bounty by Elizabeth Jensen. Interweave Press, 1991.

Earth Basketry: Weaving Containers with Nature's Materials by Osma Gallinger Tod. Schiffer Publishing, 2017.

Finding Form with Fibre: Be Inspired, Gather Materials, and Create Your Own Sculptural Basketry by Ruth Woods. Craft School Oz, 2022.

Rib Baskets by Jean Turner Finley. Schiffer Publishing, 2012.

Specific Basketry Materials

The following books will deepen your knowledge of specific commonly used basketry plants, including some that are covered in this book and a few that are not.

Willow Basketry

Willow: A Guide to Growing and Harvesting by Jenny Crisp. Jacqui Small, 2018.

Willow Basketry, by Bernard Verdet-Fierz and Regula Verdet-Fierz. Interweave Press, 1994.

Rivercane Basketry

Cherokee Basketry: From the Hands of Our Elders by M. Anna Fariello. History Press, 2011.

Black Ash Basketry

Black Ash Basketry: Tips, Tools, and Techniques for Learning the Craft by Jonathan Kline. Stackpole Books, 2011.

Birch Bark Basketry

Plaited Basketry with Birch Bark by Vladamir Yarish, Flo Hoppe, and Jim Widess. Sterling, 2009.

Rush Basketry

Rush Basketry: Weaving with Eight Makers, edited by Clair Murphy. Basketmakers' Association, 2018.

White Oak Basketry

Appalachian White Oak Basketmaking: Handing Down the Basket by Rachel Nash Law and Cynthia W. Taylor. University of Tennessee Press, 1991.

Botany and Plants

Botany in a Day: The Patterns Method of Plant Identification, 6th ed., by Thomas J. Elpel. HOPS Press, 2013.

A Field Guide to Trees and Shrubs by George A. Petrides. Houghton Mifflin (Trade), 1990.

"Find a Plant." North Carolina Extension Gardener Plant Toolbox.edu, https://plants.ces.ncsu.edu/find_a_plant

Lady Bird Johnson Wildflower Center https://wildflower.org/plants/index.php

Native American Ethnobotany by Daniel E. Moerman. Timber Press, 1998.

Native Ferns, Moss, and Grasses: From Emerald Carpet to Amber Wave: Serene and Sensuous Plants for the Garden by William Cullina. Echo Point Books & Media, 2020.

Native Trees, Shrubs, and Vines: A Guide to Using, Growing, and Propagating North American Woody Plants by William Cullina. Echo Point Books & Media, 2019.

Plants of the World Online https://powo.science.kew.org

The Sibley Guide to Trees by David Allen Sibley. Alfred A. Knopf, 2009.

PLANTS Database, USDA.gov, https://plants.usda.gov

ACKNOWLEDGMENTS

I owe deep gratitude to the many entities and people who came together to make this book possible. First, I want to thank the creek, the island, and the basswood trees that inspired me to dive deep into the world of basketry and who have held me both in times of joy and sadness. This thanks extends to all the plants that have been my greatest teachers and to the land on which I have learned.

Endless gratitude to everyone who has ever taken one of my classes. You have taught me so much, especially those who have been a part of the Wild Basketry Series over the past 8 years. It has been one of the greatest joys of my life to spend 9 months each year growing close to a community that is passionate about connecting to the natural world. So many friends that I have met through these classes come to mind . . . if you are reading this, thank you for changing my life. A special thanks to Rigmor and Andy Berntsen for supporting my earliest workshops at their home and being the first to encourage me to write a book! Thank you to all the teachers I've studied under, especially Matt Tommey, who have been my advocates and supporters over the years.

Thank you to every friend and student who reviewed chapters, tested projects, and answered random texts about basketry stuff. Your help was invaluable in making this book possible.

Thank you, Shasta Crombie, Rebecca Bratt, Katie Gibbons, Simone Lackey, Whitney Klann, Mary Chang, Kate Litteral, and Meegan Veeder-Shave, for going above and beyond in your project testing. Thank you to Alyssa Sacora for the basketry materials support and to Levi O'Brien for answering my random botany questions.

Thank you so much to the team at Storey for bringing this book to life and having faith in a first-time author. So much gratitude, in particular, to Alethea Morrison for doing the best editing and design for this book that I could have imagined and for being an organizational and communication pro. Thanks to Mars Vilaubi for taking amazing photos and making long days of project photography in the studio fun while we chatted about birds and plants.

Many thanks to Melanie Falick, for helping me write an incredible book proposal, giving me so much advice, and encouraging me to take my writing to a new level in the beginning stages.

A profound thanks to my parents, Jon and Shelly Grove, who have always supported my artistic endeavors and encouraged me to dance to the beat of my own drum. I would not be the person I am today without them, and I am incredibly lucky to have such love and support in my life. Profound thanks to my ancestors, whom I think of often while continuing to explore the ancient techniques of basketry.

Lastly, I want to express my deepest gratitude toward my partner in life, Keith Gould, for his endless support, love, and encouragement throughout the entire process. From the sunset walks on Playa Tortuga, where the seeds of this project began to sprout, to the last push of finishing the manuscript in the snowy valley of our home in New York, he made this book possible.

INDEX

Page numbers in *italics* indicate photos; numbers in **bold** indicate charts.

D

E

F

T

V

W

Y

Z